William Blake
in a Newtonian World

Oklahoma Project for
Discourse and Theory

Series for Science and Culture

William Blake in a Newtonian World

Essays on Literature as Art and Science

by Stuart Peterfreund

UNIVERSITY OF OKLAHOMA PRESS: NORMAN

Also by Stuart Peterfreund

The Hanged Knife and Other Poems (Ithaca, 1970)
Harder Than Rain (Ithaca, 1977)
Critical Theory and the Teaching of Literature (Boston, 1985)
Culture/Criticism/Ideology (Boston, 1986)
Literature and Science: Theory and Practice (Boston, 1990)

Library of Congress Cataloging-in-Publication Data

Peterfreund, Stuart.
    William Blake in a Newtonian world : essays on literature as
art and science / by Stuart Peterfreund.
        p.   cm. — (Oklahoma project for discourse and theory.
Series for science and culture ; v. 2)
    Includes bibliographical references and index.
    ISBN 0–8061–3042–3 (alk. paper)
    1. Blake, William, 1757–1827—Knowledge—Science.
2. Literature and science—England—History—18th century.
3. Newton, Isaac, Sir, 1642–1727—Influence.   4. Enlightenment—England.   I. Title.   II. Series
PR4148.S35P48   1998
821'.7—dc21   97–40080
                                                                                CIP

William Blake in a Newtonian World is Volume 2 of the Oklahoma
Project for Discourse and Theory, Series for Science and Culture.

The paper in this book meets the guidelines for permanence and
durability of the Committee on Production Guidelines for Book
Longevity of the Council on Library Resources, Inc. ∞

1   2   3   4   5   6   7   8   9   10

Contents

Illustrations

Editors' Foreword

Since its inception in 1987, the Oklahoma Project for Discourse and Theory has challenged and helped to redefine the boundaries of traditional disciplinary structures of knowledge. Employing various approaches, ranging from feminism and deconstruction to sociology and nuclear studies, books in this series have offered their readers opportunities to explore our postmodern condition. In the Series on Science and Culture, the Oklahoma Project extends its inquiries into the postdisciplinary areas of the complex relations among the humanities, social sciences, and sciences. The term *postdisciplinary* is meant to suggest that we have entered an era of rapid sociocultural and technological change in which "common sense" divisions between, say, physics and literature no longer seem as sensible as they once did. The values and assumptions, methods and technologies, that we had been taught were "natural" and "universal" are being challenged, reworked, and demystified to demonstrate the ways in which they are culturally constructed. All coherence may not be gone, but what counts as coherence is being redefined in provocative ways.

In recent years, the study of science, both within and outside of the academy, has undergone a sea change. Traditional approaches to the history and philosophy of science treated science as an insular set of procedures concerned to reveal fundamental truths or laws of the physical universe. In contrast, the postdisciplinary study of science emphasizes its cultural embeddedness, the ways in which particular laboratories, experiments, instruments, scientists, and procedures are historically and socially situated.

Editors' Foreword

Science is no longer a closed system that generates carefully plotted paths proceeding asymptotically toward the truth, but an open system that is everywhere penetrated by contingent and even competing accounts of what constitutes our world. These include—but are by no means limited to—the discourses of race, gender, social class, politics, theology, anthropology, sociology, and literature. In the phrase of the Nobel laureate Ilya Prigogine, we have moved from a science of being to a science of becoming. This becoming is the ongoing concern of the volumes in the Series on Science and Culture. Their purpose is to open up possibilities for further inquiries rather than to close off debate.

The members of the editorial board of the series reflect our commitment to reconceiving the structures of knowledge. All are prominent in their fields, although in every case what their "field" is has been redefined, in large measure by their own work. The departmental or program affiliations of these distinguished scholars—Sander Gilman, Donna Haraway, N. Katherine Hayles, Bruno Latour, Richard Lewontin, Michael Morrison, Mark Poster, G. S. Rousseau, and Donald Worster—seem to tell us less about what they do than where, institutionally, they have been. Taken together as a set of strategies for rethinking the relationships between science and culture, their work exemplifies the kind of careful, self-critical scrutiny within fields such as medicine, biology, anthropology, history, physics, and literary criticism that leads us to a recognition of the limits of what and how we have been taught to think. The postdisciplinary aspects of our board members' work stem from their professional expertise within their home disciplines and their willingness to expand their studies to other, seemingly alien fields. In differing ways, their work challenges the basic divisions within Western thought between metaphysics and physics, mind and body, form and matter.

ROBERT MARKLEY

University of West Virginia

ROBERT CON DAVIS
RONALD SCHLEIFER

University of Oklahoma

Preface

When I began my close study of Blake, working on him in my dissertation some twenty-five years ago, I was determined to bring together faithful historical scrutiny of Blake and his times with what then passed for literary theory. The result was a study heavy in its quest for Blake's sources and his transformations of these, and light in its engagement with larger questions of theorization or cultural history, the question of how accurate our understanding of the Enlightenment was being foremost among these.

In the half decade from finishing my Ph.D. to the acceptance of the article reprinted here as chapter 1, "Blake and Newton: Argument as Art, Argument as Science," I became acquainted with a number of books that helped me to redirect the historical component of my critical project, among these Donald Ault's *Visionary Physics*, Margaret C. Jacob's *Newtonians and the English Revolution, 1689–1720*, and Hayden V. White's *Metahistory* (1976) and *Tropics of Discourse* (1978).

A summer fellowship at the School of Criticism and Theory, then at the University of California, Irvine, immersed me in the proliferating field of critical theory in a way that no graduate school seminar could have done. With the potential for writing a far more thickly descriptive kind of Blake studies/cultural studies essay than I had been capable of previously, I returned to the question that I had had to pass over in the dissertation: To what extent is Blake's reaction to the unholy trinity of Bacon, Newton,

xi

and Locke, if not justified, at the very least based on an informed understanding of Enlightenment premises in general and Newtonian thought in particular?

In engaging this question, I found myself reading extensively in the field of literature and science, particularly in the work of Herbert Butterfield, A. O. Lovejoy, Marjorie Hope Nicholson, and G. S. Rousseau. As Rousseau was then arguing, in 1978, the old history-of-ideas and source-and-analog approaches to the field had reached the limits of their usefulness. Because of dwindling division membership and dwindling interest, the Modern Language Association was considering disbanding the Division on Literature and Science. Rousseau appropriately asked, in an article in *Isis*, the journal of the History of Science Society, and in a 1978 MLA Division meeting, what next? The essays in this collection, along with several others not included, have been my answer in part.

In Chapter 1, "Blake and Newton: Argument as Art, Argument as Science," I began from the premise that Blake held that Newton was not so much a poet *manqué* as a poet *soi-décevant*—Newton is, as was noted above, brought back as a poet at the close of *Jerusalem*, apparently cured of his delusions about the nature of matter, space, time, and motion. But since, as Blake knows, one speaks into existence and observes the universe that one inhabits, the focus of the study was on what sort of world Newton predicts (and prescribes) into existence and how, from Blake's perspective, it feels to live there. Chapter 2, "Blake and Anti-Newtonian Thought," originally drafted for a 1982 conference but not published until much later, and with substantial revision, continued this exploration.

The preemptive, predictive, and prescriptive turn of Newtonian thought (and the parallel development of Lockean epistemology) had an unforseen and paradoxical effect: the more these discourses sought to render the subject passive, whether as projected, corpuscular matter, or as mind-as-tabula-rasa, the more the discourses called attention to the status of the perceiving subject. Margaret C. Jacob's *The Radical Enlightenment: Pantheists, Freemasons, and Republicans* (1981) puts the case forcefully for linking a range of social, political, and religious movements to the impulse to posit an anti-Newtonian or counter-Newtonian subject, even in circles nominally hospitable to Newtonian discourse.

Freemasonry was one such movement. In chapter 3, "Blake, Freemasonry, and the Builder's Task," I undertake to show how Blake fastened upon Freemasonry and the sponsoring mythos that underwrites it to venture a critique of a line of prescriptive thought that he sees stretching from Moses, arguably the first cosmologist and lawgiver in the Judeo-Christian line, to Newton, arguably among the most recent cosmologists and lawgivers in Blake's own time. Blake deconstructs Freemasonry and its sponsoring mythos, not for the purpose of repudiating Freemasonry, but for the purpose of pointing out the movement's moral: that human fulfillment derives from an unending, uncompromising engagement of the imagination in the service of art— the "builder's task" of my title.

Freemasonry was not the only movement that reinterpreted biblical texts in the eighteenth century. Although it did not gain its current widespread scholarly interest until the translation and publication of the Nag Hammadi Codices, rediscovered in 1945, gnosticism was a reinterpretive movement that enjoyed a revival of interest in the seventeenth and eighteenth centuries—in England usually among radical artisans or other groups unhappy with the concept of an established church and state, an apostolic succession, a trinitarian God, or more than one of these concepts. Characterized in its operation by immanent rather than transcendent causation, the gnostic model of how things happen in the world of lived experience attracted a broad spectrum if not a large number of followers, ranging from the interested and the sympathetic to out-and-out adherents. The fourth chapter, "Blake, Priestley, and the Gnostic Moment," proposes Blake's time as a period of intense interest and argues for the chapter's two namesakes as being foremost among those who responded during the period.

Chapters 5 ("Blake on Charters, Weights, and Measures as Forms of Social Control") and 6 ("Power Tropes: 'The Tyger' as Enacted Critique of Metonymic Logic and Natural Theology") focus closely on individual poems from the *Experience* section of *Songs of Innocence and Experience* (1794) to demonstrate in detail how characteristically Newtonian linguistic turns serve to predict and prescribe a world of matter, motion, and force that deprives the languaged subject of the opportunity to unsay that world, or to say it otherwise. The former chapter focuses on situating historically the English understanding of standardized measure, which is a prerequisite for the sort of instrumentation necessary to conduct rational, instrumental (predictive) scientific experimentation, but which also subverts human identity and individuality. The latter chapter unpacks the sort of argument that posits scientific cause and effect in terms of tropes that may then be used in the service of natural theology, and above all in the service of that discourse's argument from design.

Repetitions of the argument from design over time have the long-term effect of positing nature as the effect of a certain myth of creation and constructing the natural philosopher, or scientist, as one who observes nature, his passive and compliant object, to extract from her the truths and laws invested in her by God at the time of the Creation. Chapter 7, "Blake and the Ideology of the Natural," extends chapter 6's focus on characteristic Newtonian linguistic turns to show how such tropes collectively serve to contruct a nature that is the reified, ideological effect of those tropes.

Chapter 8, "The Din of the City in Blake's Prophetic Books," brings the project to the verge of another argument. If the Newtonian speaker, or some other group of speakers in positions of authority, is authorized to use tropes in particular—and language in general—to predict and prescribe nature in a certain manner, then it follows that other speakers, who are not in positions of authority, are deprived of the freedom to use language to predict and prescribe according to their own lights. It is the case, in fact, that for most of the last decade of the eighteenth century and most of the first two decades of the nineteenth—the period of Blake's artistic maturity—the vast majority of England's laboring poor and artisans strove to make known their desire for universal suffrage, fair and stable food prices, and uncompromised freedom of expression, but were rebuffed by those in positions of authority, who both "owned" polite discourse and denied those who petitioned for their rights access to that discourse, in the very act of using that discourse to prescribe and reify the social patterns that that discourse authorizes. As a result, the laboring poor and artisans found themselves at a disavantage, possessing the voice with which to express their misery, but not the language with which to petition for its alleviation. Much of the din and drama of *Milton* and

Jerusalem focuses on this situation as a figment of the Mosaic-Newtonian frame of mind, and on Blake's imaginative rectification of the situation.

As I note in the introduction, a recurrent theme throughout Blake's work, picked up throughout all of these essays, is that there cannot be an epistemology that is independent of a highly specific ontology, and that the arts in general and poetry and the visual arts in particular give form to that ontology projected as desire: form is the shape desire takes. What prevents these postulates from creating conditions of incommensurability at best, or of solipsism at worst, is Blake's article of faith that the soul, in enacting desire's dynamic—what he calls "Poetic Genius" in *All Religions Are One* (1788; *CPP*, p. 1)—operates recognizably and similarly in all human beings. Newton may claim special knowledge of things cosmological and theological, may even claim insider's status as the son of an absconded Unitarian father-God, but the workings of his "Poetic Genius," however repressed or self-deluded, are recognizable to Blake as what they are. His goal is to contest these workings, and in so doing to situate them among other such workings as part of the great conversation that will become Jerusalem in England's green and pleasant land.

William Blake
in a Newtonian World

Abbreviations

CPP	*The Complete Poetry and Prose of William Blake*
MHH	*The Marriage of Heaven and Hell*
M	*Milton*
J	*Jerusalem*
U	*The Book of Urizen*
KE3	*King Edward the Third*
FZ	*The Four Zoas*
SE	*Songs of Experience*
SI	*Songs of Innocence*
VDA	*Visions of the Daughters of Albion*
NNR[b]	*There Is No Natural Religion [b]*

Introduction:
Blake and the Case for
Situated Knowledge

When this essay collection was in the final stages of the review process, and with its acceptance all but certain, I had occasion to attend the annual meeting of the Society for Literature and Science (SLS), a learned society that I helped to found in 1985, and of which I currently serve as president (1995–97). Far from being an organization entirely devoted to the "science studies" roundly denounced by Paul R. Gross and Norman Levitt,[1] SLS numbers among its members scholars whose research programs stress the certainty and universality of scientific knowledge. Joseph Carroll is one such member. I attended a session in which Carroll gave a paper that argued against viewing science as culturally constructed and in favor of science as T. H. Huxley understood it. "For Huxley," writing in "Science and Culture" (1880, 1881), "the authority of science is secured by three fundamental propositions: that science forms a unitary order, that science forms a unitary field of knowledge concordant with the order of nature, and that science is a progressive, cumulative enterprise." For Carroll, cultural construction is on the verge of giving way to "a realist, rationalist, and empirical form of literary study" that will affirm "Huxley's three central principles: the

3

unity of nature, the unity of science, and the progressive nature of scientific understanding." While he is candid enough to characterize Huxley's position as an "ideology," Carroll nevertheless holds that "this ideology should influence the study of literature and culture at the present time."[2]

As I sat listening to Carroll's presentation, I began to experience a very Blakean discomfort. Moreover, I came to understand my discomfort with the certainties that the paper proclaimed and the universalities it espoused, and as I began testing this understanding across the sweep of Western civilization from Plato onward, I realized that my reservations sprang from the fact that those who proclaim such certainty and universality do so on the basis of the undiscussed but nevertheless powerful assumption that it is possible to have an epistemology without an ontology— that it is possible to have a theory of knowledge without a narrative of coming to knowledge by traversing a certain cultural and intellectual terrain in the company of, or in opposition to, others who are either traversing that same terrain or at the very least populating it and who are, under certain circumstances, resisting the individual's attempt at traversing that terrain.

The attempt to suppress such a narrative is central to the project of what has, over time, passed for a "scientific," that is, universal and universalizable, epistemology. As stated above, one of the project's starting points is with Plato. On a number of occasions in the Socratic dialogues, someone travels to the site of dialectic from elsewhere—often, from outside the *polis*—to engage in a dispute in which the importance of the narrative of travel is held by Socrates to be secondary to the "big" truths that he pursues. It is interesting, but most emphatically not coincidental, that these are dialogues in which the Socratic interlocutor does not prevail so readily as he does on other occasions.

In the *Cratylus*, for example, Cratylus comes to Athens from outside the city walls to argue, as Hermogenes puts it, that names "are natural and not conventional; not a portion of the human voice which men agree to use; but that there is truth or correctness in them, which is the same for Hellenes as for barbarians" (383a). Unable to argue down Cratylus, a disciple of Heracleitus (and a proponent of a world of flux and process) in the matter of whether the beautiful and the good may ultimately be known by a languaged, name-using, name-giving human being, Socrates commends Cratylus to his travels. "Then, another day, my friend, when you come back, you shall give me a lesson; but at present, go into the country, as you are intending, and Hermogenes shall set you on your way" (440b).

In the *Symposium* it is Diotima, the Mantineian woman, who journeys from there to the Athenian house of Agathon—not coincidentally, a pun on *he tou agathon*, "the good," which is the goal of Socratic dialogue—to disrupt Socratic dialectic on the nature of love.[3] In his leave-taking tale to the revelers, Socrates tells the tale of his own defeat at Diotima's hands. He attempts, by means of dialectic, to get Diotima to take the stance that love is either fair or foul. " 'Hush,' she cried; 'must that be foul which is not fair?' 'Certainly,' I said. 'And is that which is not wise, ignorant? do you not see that there is a mean between wisdom and ignorance?' 'And what may that be?' I said;' 'Right opinion,' she replied" (201b–202a). Diotima goes on to construct love as such a mean. "He is a great spirit (daimon), and like all spirits he is intermediate between the divine and the mortal" (202b), she argues.

It is hardly surprising or coincidental that in pleading the case for the truth of lived experience, Diotima bases that truth on the mean between the dialectical extremes, one of which Socrates would have her choose. The mean is the ontological site that poses the gravest threat of all to the project of a universal and universalizable epistemology. Plato's *Republic* presents a society and system of dialectical education completely self-sufficient and self-enclosed, a *polis* that is at once utopia (no place) and pantopia (every place) precisely because it excludes the likes of poets, who in celebrating such human undertakings as love between a man and a woman drag human contemplation back to the mean. As Gerry O'Sullivan demonstrates, Aristotle mobilizes the law of the excluded mean in Aristotle's *Poetics* to devalue the middle voice and create hierarchies of genre and genre-based knowledge.[4] Michel Serres notes that the scientific project is inconceivable if the partners in dialectic toward scientific knowledge are unable to exclude "the third man," who is, as Serres characterizes him, "the *demon*, the propopoeia of noise,"[5] precisely because he threatens to reduce dialectically (or digitally) configured information ($+ \neq -$, $1 \neq 0$) to the entropic mean.

Stephen Toulmin's reading of how the meaning of the Greek word *theoros* evolved over time offers a parallel account of how the ontological narrative came to be suppressed in favor of the noncontingent, unmediated theory of knowledge. "In classical Greece, the word *theoros* was originally used for an official delegate who was dispatched from the city-state to consult the Oracle about some problem of city policy." Both the journey to the Oracle and the return journey colored the consultation, the events on the journey there conditioning the suggestibility and receptivity of the *theoros*, the events on the return journey coloring the *theoros*'s memory of the Oracle's words and actions, as well as his interpretation of those.

"Eventually," as Toulmin notes,

> the word was generalized . . . and used to refer to any spectator at the [Olympic or intercity athletic] Games, official or unofficial, as contrasted with a participant: correspondingly, the abstract noun theoria began by denoting the activity of spectating, onlooking, or observing any activity or process, by contrast with intervening participating, or being an agent in it. As a final step, the word achieved its familiar Aristotelian status: *theoria* came to refer to the detached intellectual posture, activity, and product associated with the philosopher's study, observation, and reflection about the world, by contrast with the praxis of the carpenter, the farmer, or the fisherman.[6]

Not surprisingly, Toulmin implicates the posture of theoria in "the central leitmotif of much self-consciously 'progressive' science and philosophy . . . the need to pursue 'rational objectivity' of a kind that could only be arrived at by a detached and reflective observer." Ultimately, in the aftermath of the Cartesian dualism, "the human mind had the task of observing (and syllogizing about) the world of material objects and mechanical processes, but always did so *from outside it*."[7]

Although this extended exposition is necessary for the discussion of situated knowledge that follows, its connection to Blake's place in a Newtonian world may not be immediately clear. To offer but one glimpse at that connection before turning from the Hellenic background to the Hebraic: as Toulmin himself notes, after duly crediting Alexandre Koyré with the insight, the Cartesian theorist's position as *spectator ab extra* is also that of the Newtonian natural philosopher, all other disagreements about the nature of matter and the motions of the planets duly noted.[8] In the "General Scholium" at the end of the *Principia*, for example, Newton tantalizingly tropes himself as the Socinian God with who he personally identified.[9] Of that God, Newton observes, "In

6

him are all things contained and moved; yet neither affects the other: God suffers nothing from the motion of bodies; bodies find no resistance from the omnipresence of God."[10] This is the Newton that Blake depicts deploying his calipers to measure the world in the middle of a blue-green nowhere, the Newton that Blake, with a knowing wink at the Gnostic cosmogony, figures in *The Book of Urizen* (1794) as "unknown, abstracted / Brooding secret."[11]

As Blake reads it, a similar scenario was being played out in the deserts beyond the Red Sea where the Israelites spent forty years wandering. When Moses ascended Sinai, he not only left the realm of a fallen humanity to talk, by his account, directly to God, who "came down . . . on top of the mount" (Exodus 19:20), but he also left and denied the ontological space and journey that defined him as a leader of his people. Moses represents the voice of God as saying, "Away, get thee down, and thou shalt come up, thou, and Aaron with thee: but let not the priests and people break through to come up unto the LORD, lest he break forth upon them" (19:24).

The written result of this encounter is the Ten Commandments (20:1–17), followed by their fuller articulation as the laws of Israel, which regulate every aspect of human conduct. Unlike the Greek *polis*, where the attempt to legislate the good by means of dialectic was at best a mixed success, the polity of the Ten Tribes was governed, with varying degrees of success, by this codification of self-proclaimed absolute knowledge and authority until the event encoded in God's threat to "break forth" came to pass, albeit with a different outcome than the implied threat in the Mosaic account.

In that acount, God is figured as divine, ineffable radiance, whether that be the radiance of the sun or the radiance of a mighty fire, covered by clouds or a pall of smoke, respectively (Exodus 19:16, 18). In the terms of the extended metaphor, then, to "break forth" is to shine like the sun or blaze like a mighty fire. But for a Blakean reader of Exodus such as I, there is a problem with the unquestioned implication that to "break forth" is to manifest destruction. For example, when God makes himself manifest to Moses in the form of the burning bush, specifically situated in a "place [that] . . . is holy ground," the bush is "not consumed." Moreover, Moses, who is himself not harmed, does not hide his face, "afraid to look upon God," until God identifies himself as the "God of Abraham . . . Isaac . . . and . . . Jacob" (Exodus 3:2–6). Terrifying though he ultimately may be to Moses, the God of this encounter is pure, radiant, unmediated being, calling himself "I AM THAT I AM," or Jehovah (3:14), and his destructiveness acts only on those who resist him, not on those who accept him. In the case of the Egyptians and their Pharaoh, Rameses II, the resistance, which takes the form of what Blake would call "hindering" the Israelites, is obvious; the opportunities to cure the behavior, numerous; the consequences of failing to do so, overdetermined.

But in the case of Moses and his people, it is an entirely different matter. Moses universalizes and naturalizes his own ontology, making his own fear of God the normative condition of all numinous encounters, and he creates extended structures, such as the Ark of the Covenant, and extended codes, such as the Ten Commandments, to serve as mediators of that unmediated being. A close Blakean reading of Exodus makes it readily apparent how Moses goes about universalizing and naturalizing his own ontology. God, as Moses encounters him, instructs Moses to "say unto the children of Israel, I AM hath sent me unto you. . . . The LORD God of your fathers, the God of Abraham, the God of Isaac, and the God of Jacob, hath sent me unto you: this is my name for ever, and this is my memorial unto all generations" (3:14–15).

This is the God who promises to bring the Israelites to a situated, pastoral existence, "unto a land flowing with milk and honey," and the only condition that he imposes is a three-day journey into the wilderness in order to "sacrifice unto the LORD our God" (3:17–18)—again, an event partaking of situated worship and situated knowledge. However, when Moses returns to Egypt to ask the Pharaoh's leave to make this journey, he and his brother Aaron embellish God's condition somewhat. "And they said, The God of the Hebrews hath met with us: let us go, we pray thee, three days' journey into the desert, and sacrifice to the LORD our God; lest he fall upon us with pestilence, or with the sword" (5:3). Moses is in the desert when he encounters I AM THAT I AM, it should be noted, because he himself has done what he represents God as being liable to do: Moses has killed an Egyptian overseer, presumably with his sword (2:12). It is important to note that Moses does not at first flee, believing that no one saw him commit the deed and having buried the body in the sand. The next day, however, when Moses encounters two Israelites who are fighting, a telling exchange occurs. Moses asks one of the two, "Wherefore smitest thou thy fellow?" The aggressor replies, with telling point, "Who made thee a prince and a judge over us? Intendest thou to kill me, as thou killedst the Egyptian?" (2:14–15). It is also important to note that what is proposed as a three-day journey to an event partaking of situated worship and situated knowledge becomes a forty-year errancy, the symbolic complement to Moses' attempt at normalization, universalization, and above all, dissituation.

Blake reprises both the fear that accompanies the numinous encounter and the Mosaic mind-set in *Milton* (1804). A numinous encounter takes place between the Blakean speaker and Los, who makes a Christlike redemptive descent to the end of restoring that speaker to his prophetic preeminence. Tellingly, the numinous encounter is highly situated—and is resituated by Los himself.

> While Los heard indistinct in fear, what time I bound my sandals
> On; to walk forward thro' Eternity, Los descended to me:
> And Los behind me stood; a terrible flaming Sun: just close
> Behind my back; I turned round in terror, and behold.
> Los stood in that fierce glowing fire; & he also stoop'd down
> And bound my sandals on in Udan-Adan; trembling I stood
> Exceedingly with fear & terror, standing in the Vale
> Of Lambeth: but he kissed me, and wishd me health.
> And I became One Man with him arising in my strength.
>   (*M*, pl. 24 [24], ll. 4–12)

Los represents the operation of "the Poetic or Prophetic character," as Blake discusses it in *There Is No Natural Religion [a–b]* (1788). The conclusion of *b* is particularly pertinent: "Therefore God becomes as we are, that we may be as he is" (*CPP*, p. 3). By this conclusion Blake means that God's eternal becomingness, which is the only characteristic by which those who live in a world of flux, mutability, and process may know him, is made manifest in the world in the form of his radiant Son, who both becomes human and is becomingly human, so that by gaining knowledge of God through his Son, one may aspire to God's own status of pure unmediated being. To attain such status is to transcend ontological situatedness and contingency and to achieve not only unmediated being but unmediated knowledge (omniscience) as well. But pure unmediated being is not attainable in this life. Read in a slightly different manner, "Therefore God becomes as we are, that we may be as he is" suggests that the Son becomes a perishing, mortal, exemplary human being to teach one that it is only by accepting one's ontological situatedness and contingency—indeed, it is only by dying as the result of that situatedness and contingency—that one lives forever and attains pure unmediated being and knowledge. Near the end of *Jerusalem* (1804–20) Jesus makes precisely this point to Albion, who asks,

> Cannot Man exist without Mysterious
> Offering of Self for Another, is this Friendship & Brotherhood
> I see thee in the likeness & similitude of Los my Friend

> Jesus said. Wouldest thou love one who never died
> For thee or ever die for one who had not died for thee
> And if God dieth not for Man & giveth not himself
> Eternally for Man Man could not exist! for Man is Love:
> As God is Love: every kindness to another is a little Death
> In the Divine Image nor can Man exist but by Brotherhood.
> (*J*, pl. 96, ll. 20–28)

It is important not to underestimate the importance of Blake's parable of becoming and being for his analysis of how Western civilization has strayed from the truth of the matter as he understands it. The errors of the Hellenic account, as these are manifested in Plato's writings, and the errors of the Mosaic account, as these are manifested in the Pentateuch, spring from a misunderstanding of how God becomes human, so that humanity may be as God is. Both what Blake calls "The Stolen and Perverted Writings of Homer & Ovid: of Plato and Cicero" (pl. 1) in the preface to *Milton*, and what he calls "the primeval Priests assum'd power" (*M*, pl. 2, l. 1) in the "Preludium" to the quasi-Mosaic *Book of Urizen* (1794), turn on the assumption that one can transcend ontological situatedness and contingency and achieve unmediated knowledge (omniscience), if not necessarily unmediated being, *in this life*, without the sacrificial and sacramental conditions that Blake places on such transcendence.

To return to the way that "God becomes as we are, that we may be as he is": it is no coincidence that Los, who in the passage from *Jerusalem* cited above is figured as Jesus "in the likeness

& similitude of Los my Friend,"[12] at first appears as "a terrible flaming Sun," the sun-son pun being fully operative here as elsewhere throughout the poem.[13] But unlike the Mosaic God, who first appears in a very similar form, and whom Moses subsequently turns away from and would segregate from the Israelites, Los appears to someone who turns toward him, not away from him, thus allowing Los to bestow a kiss of peace that is at the same time a gesture of prophetic reensoulment and reempowerment. In becoming "One Man with him arising in my strength," the Blakean speaker locates his true identity as that of "that Shadowy Prophet who Six Thousand Years ago / Fell from [his] station in the Eternal bosom" (*M*, pl. 22 [24], ll. 15–16). Whether he jumped owing to a loss of artistic nerve or was pushed by urizenic connivance is beside the point: the absence of the prophetic element from the eternal conversation that Blake figures beginning anew at the end of *Jerusalem* occasioned the fall into Bishop Ussher's six-thousand-year interregnum between the Creation and the Second Coming.

The antithesis of poetic genius is selfhood. As Blake argues in the "Application" that precedes the conclusion of *No Natural Religion [b]*, "He who sees the Infinite in all things sees God. He who sees the Ratio only sees himself only" (*CPP*, p. 3). But there is an element of bad faith that the gnomic "Application" does not fully capture. With the projection of selfhood come the twinned acts of denial-as-othering and dissituation. Selfhood in these terms is synonymous with what Blake sees as the Mosaic mind-set.

Before undertaking his own redemptive descent, Blake gives us the Milton of the prose works. In writing about "the cruelties of Ulro" (*M*, pl. 17 [19], l. 9), the land of "the Ratio"—the England of the Civil War and the Commonwealth—as though it were transcendently real, and in displacing the act of writing onto his wives and daughters, who are also his amanuenses, Milton is figured as being subject to the Mosaic mind-set described above.

He saw the cruelties of Ulro, and he wrote them down
In iron tablets:[14] and his Wives & Daughters names were these
Rahab and Tirzah, & Milcah & Malah & Noah & Hoglah.[15]
They sat rang'd round him as the rocks of Horeb round the land
Of Canaan: and they wrote in thunder smoke and fire
His dictate; and his body was the Rock Sinai; that body,
Which was on earth born to corruption. (*M*, pl. 17 [19], ll. 9–15)

At this point in the poem, Milton's Mosaic mindset creates both the inner and the outer landscape. "The Rocks of Horeb"—the place where Moses announces the covenant by means of which God makes Israel his chosen people (Deuteronomy 5:2)—is the place where Moses, by standing between Israel and its fiery God ("for ye were afraid by reason of the fire, and went not up into the mount" [5:5]) and dispensing "the word of the LORD" (5:5), is the most opaque, hence the most satanic, that he can be.[16] As Blake reads it, this unsolicited interposition between God and Israel—once again ostensibly to protect the latter from the presumptively destructive effects of fire—causes Moses to turn his back on his God,[17] and so alienates Moses from the true nature of the God for whom he presumes to speak that he first refuses, then denies, the prospect of transcendence that that God holds forth. Hence Moses can never pass through that ring of rocks that encircle his bosom to seek his prophetic inner being, can never cross "the rocks of Horeb," cross the Jordan, and enter into the Promised Land, Canaan, where the grand theodical resituation is about to begin. Not surprisingly, Moses disclaims any responsibility for his being barred from the Promised Land, attributing the exclusion to the fact, as he sees it, that "the LORD was wroth with me for your [i.e., Israel's] sakes, and would not hear me" (3:26).

Whatever the effects of his prideful selfhood, and however much his Mosaic/satanic aspect causes him to construct his mind as its own place, Milton is neither Moses nor Satan. The errors of his ways cause "Milton's Human Shadow" to continue "journeying above / The rocky masses of The Mundane Shell" (*M*, pl. 17 [19], ll. 18–19), through a set of Cartesian-Newtonian coordinates "Enlarg'd into dimension & deform'd into indefinite space" (*M*, pl. 17 [19], ll. 23).

Again, Milton is not Moses, and Milton's journey "In that Region calld Midian, among the Rocks of Horeb" (*M*, pl. 17 [19], l. 28), ultimately proves to be the inside passage to a promised land, at least insofar as everlasting life ("Eternity") is such a site. Midian is presented as the site of a Blakean vortex connecting the world of space and time to the world of eternally fused being and becomingness, through which "travellers from Eternity. pass outward to Satans seat, But travellers to Eternity. pass inward to Golgonooza" (*M*, pl. 17 [19], ll. 29–30).[18]

Figuring the site of the vortex as Midian rather than Canaan is not incidental. Blake has in mind not merely the fact that Israel visited terrible slaughter upon the Midianites, exterminating the race save for the virgins (Numbers 31:7–18), but that among those slain was "Balaam . . . the son of Beor" (31:8). The story of Balaam (Numbers 22–24) is in some respects an anticipation of Christ's story, in that Balaam speaks God's parables, not humanity's decrees, and he not only refuses to curse but blesses those who ultimately come to kill him. And Balaam is a godly man. Asked by Balak, king of Moab, to curse Israel and unite in defense against it after its slaughter of the Amorites, Balaam seeks God's wisdom. God's word is, "thou shalt not curse the people: for they are blessed" (22:12). Accordingly, Balaam initially tells the princes of Moab, "Get you into your land: for the LORD refuseth to give me leave to go with you" (22:13). God subsequently modifies his stance, saying, "If the men come to call thee, rise up, and go with them; but yet the word which I shall say unto thee, that shalt thou do" (22:20).

Even though Balaam is only following God's orders, he literally loses sight of God in so doing. Angered, God sends his angel to delay his journey with Balak and the other princes of Moab by appearing to Balaam's ass and effectively preventing the animal from following the path until "the LORD opened the eyes of Balaam" (22:21–31). Set right and rededicated to his mission, Balaam rejoins the others and calls for the large sacrifice prescribed by God, on which occasion Balak and the others expect him to curse Israel. Balaam does otherwise. In Balak's words, on the first of the three occasions that Balaam blesses Israel rather than cursing it, "I took thee to curse mine enemies, and, behold, thou hast blessed them altogether" (23:11).

Balaam subsequently takes up "his parable," singing a long hymn of praise to Israel that begins, "How goodly are thy tents, O Jacob, and thy tabernacles, O Israel!" (24:5–9).[19] Despite Balak's anger, Balaam refuses to curse those who will later kill him, and he and Balak go their separate ways, to be reunited by death.

To return to why Blake situates the vortex in Midian: "travellers from Eternity . . . to Satan's seat" travel in the service of Satan, who is Blake's God of this world. Balak is one such, but so is Moses, who, ostensibly under God's tutelage, sees the Midianites,

13

and especially the sexually active women, as nothing more than the carriers of a venereal "plague" (25:8) that cannot be eradicated save by the eradication of Midian outright. To see in this manner is to reduce the infinite and universal to the finite and particular, to see as the humanity characterized in *No Natural Religion [a]*, whose "desires are limited by his perceptions" (*CPP*, p. 2). Conversely, "Travellers to Eternity" who "pass inward to Golgonooza" travel in the service of God. Balaam is one such, but so is Milton about to embark on his redemptive descent, and so are Jesus and the prophetic line that precedes him, all of whom are able to see the infinite and universal in the finite and particular. Balaam is able to overcome the selfish fear and enmity that strike Balak and the other Moabite princes by selflessly seeing Israel not as a numerous and powerful conquering people, but as the instrument of God's plan for humanity. To recall the words of the "Application" of *No Natural Religion [b]*: "He who sees the Infinite in all things sees God. He who sees the Ratio only sees himself only" (*CPP*, p. 3). Thus the reference to "Golgonooza," the New Golgotha, or Hill of Skulls, where one strives continually to put off selfhood to see beyond oneself—if not by dying on the cross there, as Jesus did, then by killing off and transcending the limits of self-interested thinking by symbolically escaping one's skull by adding it to the pile of skulls that forms the hill, while at the same time understanding that what makes such transcendence possible is precisely the fact that it goes forward only out of a specific situation symbolized (but not totalized) by the geographical references that permeate Blake's poetry.

Situation is an essential constituent of prophetic discourse generally and of the discourse of Jesus and his disciples in particular. To glimpse forward to the New Testament briefly: the life of Jesus, as set forth in the Gospels, is always situated. Place figures prominently, whether one thinks of the Sermon on the Mount (Matthew 5–7), the healing at the pool of Bethesda (John 5), or the conversion of Saul to the Apostle Paul on the road to Damascus (Acts 9:1–8), for example. And Jesus's parabolic discourse is always articulated with a care to who the listeners at a specific site are. So, too, the miraculous acts that emanate from such places are always site specific, the healing of the infirm in the waters of the pool at Bethesda being a case in point. Similarly, the disciples are always situated, and they mend their discourse to the local audience. Paul deals with the Romans differently than he does with the Corinthians, for example, articulating the fine points of Christianity versus Judaism to Romans interested in questions of religious doctrine, and laying down the law on marriage for the sexually preoccupied Corinthians (1 Corinthians 7).

The issues that Blake sees as underwriting Plato and his successors, as well as the Old and New Testaments and the conflicting epistemes that they give rise to, are not merely textual. These same issues fueled much of the intellectual debate of Blake's time.[20] As Michel Foucault observes, the period of the end of the Enlightenment and the beginning of the nineteenth century—the period in which Blake lived, not coincidentally— saw the development of what Foucault calls the "analytic of finitude."[21] In David Simpson's careful analysis of this analytic, he notes its significance as being that "all knowledge is thus positioned as both knowledge 'in itself' (all that we have of it) and knowledge production from within bodies and minds in times and places."[22] Although not without its own problems (and problematic), the "analytic of finitude" is in some measure responsible for what Simpson calls "localism," borrowing and extending the concept from Clifford Geertz's twinned concepts of "thick description" and "local knowledge."[23] Not only is localism one of the defining characteristics of English romanticism, but it is, moreover, "a sign of literature's being refigured by the pressures of a crisis in the entire system of modern history."[24]

Simpson and those he cites are not necessarily the first contemporary commentators to engage and discuss these issues. Hayden V. White, in his essay "The Irrational and the Problem of Historical Knowledge in the Enlightenment," captures finely the moment of struggle and transition that Foucault cites, as that moment plays out in historiography. Opposing "the main line of rationalism—Bayle, Montesquieu, Voltaire, Robertson, Hume, and Gibbon—" are "representatives of the variant convention— Leibniz, Vico, Moser, and Herder." The former, while granting the primacy of what Simpson calls "knowledge 'in itself,'" will suffer no claims concerning "knowledge *production* from within bodies and minds in times and places." This tension gives rise to what White terms an important hidden assumption in Enlightenment historiography, a contradiction which hindered the efforts of its best historians to deal with the main problems of historical representation, whether irrational or anything else. This contradiction is caused by Enlightenment historians' dependence upon the rules of classical rhetoric and poetics as the methodology of historical representation and a simultaneous suspicion of the figurative language and analogical reasoning required for their proper application.[25]

When White discusses the case of Voltaire, an exemplar of his "main line of rationalism," he reveals the philosopher-historian as someone under a certain amount of intellectual duress, poised on, but endeavoring to retreat from, the brink of the abyss of subjectivity—as someone who accepts "knowledge 'in itself' " but rejects "knowledge *production* from within bodies and minds in times and places," in other words. Citing Voltaire's observation, in the *Philosophical Dictionary* (1764), that "too many metaphors are hurtful, not only to perspicuity, but also to the truth, by saying more or less than the thing itself," White remarks that Voltaire's is a failure "to see . . . that figurative language is just as often a way of expressing a truth incompletely grasped as it is of concealing an error or falsehood incompletely recognized."[26]

It is precisely White's "representatives of the variant convention," perhaps none more so than Vico, who are able to see the importance of historically situated "figurative language and analogical reasoning" where these occur, and to engage in analyzing them. Discussing the last (1744) edition of Vico's *New Science*, White notes that

> It was by *metaphorical projection* of his own nature onto the world, Vico theorizes, that primitive man was able progressively to *humanize* it. By identifying the forces of nature as manlike spirits, primitive man invented religion. By the progressive tropological reductions of those forces—by metonymy and synecdoche especially—primitive men gradually came to the realization of their own godlike natures.[27]

To understand the primacy of situated knowledge as it is discussed above for Blake is to gain some insight into his locolalia—the interminable lists of London neighborhoods, English cathedral towns, English counties, modern nations, biblical nations, English geography, and biblical geography that one finds in the Prophetic Books. To understand the primacy of situated knowledge is also to understand how the metaphor of travel operates in Blake's poetry. Using Milton as a case in point, one discerns at least three sorts of travel: deluded travel (from "Eternity . . . to Satan's seat"), inspired travel (from Midian to Golgonoonza), and Newtonian errancy ("journeying above / The rocky masses of the Mundane Shell"). Moreover, to understand the primacy of situated knowledge is to understand Blake's distrust for any universalizing, totalizing "official version" of any discourse, be it history, poetry, religion, science, or the visual arts. To stand Voltaire on his head: if "unofficial versions" such as Freemasonry, the Gothic as Blake understands it, gnosticism, and radical Protestantism had not existed, Blake would have found it necessary to invent them.

In the final analysis, what situated knowledge foregrounds and celebrates above all else is the deployment of metaphor in the act of invention. Invention, as Blake understands it in his infernal sense of the classical term (*inventio*), can mean preparing to speak (or draw)[28] by choosing ideas appropriate to the subject, and for the audience and occasion. In "To the Public," his preface to *Jerusalem*, for example, Blake, echoing Milton's strictures against "the modern bondage of Rhyming," states that "Every word and every letter is studied and put into its fit place: the terrific numbers are reserved for the terrific parts—the mild & gentle, for the mild & gentle parts, and the prosaic, for the inferior parts: all are necessary to each other" (*J*, pl. 3). In the poem itself, the Blakean speaker glosses the meaning of the agonists named by his nomenclature, observing,

(I call them by their English names: English, the rough basement.
Los built the stubborn structure of the Language, acting against
Albions melancholy, who must else have been a Dumb despair.)
   (*J*, pl. 36 [40], ll. 58–60)

But invention in the infernal sense can just as easily mean testing the very limits of appropriateness of ideas for a given audience and occasion by choosing and uttering those ideas, in apparent defiance of the canons of appropriateness, to the end of transforming both the audience and the occasion. The Jesus of sermons, and especially of parables, is Blake's paragon of invention in its infernal sense, but so, too, are the precursor-exemplars of the prophetic line, such as Isaiah and Ezekiel. In words of the former, in *The Marriage of Heaven and Hell* (1790–93), who "was then perswaded. & remain confirm'd; that the voice of honest indignation is the voice of God, I cared not for consequences but wrote" (pl. 12).

Nor is Blake oblivious to one possible etymology of *invention* (*inventio*, from L. *inventus*, pp. discovered, found out). *Ventus* is the Latin word for wind, and invention (or in-vention) for Blake is, in one sense, the subject breathing into the object, that act which recaptures the moment of ensoulment, when God "breathed into his nostrils the breath of life; and man became a living soul" (Genesis 2:7).[29] In this sense, invention is not metaphor but metalepsis—a metaphor for the transferential power of metaphor. The operation of invention in this world is exemplified by the prophetic line, and above all by Jesus, who, by means of continual invention—continually breathing "the breath of life" into the nostrils of a fallen humanity, continually reensouls its members. It is this operation Blake refers to in "To the Public" when he declares, "The Spirit of Jesus is continual forgiveness of Sin" (*J*, pl. 3).

Set free and at large by dint of Los's efforts, invention is figured as "The Breath Divine" (pl. 94, l. 18) at the end of *Jerusalem*. By its operations, this agency reinvents not only Albion but all of his members, as it were, showing these for the inventors that they in turn are. Among the occupants of "The innumerable Chariots of the Almighty [that] appeard in Heaven" near the end of *Jerusalem* are "Bacon & Newton & Locke, & Milton & Shakspear & Chaucer" (pl. 98, ll. 8–9), a trio of would-be natural philosophers and a trio of poets grouped together and seen for the inventors that they ultimately are for Blake.[30] Epiphanic though this moment may be, it too is situated: "Heaven" is, for Blake, no less a place than a state of mind, and in it, under the proper conditions, as Blake states at the end of *The Four Zoas* (1797), "intellectual War The war of swords [is] departed now / The dark Religions are departed & sweet Science reigns" (p. 139, ll. 9–10).

CHAPTER 1

Blake and Newton: Argument as Art, Argument as Science

There has been a good deal of discussion recently, by George S. Rousseau and others, about the status of the relationship between literature and science as modes of discourse.[1] Interestingly enough, much of what has been written about literature and science has been focused on the relationship of the two modes as viewed in the context of the eighteenth century, when the relationship of the two, clearly defined or otherwise, seems to have been the strongest. Problems with defining the status of the relationship seem to have arisen from the variety of its "surface" manifestations. These range from the implicit relationship of book 3 of *Gulliver's Travels* to *Philosophical Transactions of the Royal Society*, so astutely perceived and documented by Marjorie Hope Nicolson,[2] to the highly explicit relationship of Blake's *Milton* to Newton's *Principia*, with which this essay will be principally concerned. But before entering into the substance of the discussion, it would seem proper to raise a question begged by the preceding remarks: On what basis or common ground may literature and science be discussed, with the purpose of understanding their relationship?

One answer to this question is that literature and science may be viewed as artifacts of rhetoric—as arguments, in other words. One who begins from such a view proceeds in the study of the relationship between literature and science with the understanding that, when any argument, either literary or scientific, speaks to the issues raised by another argument with the goal of overturning that other argument, the critical argument in question proceeds from a rhetorical position no less well defined and interested than that of the argument it seeks to overturn. Seen in this perspective, the "General Scholium" of the *Principia* differs from the "conversation" of the "Visionary forms dramatic" that takes place at the end of Blake's *Jerusalem* (pl. 98, ll. 27ff.) not so much in terms of what it argues for as in terms of its refusal to acknowledge its status as argument—with the corollary refusal to acknowledge that what is being said, or argued for, must ultimately be reflexive to the interested position of the person mounting the discussion. Newton, for example, having disposed of the Cartesian model of vortical planetary motion, is not content to rest on his calculations, nor is he content to regard those calculations as evidence brought forth in support of his argument. Instead, by disclaiming any personal interest in elaborating the model of the solar system based on the principle of elliptical rotation, Newton is able to deny that there is any argument on his part in the first place, averring instead that "this most beautiful system of the sun, planets, and comets, could only proceed from the counsel and dominion of an intelligent and powerful Being."[3] This "Being," happily enough for Newton, is also the source of the language and rhetoric that Newton "discovers" for the purpose of propagating his (His?) celestial mechanics, just as Newton "discovers" the system of mechanics itself. Blake's Four Zoas, by way of contrast, do not discover, in their use of language, the space and time that are the parameters of Newton's system. Rather, the Zoas are seen "Creating Space, Creating Time according to the wonders Divine / Of Human Imagination." The consequence, which would be an abhorrence to Newton, with his allied conceptions of absolute time and absolute space, is the "variation of Time & Space / Which vary according as the Organs of Perception vary."[4]

To be sure, many of the eighteenth-century writers active before the 1790s, when Blake came to intellectual and artistic maturity, recognized the rhetorical and ontological status of Newtonian argument as *argum ent*and they evinced a shared concern about the full significance of that argument and the limits to which it might be made, by analogy, to serve in other fields of inquiry. Writers as far apart in politics as Addison and Pope and as far apart in temperament as Desaguliers and Dr. Johnson all had something to say about the impact of Newtonian mechanics and optics and the implications to be derived therefrom, These responses have already been dealt with in several fine studies, including book-length treatments by Nicolson, Richard B. Schwartz, and Margaret C. Jacob, and need only be mentioned here in passing to emphasize the crucial difference between Blake's response to Newton and the responses of English writers before him.[5] Addison, Pope, Desaguliers, Johnson, and others may have disagreed over the extent to which Newtonian physics could, by argument from analogy, be used to help see the "subjective" aspects of the universe in an orderly manner. But these and other writers of the eighteenth century were of one mind concerning the "objective" truth of Newtonian physics *per se*. Pope may have taken issue with Addison over how far Newtonian argument might be extended in the areas of perceptual psychology and political economy, but both writers agreed on the paramount importance of the physics itself to Western thought. And although Johnson may have placed less emphasis on the discovery of physical truths than on the discovery of moral and religious ones, he still considered Newton a model of scientific thought and conduct.[6] Up to Blake's time, the response of eighteenth-century literature to Newtonian science is unanimous in its belief that Newton's mathematics and physics are fully disinterested, inductive, impartial, and authoritative. It is only in the question of how far Newtonian thought might be extended into other spheres of inquiry that there is any real debate.

For Blake, however, the painful and oppressive conditions of human existence, which he viewed as being in part descended from the "reasonable" assumptions of Newtonian physics, translated into Newtonian metaphysics and implemented as social policy, meant that there was something wrong with the physics itself. Blake seems to have understood, as we now do, that the metaphysics might precede the physics as well as follow from it. Accordingly, Blake undertook the critique and demonstration, whose record is to be found throughout the Prophetic Books, especially in *Milton*, a critique and demonstration anticipatory, in the essentials, of the insights set forth by relativity physics concerning the space-time continuum and other matters in the latter physics' correction of the Newtonian model of the universe.[7]

Lest it be objected, however, that the present strategy is to turn Blake into an *ur*-Einstein, the point should be made that Blake's insights about and critique of Newtonian physics—indeed, his critical responses to many of the language-bound activities of the age—owe a good deal to his grasp of the nature and function of language, as well as of how one reads that language. Blake's senses of language and reading depend upon his understanding that all texts, as the artifacts of specific individuals writing in specific contexts of time and place, are rhetorical, or argumentative, and that the situation could not be otherwise, since all language is produced by individuals speaking from positions more or less clearly defined, but always definite.[8] Accordingly, there is no such thing as disinterestedness, only concealed or dissembled interest; no such thing as pure induction, only induction with a concealed or impure hypothesis, usually disguised as an "axiom" or "truth"; no impartiality, only imperfectly revealed partiality; and no authority, only usurped freedom.

Blake's idea of language has been discussed at some length previously by Robert F. Gleckner and this writer. These discussions emphasize that fallen humanity uses a fallen language that is at best partial in its grasp of phenomena and at worst tyrannous in its insistence on the authority of that partial grasp.[9] But neither of the discussions deals with the relationship between language and reading, or with the role of reading as an instrument of language reform. Blake has a vision of how language functions when properly used, and that vision is closely tied to his idea of how one should read. Before turning to the question of how Blake reads and responds to Newtonian language specifically, it might be helpful to develop an understanding, in general terms, of Blake's conception of the relationship between language properly spoken and reading properly practiced.

Blake's most complete account of language properly spoken is found at the end of *Jerusalem*, in his rendering of the "conversation" dealt with briefly above. The Four Zoas

conversed together in Visionary forms dramatic which bright
Redounded from their Tongues in thunderous majesty, in Visions
In new Expanses, creating exemplars of Memory and of Intellect
Creating Space, Creating Time according to the wonders Divine
Of Human Imagination, throughout all the Three Regions immense
Of Childhood, Manhood & Old Age [;] & the all tremendous
   unfathomable Non Ens
Of Death was seen in regenerations terrific or complacent varying
According to the subject of discourse & every Word & Every Character
Was Human according to the Expansion or Contraction, the
   Translucence or
Opakeness of Nervous fibres such was the variation of Time & Space
Which vary according as the Organs of Perception vary. (*J*, pl. 98,
   ll. 28–38)

The language spoken by the Four Zoas creates what it refers to rather than merely describing something thought to have been created previously. "Exemplars of Memory and of Intellect," up to and including space and time themselves, are created in the course of such speech. But the overall qualities of any given "exemplar" are entirely reflexive to the qualities of the speaker in question: "Human Imagination," the speaker's age, "the subject of discourse," and the variables having to do with differences in "the Organs of Perception" from speaker to speaker. In a "conversation" of the sort described by Blake, no one speaker lays claim to, or is accorded, the authority that would make that speaker's position the only "right" or "reasonable" one among other "wrong" or "unreasonable" alternatives. Authoritative meaning under such circumstances is comprehensive meaning, which takes the form of a living body of utterance, augmented by each additional utterance but never completed by it. Thus the sense of the verb *redounded*, as Blake uses it, meaning in the context of *Jerusalem*, pl. 98, "to add, yield, cause to accrue."[10]

In order to use language as the Four Zoas do at the end of *Jerusalem*, it is necessary to relinquish the coercive authority implicit in point of view and usually identified in Blake's lexicon as *selfhood*. Selfhood is Blake's cardinal sin, replacing the more usual pride and posing a threat to the individual far greater than might be posed by pride alone, since selfhood is an amalgam of pride and deceit that denies the existence of that very pride, a powerful amalgam indeed. As Albion faces the prospect of putting off his selfhood, for example, he comments on the powerful bond between pride and deceit, a bond that gives the resultant selfhood the power of a mighty army.

> O Lord what can I do! My Selfhood cruel
> Marches against thee deceitful from Sinai & from Edom
> Into the Wilderness of Judah to meet thee in his pride. (*J*, pl. 96, ll. 8–10)

Albion must put off selfhood to be united with the paragon of selfless energy, Jesus. The goal of doing so is one proposed by Blake for all of creation in the Greek epigraph to *Jerusalem*, μόνος ὅ Ιεσους (Jesus alone), and describes as occurring at the end of the epic, when the triumphant "All Human Forms identified" is pronounced and those forms are described as "Awaking in his [i.e. Jesus'] Bosom in the Life of Immortality" (*J*, pl. 99, ll. 1, 4).

As Enitharmon notes slightly earlier in the poem, the putting off of selfhood must necessarily entail the repudiation of Bacon, Newton, Locke, and others like them—those who worship a "natural" order they both have created and have refused to take responsibility for creating.

> We shall not die! we shall be united in Jesus.
> Will you suffer this Satan this Body of Doubt that Seems but Is Not
> To occupy the very threshold of Eternal Life. if Bacon, Newton, Locke,
> Deny a Conscience in Man & the Communion of Saints & Angels
> Contemning the Divine Vision & Fruition, Worshiping the Deus
> Of the Heathen, The God of This World, & the Goddess Nature
> Mystery Babylon the Great, the Druid Dragon & hidden Harlot[,]
> Is it not the Signal of the Morning which was told us in the Beginning.
>   (*J*, pl. 93, ll. 19–26)

How does one go about repudiating those who not only champion the empirical mode of observation and the argument by induction, but also worship the horrible Antichrist under its several names and guises? Blake's answer is that one reads the texts produced by these and other usurpers—all texts, for that matter—in what he calls the "infernal or diabolical sense." This reading strategy is described in *The Marriage of Heaven and Hell*.

The speaker of Blake's mixed-media polemic has just shown an "Angel" that the Gospels, although written by men of genius about a man of genius,[11] have been misread consistently because of the interpositions of the priesthood in the reading process. These interpositions have perverted Christianity, until it has become an organized religion along typically tradition-bound lines.

> . . . a system was formed, which some took advantage of & enslav'd the vulgar by attempting to realize or abstract mental deities from their objects; thus began Priesthood.
> Choosing forms of worship from poetic tales.
> And at length they pronounced that the Gods had orderd such things.
> Thus men forgot that All deities reside in the human breast. (*MHH*, pl. 11)

In the sense that both are attempts to exercise spiritual sovereignty in the name of an absent, originary "other," priesthood and selfhood are synonymous. Both are interested points of view that pretend to disinterestedness, calling on "Jehovah," "Nature," or suchlike to bear witness to the impartiality with which they hold sway. Both priesthood and selfhood are in fact argumentative positions that deny the existence of any argument whatsoever, in light of their self-image of authoritativeness and permanence.

Priesthood and selfhood have their antithesis in the authentic voice of religious vision, that of the prophet. The nature of the antithesis is made clear in Blake's account of a "dinner conversation" with Isaiah and Ezekiel, in which Blake asks the two prophets why they should not be charged with the same crime of selfhood attributed to the priests. Isaiah answers that he "was then perswaded, & remain[s] confirm'd; that the voice of honest indignation is the voice of God, I cared not for the consequences but wrote" (pl. 12). Thus emerges the doctrine of "firm perswasion," which furnishes a useful gloss on Blake's statement, also in *The Marriage*, "that all deities reside in the human breast" (pl. 11). As a state of mind, "firm perswasion" is characteristic not only of Isaiah and Ezekiel but of the Four Zoas at the end of *Jerusalem* as well. In such a state, the fact that language is always argument, always coming from an interested position, is openly acknowledged, and the creative, verbal energy liberated by that very acknowledgment is of a magnitude comparable to that of the Zoas as they create and recreate space and time in their respective images. Blake inquires as to the potential for such energy through the acknowledgment of one's interested position, and Isaiah tells him that there is no reality without that acknowledgement.

Then I asked: does a firm perswasion that a thing is so, make it so?
He replied. All poets believe that it does, & in ages of imagination this
firm perswasion removed mountains; but many are not capable of a firm
perswasion of any thing. (*MHH*, pl. 12)

Reading in "the infernal or diabolical sense" proceeds on the understanding that the primary difference between prophecy (inspired poetry) and the literature of doubt ("philosophy," "rational discourse," "dogma," etc.) is that the former affirms, even celebrates, its "perswasion," or interested position, while the latter denies the very existence of such a position. Blake's venture in reading, then, is to "converse" with the text in order to locate and identify the human form responsible for producing it and its point of view. This venture is made clear in *The Marriage* and even clearer in Blake's Annotations of various authors, where his designedly ad hominem stance is aimed at producing from behind his words the writer who has refused to take full responsibility for the substance and implications of his text. "Conversing" in this context is Blake's reading strategy for prophecy and the literature of doubt alike, for the locus of rhetorical interest in each is alike in its need for elaboration and clarification. Blake therefore reads prophecy and the literature of doubt in precisely the same way, and in each case he fully acknowledges the status of his own discourse in the process of doing so. With specific reference to Blake's reading of Newton, it should be noted that Blake's adversary position is not held with the hope of "destroying" Newton. Blake acknowledges the power of the scientist's intellect; moreover, he wishes to "save" the intellect in much the same way that he wishes to "save" Milton's creative genius: by having both Newton and Milton acknowledge that their texts are the creations of a self-interested position, then having them cast off the selfhood that ordains and disguises the self-interest inherent in the position.

Blake does indeed "save" Newton in much the same way that he "saves" Milton. In the case of the latter, the process of this "salvation" is clearly chronicled in the brief epic that bears his name. In the case of Newton, however, the process is less clear, being carried forward by means of what might be termed "Christian association": the use of Christlike, visionary avatars, whose putting off of selfhood is done both for their own good and, by example, for the good of others. Milton functions as one such avatar for Newton, as does Albion, who functions in this capacity for Milton and Newton alike. Near the end of *Jerusalem*, shortly after Albion has confronted Jesus and participated in the "Mysterious / Offering of Self for Another" (pl. 96, ll. 20–21), the time of the fallen world ends, and all those immured in that time reappear in their eternal forms. "The innumerable Chariots of the Almighty appeard in Heaven / and Bacon & Newton & Locke, & Milton & Shakspear & Chaucer" (pl. 98, ll. 8–9).

Salvation of the sort Blake practices and preaches depends upon criticism, the sort of "Opposition" that "is true Friendship" (*MHH*, pl. 20). Blake's criticism of Newtonian physics is one instance among many of Blake's friendly opposition to what he conceives of as deluded thinking. At this point it is time to turn to an examination of Blake's criticism of Newton, in order to see how well the former understands the latter's physics and metaphysics. If Blake's criticism is to be considered cogent, it may be so only if his understanding is equal to Newton's, in much the same way that the unceasing "Mental Fight" that Blake announces in *Milton* (pl. 1, l. 13) must occur between equally matched antagonists if it is to be successful in redeeming them from error.

The evidence for Blake's having read widely and deeply in Newtonian literature is extensive, both in Blake's own writing and in discussions of it by Donald D. Ault and F. B. Curtis, among others.[12] There is accordingly no need to reargue the issue of Blake's degree of familiarity with Newtonian thought. What does need to be argued, however, is that Blake's reading of Newton led him to focus on the *Principia* as much if not more so than on the *Optics*, the primary source of Newtonian thought for Blake, according to Ault and Nicolson before him.[13] The importance of Blake's knowledge of the *Principia* for the creation of *Milton* will be demonstrated in the discussion below. A general reason for such having been the case may be ventured at this point, however. The reason "that the English poets who wrote about science in the eighteenth century put greater emphasis on the *Principia* than on the *Optics*," according to William Powell Jones, is that "the poets knew . . . that Newton had mathematically demonstrated the order of the universe. . . . They used this idea over and over in numerous variations, not only when they mentioned Newton by name but when, in their illustrations of various branches of science they devoted more space to celestial order . . . than to the physics of light and color."[14] It is precisely on this issue of celestial order—where ideas of it come from and what force they ought and do have—that Blake confronts Newton. Blake's understanding is that such "celestial order" is in fact the order of Newton's mind, projected outward and argued for subtly but powerfully for the purpose of compelling the very consensus of opinion commented on by Jones.

As Blake assesses it, the net effect of the Newtonian argument in the *Principia* is to create the universe in Newton's image, an act of creation for which Newton refuses to take responsibility, assigning it instead to a God with whom Newton and no one else is able to communicate on an intimate, father-son basis.[15] It is in response to this Newtonian move and all the implications to be derived from it that Blake frames the narrative of *Milton*, in which the poem's namesake must fight off not only the implications of the Newtonian model of the universe, but also the implications of the continuing cast of mind that is always ready to fabricate such models. That cast of mind may be viewed in the context of a tradition that embodies it, a tradition known as the *prisca sapientia*, or *prisca theologia*, and discussed by Ault in relation to Blake.[16] This tradition of ancient or pristine wisdom or theology is what Blake has in mind when he derides "The Stolen and Perverted Writings of Homer & Ovid: of Plato & Cicero. Which all Men ought to contemn" (*M*, pl. 1). Milton's goal in condemning this ancient tradition is to be reunited with his "emanation," Ololon, who represents space just as Milton represents time. Ololon, for example, is described as being "Six-fold" (*M*, pl. 2, ll. 19), a multiple unique to her in all of Blake's number symbolism, at least in part because Blake associates her spatialized being with Newton's conception of the six primary planets.[17] Seen in a larger frame, the reuniting of Ololon with Milton is but one in a series of similar reunions, including those of Enitharmon with Los, Vala with Luvah, and Jerusalem with Albion, the overall purpose being to reunite fallen time, which Blake sees as being male, with fallen space, which Blake sees as being female and somehow being "generated" by time. Out of this multiple reconstitution of the space-time continuum Blake hopes to see established conditions under which space and time, energy and matter, approach identity at the speed of light itself.[18]

But any such reconstitution must begin with a taking stock of what conditions are like in the fallen world and how they have come to pass. Blake does so in *Milton* by retelling the story of the Creation, which he had told several times previously, for example, in *The Book of Urizen* and *The Four Zoas* (1794, 1797). Implicit in such a retelling is the awareness that the Creation and Fall have been as fully multiple as the reconstitution that corrects them must be. For Blake, the story of the Creation is the story of a fall into finitude, brought about by the sort of God Newton talks about in the "General Scholium" of the *Principia*. Creation in *Milton* begins when Los, Blake's avatar for all poets and prophets, is unable to "identify" Urizen, whom Ault associates with Newton,[19] such "identification" being a matter of giving Urizen an eternal form or an eternal name.

> Los siezd his Hammer & Tongs; he labourd at his resolute Anvil
> Among indefinite Druid rocks & snows of doubt & reasoning.
> Refusing all Definite Form, the Abstract Horror roofd. stony hard
> And a first Age passed over & a State of dismal woe! (*M*, pl. 3, ll. 7–10)

Urizen's "Refusing all Definite Form" cuts at least two ways, given the Newtonian background of *Milton*. On the more obvious level, Urizen is Newton's God, "utterly void of all body and bodily figure" (*Principia*, 545). But on a subtler level, Blake's description—or non-description—goes right to the core of the Newtonian argument. Blake senses the relationship between the attributes of Newton's God and the habits of Newton's thought. "Refusing all Definite Form" is also a gibing reference to Newton's claim to "frame no hypotheses" (*Principia*, 545). Blake, who by his own account knew how to read Latin tolerably well by 1803, seems to have in mind a pun on the Latin original of Newton's statement about framing hypotheses: "*hypothese non fingo*."[20] "I frame no hypotheses" is an adequate translation of the Latin, but it is by no means the only adequate one. *Fingo* may mean "to form" or "to frame" in the sense usually understood of Newton, but two other translations of the verb are also possible on the basis of the definitions of the Latin root, which discuss it in terms "of the plastic art, to *form* or *fashion by art . . . to mould or model*, as a statuary," and "with the access. notion of untruth, to alter, change, for the purpose of dissembling."[21]

The net effect of such a pun is to show that Newton's God and Newton are one and the same, and that a God who refuses definite form is the creation of a man who dissembles about the fact that he has created God in his own image and refuses to acknowledge the responsibility for exercising the creative initiative that would lead him to do so, since by the standards of such a mind being found out would mean being caught lying, not caught in the act of creating art. This particular set of circumstances accounts for Urizen's continual disavowal, here and elsewhere throughout the Prophetic Books, of form. It also accounts for the confrontation that occurs later in *Milton* proper, in which Milton marches against Urizen at the River Arnon and attempts to give him form through the sculptorly act of molding to his formless bones the red clay of Succoth (pls. 19–20). Urizen must realize his own full presence, of body as well as of mind, before he can experience the full presence of the God he creates—and realize that such a God is only as powerful and good as its creator. The applicable text, from Blake's "The Everlasting Gospel," is "Thou art a Man God is no more / Thy own humanity learn to adore" (pp. 52–54, ll. 71–72).

A far cry from the Four Zoas who, at the end of *Jerusalem*, freely create space and time in their own images with dazzling rapidity, Urizen/Newton denies responsibility for creating what is "out there," much as Newton before him had denied responsibility for the hypothesis that placed God, invisible, at the center of a universe composed of very visible, very dead, atomistic matter. Somehow, even though he wishes to disavow any knowledge of or responsibility for it, creation—or anticreation—of a universe of dead matter centered by a materialistic sun possessed of invisible force(s) is a direct result of Urizen's refusal to assume form. After the "first Age," in which Urizen is characterized as "Refusing all Definite Form,"

> Down sunk with fright a red round Globe hot burning. deep
> Deep down into the Abyss. panting: conglobing: trembling
> And a second Age passed over & a State of dismal woe.
> (*M*, pl. 3, ll. 11–13)

Because he disavows any responsibility for voluntarily creating a centered, materialistic universe, Urizen suffers the fate of all Blake's self-denying artificers who refuse to take responsibility for their creations: the process appears to be reversed, and the created appears to have created the creator. Nor will the creator correct this misapprehension, owing to his ulterior motives. Thus Urizen/Newton postulates a universe that is centered by "a round red Globe hot burning," denies responsibility for doing so, and instead appears to become what he beholds, his organs of vision appearing to have been formed by the sun at the center of that postulated universe, when that sun in fact has been looked into place by eyes that do the bidding of a will. And that will exercises a *fiat* every bit as powerful, within its own sphere, as the first such *fiat: fiat lux.*

> Rolling round into two little Orbs & closed in two little Caves
> The Eyes beheld the Abyss: lest bones of solidness freeze over all
> And a third Age passed over & a State of dismal woe. (*M*, pl. 3, ll. 14–16)

The "creation," which is in fact a fall into a state of fragmented materialism, continues apace. Urizen/Newton's failure to assume responsibility for framing the first hypothesis causes the division of the creative consciousness into a fragmented, materialistic world "out there" and five contracted senses with which to perceive it. Stunned momentarily by doubt, Los believes that the "creation" taking place "out there" has a spiritual as well as a material reality. His doubt leads to Los's recapitulation, willy-nilly, of the fall of Urizen into generation. With no sense, momentarily, of his own creative energy, no sense that voids and absolute space exist only for those who do not fill them with plenitude by perceiving *through* them to the infinite, Los becomes fearful. As Blake elsewhere notes, "One thought fills immensity" (*MHH*, pl. 8, l. 36). But when fear leads the individual to cease thinking creatively, the process reverses and immensity fills the thinker. In this particular case, instead of Los filling the void, the void fills Los, fragmenting him into the fallen categories of Newtonian space and time.

> Terrified Los stood in the Abyss & his immortal limbs
> Grew deadly pale: he became what he beheld: for a red
> Round Globe sunk down from his Bosom into the Deep in pangs
> He hoverd over it trembling & weeping. suspended it shook
> The nether Abyss in tremblings. he wept over it, he cherish'd it
> In deadly sickening pain: till separated into a Female pale
> As the cloud that brings the snow: all the while from his Back

31

A blue fluid exuded in Sinews hardening in the Abyss
Till it separated into a Male Form howling in Jealousy.
(*M*, pl. 3, ll. 28–36)

The "Female pale" is Enitharmon. She is "pale," as is Los, because of an act of self-deception fundamental to the process of "creation" in which both are involved. When the void fills and fragments Los, it causes him to fragment into his likeness. Paleness in Blake usually connotes desire restrained or repressed.[22] In restraining his creative energies, Los does not totally abdicate his role as a creator—no more than Urizen/ Newton does, in fact. Instead, Los creates Enitharmon in the image of his restrained desire—pale creator, pale creation. His "trembling & weeping" are also symptomatic of the creative drive sublimated, and these symptoms are likewise passed along in the creation of a female who shakes "the nether Abyss in tremblings."

The creation/fragmentation that occurs leads Los to believe that he and Enitharmon are separated by some insurmountable obstacle, a "Male Form howling in Jealousy." Like Enitharmon, however, this male form is the creation of Los's own mind and body and is separated from Los when, because of fear, he refuses to do anything to halt or control the fragmentation. In this particular case, the specter that is created bears a striking resemblance to Newtonian absolute space, a resemblance that is hardly accidental. The idea of "A blue fluid . . . hardening in the Abyss" is derived from at least two of Newton's concealed axioms concerning the nature of space. The first of these states "*That the centre of the system of the world is immovable*" (p. 419), that is, that absolute space is rigid.[23] The second of these states that "the matter of the heavens is fluid" (*Principia*, 549). The fact that the *locus maledictus* of Los's activity is described alternately as an abyss or a void has to do with Newton's description of absolute space as being "void of resistance" (*Principia*, 68). Space, absolute or otherwise, of course appears to be blue to the earthbound observer.

Los assumes, as Newton seems to assume, that all the materialistic fragmentation he encounters is "really" going on "out there," that is, that it arises because of an external, "natural" cause that is responsible for all instances of fragmentation, perceived as external, "natural" effect. In doing so, Los is only being "reasonable," in the sense of following the line of logic laid down by Newton in the "Rules of Reasoning in Philosophy" that preface the third book of the *Principia*.[24] The result of Los's being "reasonable" on the basis of his assumptions is bitterly humorous. Believing the cause to be external and doubting his ability to stem the fragmentation, the deluded Los makes fragmentation the law of the universe, using a distinctly Newtonian style of inductive reasoning to do so. And in his longing and lusting after Enitharmon as a discrete being forever fragmented and apart from him, Los participates in the further fragmentation of the universe, by begetting on Enitharmon children who add to the force of the "selfhood explosion," by means of which the universe is populated with discrete little bodies, which are, at least in this context, Blake's visionary rendering of what is implied by Newton's corpuscular theory of matter. A corpuscle is, in the root sense of the Latin, a little body. The irony underlying the whole of Los's project is that he causes additional fragmentation in the very attempt, albeit a deluded one, to end the process by somehow transcending and comprehending what is already deployed in the depths of spectral, rigid, absolute space.

> Within labouring. beholding Without: from Particulars to Generals
> Subduing his Spectre, they builded the Looms of Generation
> They Builded Great Golgonooza Times on Times Ages on Ages
> First Orc was Born then the Shadowy Female: then all Los's Family
> At last Enitharmon brought Forth Satan Refusing Form, in vain
> The Miller of Eternity made subservient to the Great Harvest
> That he may go to his own Place Prince of the Starry Wheels
> (*M*, pl. 3, ll. 37–43)

The reference to the idea of moving "from Particulars to Generals" is Blake's gibing allusion to Newtonian inductive method and summary of it as it, for example, *generalizes*, in the "Rules of Reasoning in Philosophy," about the particular, or particle-like, nature of matter. In the third rule, which seems to be the one Blake has explicitly in mind, Newton uses the inductive method to conclude that "the hardness of the whole arises from the hardness of the parts, we therefore justly infer the hardness of the undivided particles not only of the bodies we feel but of all others" (*Principia*, 399).

Satan's refusal of form is a trait that helps the reader trace his lineage back to Urizen/Newton, as indeed Los and Enitharmon do later in *Milton*, when they discover that "Satan is Urizen / Drawn down by Orc & the Shadowy Female into Generation" (*M*, pl. 10, ll. 1–2). The fact that Satan is the lastborn of Los and Enitharmon's children is significant, in the sense that his birth indicates that the limits of "particularization," of fragmentation, have been reached. As the "Miller of Eternity," Satan, who is also the most finely ground grist of his "mill," has witnessed, both in the creation of his own body and that of the world as the body-image he sees from it, the matter of the fallen world divided as finely as it can be divided. Henceforth, in Blake's theater of visionary action, the forces of particularization and fragmentation are to be made "subservient to the Great Harvest," made to look inward into living, visionary space, rather than outward into dead, Newtonian space. In so doing, all "human forms" will be "identified" and will therefore be able to put off that corpuscular identity which is selfhood. Under such circumstances, seemingly dead corpuscles will be perceived as actually being living seeds, which throw off their dead husks to become grapes and grain, which in turn throw off their individual identities, in the winepress and the mill, to become wine and bread, which in turn give up their identities in a massive and progressive Eucharist. Ultimately, all of creation becomes the flesh and blood of one body, the one seen at the end of *Jerusalem* walking "To & fro in Eternity as One Man reflecting each in each & clearly seen / And seeing" (pl. 98, ll. 39–40). The task of bringing this Eucharist to pass is the task of all of Blake's visionary avatar-heroes, Milton, Los, and Albion among them.

Until such a putting off of selfhood is made to occur, however, Satan presides over all that is to be annihilated, known as the world of the Ulro, an "ultimate ratio" of dead particles acted upon by blind forces, both particles and forces in fact being reflexive to the wills of their self-effacing, self-deceiving creators. Satan's "own place," the very phrase commenting on the solipsistic nature of such a place by echoing Satan's speech in *Paradise Lost*,[25] is that of the presiding spirit, "Prince of the Starry Wheels." This title is yet another gibing reference to the Newtonian model of the universe, in which planets, moons, and comets revolve around "fixed stars" in circular or elliptical orbits, making their motion seem wheel-like. The proprietary role connoted by the phrase "own Place" should also serve to indicate that Satan, rather than being merely the superintendent of these "Starry Wheels," is their creator as well.

The particularization and fragmentation of the universe will never be more complete in any of Blake's other poems than it is at the end of the third plate of *Milton*. It is at this point that affairs begin to reverse, with the recognition, by Los, of Satan's true identity: the latter is the Supreme Being Newton refers to in the "General Scholium," the God Newton creates in his own image through the use of concealed hypotheses and assumptions, all the while denying the existence of these hypotheses and assumptions and asserting that the will has no role in promulgating his view of the matter. In a flash of insight, Los identifies his multifaceted yet unitary enemy as Satan/Newton/the God of Natural Religion/ Locke's God revealed by Reason/Urizen.

> O Satan my youngest born, art thou not Prince of the Starry Hosts
> And of the Wheels of Heaven, to turn the Mills day & night?
> Art thou not Newtons Pantocrator weaving the Woof of Locke[?]
>   (*M*, pl. 4, ll. 9–11)

The identification of Satan as "Newtons Pantocrator" is a direct reference to the "General Scholium," in which Newton has occasion to talk of a "Being" who "governs all things, not as the soul of the world, but as Lord over all; and on account of his dominion he is wont to be called *Lord God* παντοκράτωρ, or *Universal Ruler*; for God is a relative word, and has a respect to servants; and *Deity* is the dominion of God not over his own body, as those imagine who fancy God to be the soul of the world, but over servants" (*Principia*, 544). The relevance of the idea of "Newtons Pantocrator" in a poem about Milton has to do with Blake's critique of Milton's allegiances in *Paradise Lost*, given in full in *The Marriage of Heaven and Hell* (pl. 5). In that critique, Blake argues that Milton mistook the real Satan, in all of his dissembling humility, for God, who was actually immanent not in Heaven but in the energy of the fallen angels and in the realm of art they created by dint of that energy. The reason that Milton, Los, and Blake himself are all walking about in the "Eternity" (l. 16) that frames *Milton* is to begin the task that culminates in the announcement of "All Human Forms identified" at the end of *Jerusalem*. The first step of that task seems to entail calling a pantocrator a pantocrator, thus identifying covert selfhood.

In one important sense, though Milton may have initially been deluded in his allegiances, he saw clearly enough that the Fall was fortunate. For it did lead Adam to turn his gaze from the outer world, which begins to fragment at the very moment that the angels fall, to the inner world, which may be retained as a paradise inviolate, notwithstanding the vicissitudes of "natural," external change. Adam and Eve do have to experience the self-hood that comes from the eating of forbidden fruit in order to realize the limits one faces in attempting to look outward for coherence. The outer world is a realm of fragmentation and particularization; it is the Hell depicted by Milton in book 2 of *Paradise Lost.*

> . . . many a Frozen, many a Fiery Alp,
> Rocks, Caves, Lakes, Fens, Bogs, Dens, and shades of death,
> A Universe of death. (51.620–22)

Outward lies a "Universe of death"; inward lies something else entirely. Surrounded by that universe as the result of eating the forbidden fruit, Adam, at the behest of Michael, looks inward and sees the deeds of all time spread out before him. As the result of this perception, Adam realizes the delusory nature of fallen time and fragmentation, and he heeds Michael's injunctions in the hope of possessing "A Paradise within . . . happier farr" (12.587) than the materialist Paradise he is about to leave.

Insight plays the crucial role in Adam's realization, as it does in the realizations of Milton, Los, and Blake. Jehovah the tempter must get into Adam and Eve, be ingested as the apple in what is essentially an "anti-Eucharist," in order to force them to look outward with his point of view and see the fragmentation that he sees. Similarly, Urizen must get into Milton, Satan must get into Los, and Newton must get into Blake, the last of these, at least, by means of reading, which is but another form of ingestion, witness Blake's reading of/dining with Isaiah and Ezekiel in *The Marriage.* But whereas Isaiah and Ezekiel are "wholesome," in the sense that their "firm perswasion" on issues vouchsafes against the possibility of any deception on their part, Urizen, Satan, and Newton are not "wholesome," in the sense that they do practice deception in the name of reason. One of Blake's "Proverbs of Hell" is to the point: "All wholsom food is caught without a net or a trap" (*MHH*, pl. 7, l. 13). The nature of the "poisonous" reason in question is to impose, with few or no symptoms, an alien point of view on the victim, under the guise of being "natural," thus substituting the selfhood of the "poisoner" for that of the "poisoned" and "killing" the "poisoned" individual, as is the case in "A Poison Tree."[26]

Accordingly, when Los "identifies" Satan, or when Milton and Blake do the same thing to Urizen and Newton, respectively, two steps are involved. The first of these has to do with the recognition that the figure "identified" is seen to be *outside* only because he has "poisoned," or gotten *inside*, his victim. Los sees Satan as "Newton's Pantocrator" because Satan has managed to put that "Pantocrator" *inside* Los by "poisoning" him, either with food for the body or food for the mind, if in fact a distinction can be made between the two in the world of symbolic action of Blake's poetry.

The second step involved in "identifying" Satan has to do with replacing the "poison" of another selfhood's imposing its views on its victim with the healthy food of self-nurture. Only by this means can one freely create the world in one's own image and then merge in full plenitude and likeness with that image.

Thus it is, at the point when fragmentation has reached its utmost limit and Satan is "identified" by Los, that Blake, by means of a marvelous transposition, is able to turn the dead and potentially "poisonous" Newtonian corpuscles into living seeds of the life of humanity to come. At a later point in *Milton*, Los will be able to proclaim the plenitude of those seeds, harvested as grain and grape, the stuff of bread and wine, flesh and blood. "Fellow Labourers! The Great Vintage & Harvest is now upon Earth / The whole extent of the Globe is explored" (pl. 25 [27], ll. 17–18). But at the outset of the struggle in *Milton*, the outcome seems very much in doubt. The seeds of the humanity to come must be made to grow, which means that they must be regarded and responded to as though there were a life force within their apparently lifeless exteriors, a life force in need of liberation and nurture. Only in such a manner can the collective power of the life force within be revealed, and only in such a manner can that collective life force merge so as to liberate its full apocalyptic energy, "To go forth," as Milton does at the end of the poem bearing his name, "to the Great Harvest & Vintage of the Nations" (*M*, pl. 43 [50], l. 1).

CHAPTER 2

Blake and
Anti-Newtonian Thought:
The Problem with
Prescriptive Thought

William Blake rejects the proposition that human understanding arises from dialectical logic. Faced with the question of whether to give pride of place to opposites, the practitioner of dialectical logic would proceed by assuming that a given instance is either emotional or rational, personal or universal, spiritual or material. Blake, on the other hand, would proceed by assuming that a given instance is both emotional and rational, personal and universal, spiritual and material. As he claims in "The Grey Monk," "a Tear is an intellectual Thing" (*CCP*, p. 489, l. 29). That is, among other implications of the passage, the dialectical method at best yields a half truth and at worst falsifies reality.

In the pursuit of a rational, universal, materialist understanding of reality, prescriptive thought attempts to deny the emotional, personal, and spiritual dimension of understanding through a strategy of marginalization and repression. In his letter of 11 October 1801 to Thomas Butts, Blake resists the strategy by discussing how the world prescribed by Newton and other materialists feels to the individual who lives in it: "Bacon &

Newton would prescribe ways of making the world heavier to me & Pitt would prescribe distress for a medicinal potion. but as none on Earth can give me a Mental Distress, & I know that all Distress inflicted by Heaven is a Mercy. a Fig for all Corporeal Such Distress is My mock & scorn" (716).

Clearly, Blake discredits the authority of the Newtonian model of matter, motion, and force, which explains phenomena as the result of force (*vis*) impinging on a body that either is a corpuscle (L. "little body") or is composed of such corpuscles.[1] Yet though he repudiates that model, Blake recognizes the seductive power of its half truths and imagines the effect of taking them for the whole truth. The choice of "Corporeal" over *corpuscular* suggests his awareness that the Newtonian model involves a metaphor originating with the body—a desire-motivated "bodying forth" of much the same sort that Giambattista Vico attributes to the "greater gentes."[2] The "Distress" results from denying the emotional and personal dimension. To "prescribe" in Blake's sense is to preempt the autonomy of the imagination in the name of "reason," "common sense," or "God's truth." To impose one's own model of corpuscular (or "Corporeal") matter on someone else is not only to impose the metaphor's physical "reality" but also to deny the emotional and personal dimension.

And yet Newton's model does have an emotional, personal, and spiritual dimension as well as a rational, universal, and material one—it cannot be otherwise. Indeed, all language-bound constructs are in some measure emotional, personal, spiritual, and ultimately fictive—inspired fabulations we use to talk (and write) the world and our origins in it into a provisional coherence.[3] Because Blake recognizes the personal dimension in tbe constructs of others, as well as the primacy of the inspired individual, he asserts that "none on Earth can give me Mental Distress." He understands the damaging emotional, personal, and spiritual consequences of Newton's prescriptive vision for the individual who fails to see it for the half truth, or "Single vision," that it is (*CPP*, p. 722, l. 88).

Yet even though a strong anti-Newtonian position arose during the Enlightenment, and even though its adherents stressed the primacy of immanence "bodied forth" as form—be it linguistic form or some other sort—Blake was, as an anti-Newtonian, swimming against the main current of his age, albeit in the distinguished company of Leibniz, Vico, Herder, Goethe, and others. However, Blake's response was not merely a reaction to a "reasonable" account of the world and its workings. Even if one holds that the Newtonian synthesis constitutes such an account, it manifests some notable shortcomings, both as metaphysics and as science. As described by Hans Eichner, shortcomings of the former sort include the failure to account for the "intractability of evil in a world assumed to be basically unchangeable, the . . . interaction of mind and matter, and the problem of free will."[4] Shortcomings of the latter kind include a failure to account for phenomena such as electricity, magnetism, chemical reactions, and life itself.

Indeed, Newton himself is mindful of both sorts of short-comings. He closes the *Principia* (1687; trans. 1729) by alluding to "a certain most subtle spirit which pervades and lies hid in all gross bodies" and is responsible for various phenomena, ranging from how "the particles of bodies attract each other at near distances" to how "the members of animal bodies move at the command of the will." Newton claims, however, that "these are things that cannot be explained in a few words, nor are we furnished with that sufficiency of experiments which is required to an accurate determination and demonstration of the laws by which this electric and elastic spirit operates."[5]

HOMO CORPUSCULANS IN THE EIGHTEENTH CENTURY

Living in a Newtonian universe was, as Blake suggests, "heavy" going—all matter, motion, and force, and little or no (en)lightening spirit—even for those who subscribed to the premises and explanations of Newtonianism. Moreover, the going got heavier as the century wore on. Newtonian explanations "settled" issues in fields as apparently unrelated as history, physiology, and psychology with presumptive justification, as each discourse identified causes and effects and studied the relationship of the two.[6] The Newtonian model was the model for explaining how "things happen" in that universe of cause and effect.

But such explanations also had a surprising currency in the more nearly "humanistic" realm of literature, where affect no less than effect was a salient concern. Even its staunchest supporters recognized that the Newtonian model barely conceals an abject view of humanity. Confined to a little body that is itself composed of "little bodies" (i.e., corpuscles), the individual is severely limited in any aspirations toward unmediated knowledge or transcendence. Viewed from the perspective of "Superior Beings" such as Newton's "Lord God *Pantokrator*," human beings have more in common with the apes than with those ethereal beings who inhabit absolute space. Not even Newton himself is exempt from the dilemma of inhabiting the fallen universe whose laws he has formulated. Pope, another "little body" as well as a confirmed Newtonian, observes in his *Essay on Man* (1733–34) that

> Superior Beings, when of late they saw
> A mortal Man unfold all Nature's Law,
> Admir'd such Wisdom in an earthly Shape,
> And shew'd a NEWTON as we show an Ape.[7]

"Little bodies" have nothing intrinsic except the five irreducible properties of extension, hardness, impenetrability, mobility, and inertia,[8] and are subject to no immanent cause; they exist at the pleasure of the large forces that move them and that of the creator that made them.[9] Such bodies move for purposes totally unknowable to the individuals who inhabit them.

Even a steadfast Newtonian such as Pope has problems with the Newtonian mind-body model. The fit of the model is questionable. How does such a mind govern the body as the "Lord God *Pantokrator*" governs the material universe, or even as force governs matter? If both mind and body are made up of matter, does predicating a mind endowed with priority, volition, and cognitive awareness imply an anomaly, a conflict between embodied human force and the disembodied forces to which all bodies, living or otherwise, are subject? The very existence of the human mind is troublesome, creating doubt where it might create certainty, ambiguity where it might create knowledge, frustration where it might create calm.

Taken to its extreme in the latter part of the century, the discomfort manifested by a Pope (and other poets) in response to living in a Newtonian world becomes the despair of a Cowper, for whom the Newtonian model fails to explain not only the relationship of mind to body but optical phenomena as well. William Cowper's *Truth* (1781) implicitly questions the nature of optical illusion. If light is composed of corpuscular particles propagated at a material point source, how does one account for such aberrations as mirages, for which no readily discernible point source exists? Furthermore, if appearance is at odds with reality, might it not be the case that basing human action on faith in God's providential workings is a mistake, and that the mind, acting on the basis of mirages, may be anything but providentially informed? Finally, if the mind acting on the basis of appearance is mistaken, to what extent is the very assumption of a providentially ordered universe itself mistaken?

For Blake, the entire range of theodical time is immanent in every moment of lived experience and is thereby accessible to the inspired individual. Since Blake views himself as writing in a tradition of inspired prophecy, he chooses the "inside" journey as the means of pursuing the durable truths that only God can ordain. As a source, that God exists for Blake prior to any "givers" or "rules of reasoning" characteristic of the Newtonian universe of matter, motion, and force, up to and including such apparently stable entities as matter, space, time, and the very language used to describe them. Blake is talking of an immanent cause prior to the body—indeed, prior to the "artery" that runs through that body—and prior to the poet's attempt to render it figuratively. And yet this prior entity contains within itself the potential for the immanent constitution of all variety and all forms, everything possible within the six thousand years of the Judeo-Christian theodicy delimited by Bishop Ussher. This ordering of priorities aligns Blake with such anti-Newtonian thinkers as Vico and Johann Gottfried Herder, and it provides a basis for understanding Blake's even more radical position.

THE GHOST IN THE "ROUGH BASEMENT": AN INSPIRED "STUBBORN STRUCTURE"

In the lines from *Jerusalem* (1804–20) referring to "the stubborn structure of the Language," Blake characterizes his own English as "the rough basement" that is the only alternative to "Dumb despair." He thereby suggests that for him, as for Vico and Herder, language is the basis of human knowledge and that metaphor, as typified by the metaphor *English–rough basement*, is the basis of language.[10] This view contrasts sharply with

Bacon's view of language, adopted by Newton and many of his contemporaries in the Royal Society, that the perfect, pristine language displays perfect referentiality, with an immediate and unambiguous fit between the speaker's noun and the denominated object. This perfect language has been lost to humanity as a result of the Fall.[11] In its absence, metaphor accommodates word to object while testifying to the nescience of the human condition. Even the greatest visionary is not proof against such ignorance, in part because all who live after the Fall are subject to it and in part because metaphor alone lets the fallen understand language. Thus no less a prophetic figure than Moses is forced to use metaphors, as Newton tells Bishop Burnet in a letter of January 1680/81.

> If it be said that ye expression of making & setting two great lights in ye firmament be more poetical than natural: so also are some other expressions of Moses, as where he tells us that the windows or floodgates of heaven were opened Gen 7 & afterwards stopped again Gen 8 & yet the things signified by such figurative expressions are not Ideall or moral but true. For Moses accommodating his words to ye gross conceptions of ye vulgar, describes things much after ye manner as one of ye vulgar would have been inclined to do had he lived & seen ye whole series of wt Moses describes.[12]

On the matter of what constitutes the primal metaphor, the basis of language, Blake is more radical than either Vico or Herder. They believe that such metaphor arises through a process of "bodying forth." Vico observes that "in all languages the greater part of the expressions relating to inanimate things are formed by metaphor from the human body and its parts and from the human senses and passions."[13] Herder, for his part, notes that at one time "everything was personified in human terms, as woman and man. Everywhere gods, goddesses, acting beings of evil or of good. The howling storm and the sweet zephyr, the clear source and the mighty ocean—their entire mythology lies in the treasure trove, the verbs and nouns of the old languages, and the oldest dictionary was therefore a sounding pantheon, an assembly of both sexes, as was nature to the senses of the first inventor."[14] Blake believes that the body has its role in the creation of primal metaphor. But to use the tenor-vehicle model of metaphor first proposed by I. A. Richards,[15] Blake views the body's role as the vehicle, or material completion of the metaphor, rather than its tenor, or spiritual origin.

For Vico, and for Herder as well, what is "at hand" is the body.[16] The speaker of primal metaphor bodies forth a familiar tenor in order to link it with the unfamiliar, material "other" that is the metaphor's vehicle. The implied comparison, then, is between body-as-tenor and "other"-as-vehicle. But what is primal metaphor for Vico and Herder is rather second-order metaphor for Blake. He postulates a prior metaphoric act in which the immanent principle that he calls "poetic genius" or "soul" assumes the role of tenor, with the physical body assuming the role of vehicle.

The tenor-vehicle model of metaphor has peculiar appropriateness for a discussion of Blake, who himself uses similar terminology, referring in *Milton* (1804) to "Lazarus who is the Vehicular Body of Albion the Redeemd" (*M*, pl. 24 [26], l. 27). And Blake proclaims the secondary and ultimately derivative status of the body-as-vehicle from his earliest illuminated texts. The first principle proclaimed in *All Religions Are One* (1788) states "That the Poetic Genius is the true Man. and that the body or outward form of Man is derived from the Poetic Genius. Likewise the forms of all things are derived from their Genius which by the Ancients was call'd an Angel & Spirit & Demon" (*CPP*, p. 1).

Despite its derivative status, the body-as-vehicle is utterly inseparable from the generative consciousness that projects it: primal metaphor, for Blake, is a living yet indestructibly unified entity, owing to the existence of an immanent principle that pervades body and consciousness (or soul) alike. In *The Marriage of Heaven and Hell* (1790–93) the visionary "Voice of the Devil" proclaims, "Man has no body distinct from his Soul for that calld Body is a portion of Soul discernd by the five Senses. the chief inlets of Soul in this age" (*MHH*, pl. 4). It is precisely because primal metaphor as Blake conceives of it is so indestructibly unified that one is liable to forget that it is metaphor completed by the body and that there is something ontologically prior to the body itself. Such forgetfulness is what gives rise to the "bodying forth" and the resultant birth of the gods. The individual creates the world in his image as he denies responsibility for doing so, ascribing responsibility to external and autonomous "mental deities": "a system was formed, which took advantage of & enslav'd the vulgar by attempting to realize or abstract the mental deities from their objects: thus began Priesthood. . . . Thus men forgot that All deities reside in the human breast" (*MHH*, pl. 11).

If the body is not the origin of metaphor but is rather its completion, then the visionary artist must recognize the mistake and reverse it. The task of *identifying* all human forms, of reconciling them in the unity of soul and body, is the means of reversing and offsetting forgetfulness and recognizing the true nature of primal metaphor. It is an arduous task. In a letter of 2 October 1800 Blake shares with his correspondent Thomas Butts the insight that

> Each grain of Sand
> Every Stone on the Land
> Each rock & each hill
> Each fountain & rill
> Each herb & each tree
> Mountain hill Earth & Sea
> Cloud Meteor & Star
> Are Men Seen Afar. (*CPP*, p. 712, ll. 25–32)

But it is not until some twenty years later, at the close of *Jerusalem*, that Blake proclaims, "All Human Forms identified even Tree Metal Earth & Stone" (pl. 99, l. 1). The completion of the task requires transcending bodily limits previously considered untranscendable, as, for example, when "Urizen & Luvah & Tharmas & Urthona arose into / Albions Bosom" near the end of *Jerusalem* (pl. 96, ll. 41–42). It entails working from body to soul, or poetic genius, from the second-order structures of reality to the first-order structures. Blake's procedure anticipates Paul Ricoeur's insight into the nature of metaphor: "second-order" reference of metaphor "constitutes the primordial reference to the extent that it suggests, reveals, unconceals—or whatever you say— the deep structures of reality to which we are related as mortals who are born into this world and who dwell in it for a while."[17]

A CEASELESS MENTAL FIGHT AGAINST FORGETFULNESS

The letter to Butts and the last plate of *Jerusalem* suggest that the battle against forgetfulness is the salient objective of Blake's artistic maturity—indeed, that the battle constitutes his mature artistic program. Mind's priority over matter is a given for Blake, as two of the "Proverbs of Hell" suggest. "Where man is not nature is barren" (*MHH*, pl. 10, l. 68) implies that living nature depends on the prior existence of the living and (pro)creative mind. "One thought. fills immensity" (pl. 8, l. 36) suggests that the void of Newtonian absolute space does not exist for the subject who "humanizes" its "otherness."

However, forgetting that the creative consciousness exerts absolute priority over the body in the framing of primal metaphor allows for the delusion of material priority, and with it the sort of tropaic degeneration described by Vico. The failure to understand primal metaphor as an entity grounded in the creative consciousness makes it appear that the tenor of the metaphor is the body—or worse yet, an object "out there" in the material universe. One consequence of the delusion is to conceive the creative consciousness in terms of the repetitive material proliferations of the object world rather than conceiving—or, to use Blake's term, "identifying"—the object world in terms of the unique (but hardly singular) creative consciousness. Thus the forgetfulness that leads to the delusion of material priority also sets in motion a repetitive process in which the primal metaphor degenerates further at every stage, as the vehicle of the preceding metaphor becomes the tenor of the succeeding one. In the terms of Vico's analysis the body-"other" comparison implicit in primal metaphor degenerates in the second phase of the tropaic dialectic, when the "other" that served as the vehicle of that metaphor becomes the tenor of second-order metaphor.

Although Blake is aware that a process like the one described above exists, he does not hold that such a process is either inevitable or necessary. Instead, he maintains that the process is implemented by those in power who stand to benefit the most from its continuance, those denominated by the term "Priesthood." Whatever the final issue of their task, members of the "Priesthood" go about erecting rigorous belief systems that are ultimately based on projection, denial, and most importantly, forgetfulness.[18] In *The Book of Urizen* (1794) Blake's archpriest Urizen practices such projection and denial in his mistaken demiurgic creation of the Newtonian universe of matter, motion, and force, as well as in his creation of the rigidly prescriptive and reductive book of law by which that universe is to be understood. Urizen's account of the book's origins makes clear his responsibility for world and book alike.

First I fought with the fire; consum'd
Inwards, into a deep world within:
A void immense, wild, dark & deep
Where nothing was: Natures wide womb. (*U*, pl. 4, ll. 14–17)

The passage chronicles Urizen's denial of his own immanent, creative consciousness and the projection of that denied figment onto the landscape without. Urizen must disavow that creative consciousness to proclaim himself priest and subjugate others to his authority. His internal struggle arises out of the failure to understand that the object world—and the life world as well—does not begin at the body and extend outward without there being some prior principle. Any perception or intimation at odds with the delusion of material priority is a potential threat. Thus the reference to the feral "void" that lies "within": the denial of immanence in oneself becomes the basis for denying it in the landscape, and the primal natural scene looks a good deal more like the dark "face of the deep" (Genesis 1:2) than the pleasant Edenic landscape in which "the breath of life" (2:7) is the immanent principle responsible for all manner of "bringing forth," up to and including the ensouling of Adam. An interesting gloss on Urizen's actions of denial and projection is to be found in one of the "memorable fancies" in *The Marriage*: a "satanic" (creative) speaker recalls "walking among the fires of hell, delighted with the enjoyments of Genius; which to angels look like torment and insanity" (*MHH*, pl. 6). The implication is that "Genius," "good" immanence, or internal creative fire that distinguishes the individual is perceived by the orthodox who deny its existence as "evil" immanence—"torment and insanity" indicating demonic possession.

Urizen uses the delusion of material priority to support his "priesthood," which surveys matters psychological, scientific, and political as well as religious. His book of laws subverts the creative understanding of the individual by reducing human activity to a concealed, coercive, unitive standard of measurement:

One command, one joy, one desire,
One curse, one weight, one measure
One King, one God, one Law (*U*, pl. 4.38–40).[19]

Urizen's "bodying forth" is characteristic of Blake's other natural theologians cum Newtonian villains.[20]

In *There Is No Natural Religion [b]* (1788) Blake argues that "If it were not for the Poetic or Prophetic character. the Philosophic & Experimental would soon be at the ratio of all things & stand still, unable to do other than repeat the same dull round over again" (*CPP*, p. 3). But unlike Vico, who links the cycle with poetic discourse, Blake suggests that "the Poetic or Prophetic character" can intervene in the cycle and end it. A number of recursive cycles must pass beforehand, each adjusting the relationship between the bodily tenor of Vichian first-order metaphor and the vehicle of each subsequent "bodying forth." With each successive proliferation the primal body grows smaller in relation to the new metaphoric vehicle until, in the ironic phase, the relationship between the originary body and projected other of the fourth-order metaphor grows nearly inconceivable. Thus the initial bodying forth of each subsequent *ricorso*, or cycle in the spiral, is more modest than the initial move of the preceding one. What is at first "bodied forth" as larger and more powerful than its human creator becomes ever larger and more powerful with each proliferation, whereas what is "bodied forth" as smaller and less powerful becomes ever smaller and less powerful.

The intuitive rightness of Blake's insight is suggested by the shift of scale that characterizes materialist conceptions of the universe and the fundamental constituents of matter. Each succeeding cosmological account of the universe makes the earth (and its inhabitants) less central to the cosmos—and thereby less significant and less influential in the unfolding of any given cosmology in relation to the universe as a whole and other places in it. And each succeeding theory of matter posits ever smaller subatomic constituents. In both cases the shifting of scalar relationships results from an adjustment of the relationship between the body-as-covert-standard and the universe and the fundamental constituents of matter as the projection of that standard: both the earth and that essential constituent are viewed as covert projections of the body, as being smaller in relation to the total system of bodies, which occupies ever larger domains of space and time prior to the individual creative consciousness. Another way of putting the case is to say that with each ricorso of metaphor the delusion of a material universe prior to the individual consciousness is heightened, and access to the creative consciousness that speaks the material world into coherence attains a degree of difficulty that verges on outright interdiction.

Blake is aware of such a shift of scale. But he holds out the hope, based on his "firm perswasion" (*MHH*, pl. 12), that the diminution of the individual and the delusion of material priority are self-limiting processes, and that at the point of greatest diminution and delusion each process will reverse. At that point the body will revert to its proper role as the vehicle of primal metaphor, and the creative consciousness will return to its rightful place as the tenor of such metaphor.

Milton offers a scenario of self-limitation and reversal, narrating the triumph of "the Poetic or Prophetic character" over "the Philosophic & Experimental." Blake's Satan, "Prince of the Starry Wheels" (*M*, pl. 3, l. 43), exemplifies the latter, like a wheel "unable to do other than repeat the same dull round over again." But Satan is also the limit of his kind, the last material issue of Enitharmon, who is the emanated material "bodying forth" of Los's immaterial soul as well as the emanated space of his durational time. And Satan is also the "limit" of "Opacity" (*M*, pl. 13 [14], ll. 20–21), the self-deluded corporeality that both emphasizes the importance of the bodily eye and pleads blindness by way of denying the priority of consciousness to bodily eye and bodily sense alike.

When Enitharmon "bodies forth" Satan, the last two avatars of Blake's deceased younger brother Robert and of Blake himself, Rintrah and Palamabron (*M*, pl. 9, l. 11), are laboring with "the Plow of Rintrah & the Harrow of the Almighty / In the hands of Palamabron" (*M*, pl. 4, ll. 1–2). These implements are complex symbols. They suggest that the means of reversing the diminution of the human form, with its divine origins, is to remove the delusion of material priority by "plowing" and "harrowing" it to show matter for what it is: mere inessential "din." In *A Vision of the Last Judgment* (1810) Blake offers a gloss on the symbolic actions of Rintrah and Palamabron that has distinctly theodical and cosmological implications. "Error or Creation will be Burned Up & then & not till then Truth or Eternity will appear It is burnt up the Moment Men cease to behold it I assert for My self that I do not behold the Outward Creation & that to me it is hindrance & not Action is as the Dirt upon my feet No part of Me" (p. 95).

As Blake suggests, reversing the diminution of the human form and removing the delusion of material priority entail creative "Action," not intellectual "hindrance." The recognition of this imperative brings with it two corollaries: first, "that pity divides the soul / And man, unmans" (*M*, pl. 8, ll. 19–20), that is, pity enhances diminution and delusion; and second, that prophetic wrath, characteristic of Rintrah and Palamabron, unifies the soul and confirms the spiritual essence to humanity—to "man man," in other words. "Hindrance," for its part, arises from a failure or unwillingness to recognize that the "soul," or creative consciousness, is the source of primal metaphor and that the body completes the metaphor not permanently but contingently. This failure in its turn gives rise to the misapprehension that reifies the vehicle of primal metaphor, thus dividing consciousness from body, "unmanning" the individual by duping him into thinking that the life of art resides in the body and causing him to privilege the body under the delusion that it is the source of all creative activity.

Satan himself is subject to this delusion. While "Palamabron with the fiery Harrow" of prophetic wrath returns each morning "From breathing fields" (*M*, pl. 5, ll. 1–2), whose essence is "the breath of life" that he seeks to liberate from its material, "earthen," and ultimately delusory constraints, Satan subverts the task out of what seem to him to be the best of intentions. Under the guise of assuming Palamabron's task, Satan employs not "the Science of Wrath, but only of Pity" (pl. 9, l. 46). He takes Palamabron's place behind the harrow "with incomparable mildness" (pl. 7, l. 4), protecting his material existence, his delusion of material priority, and all others under that delusion. Satan is dimly aware that these others are all, in an important sense, projected figments of himself. As the result of his pity the material component of the "breathing fields" is not obliterated by the harrow to reveal their inspirited essence; rather, his use of the harrow preserves delusive, divided materiality. If anything, Satan attempts to extend the delusion by dividing matter into ever smaller bits.

Not that Satan could do otherwise: he is himself subject to the delusion that he fosters and preserves. When his own immanent creative potential reaches wrathful intensity, Satan practices the tactics of projection and denial. In attempting to justify the usurpation of Palamabron, Satan exercises what to him is rational argument, but what is in fact the denial of his own prophetic wrath projected outward as that argument. Projection and denial gives rise to a wide range of affect, but it always locates the cause of the affect outside the bodily limits, not inside. For example, Satan "wept . . . before Los, accusing Palamabron; / Himself exculpating with mildest speech" (*M*, pl. 8, ll. 1–2). And "Satan flaming with Rintrahs fury hidden beneath his own mildness / Accus'd Palamabron before the Assembly of ingratitude! of malice" (pl. 9, ll. 19–20). But in both cases the presumed cause of Satan's affect—and his actions—is Palamabron, who is external to him, rather than Rintrah, who is the spirit of prophetic wrath that dwells within.

Those who suffer the consequences of Satan's projection and denial are not deceived. Instead, they are enraged by his unthinking imposition:

> . . . the Horses of the Harrow
> were maddend with tormenting fury, & the servants of the Harrow
> The Gnomes, accus'd Satan, with indignation fury and fire.
> (*M*, pl. 7, ll. 17–19)

As the furious affect of the oppressed—the horses and the gnomes—suggests, the strategy of projection and denial ultimately has the opposite of its intended result: it rouses in its intended object the very prophetic wrath that the satanic subject denies. The "servants of the Harrow / The Gnomes" are especially interesting in this regard. Satan's refusal to liberate what Blake in *Jerusalem* calls "The Breath Divine" from the "breathing fields" of Milton causes the welling up of breath that culminates in the gnomes' furious, fiery indignation and their accusations. The interaction is an allegory of what happens when one insists on the Newtonian model of corpuscular matter—gnomes are, after all, corpuscles, or "little bodies"—without owning the powerful generative efficacy of that "certain most subtle spirit [L. *spirare*, to breathe] that pervades and lies hid in all gross bodies," even little ones, and without entertaining the possibility that the body in such an instance may be not a material equivalent of the spirit but a metonym for it. Satan's pity is mistakenly directed at saving such metonyms, even if the project entails denying the generative efficacy of spirit and positing ever smaller irreducible bodily units to supplant the corpuscle.

Satan's self-delusions must have an end. "A Great Solemn Assembly" (pl. 11 [12], l. 15) convenes to judge his usurpation of Palamabron. The assembly's unified action is a harbinger of Blake's culminating vision of humanity as one person. Each member of the assembly, possessed of the "Science of Wrath," cooperates to set a limit to satanic delusion—the very limit of Bishop Ussher's six-thousand-year chronology that Newton himself accepts in *The Chronology of Ancient Kingdoms Amended* (1728) and elsewhere.

> Loud raging
> Thundered the Assembly dark & clouded, and they ratify'd
> The kind decision of Enitharmon & gave a Time to the Space
> Even Six Thousand years. (*M*, pl. 13 [14], ll. 14–17)

By limiting time and space, the assembly limits the temporal duration of Newtonian matter, and with it the dialectical process by which such delusory matter is proliferated. But what follows the end of this period will not be the apocalypse envisioned by John of Patmos; rather, it will be the triumph of the spirit, restored to primacy over matter. With this triumph will come the realization that the individual is rooted in a creative consciousness that the material body completes but does not originate. Blake observes explicitly in *A Vision of the Last Judgment* that one may have the Last Judgment and enjoy it, too, by recognizing the priority of the spiritual. "What are all the Gifts of the Spirit but Mental Gifts whenever any Individual Rejects Error & Embraces Truth a Last Judgment passes upon that Individual" (p. 84).

The move beyond the dialectical process in which Satan participates establishes the possibility of sustaining a spiritual existence "outside" time and space and implies as well the possibility of sustaining a spiritual existence "inside" time and space. Urizen's characterization of "Nature's wide womb" is therefore mistaken. No matter, no Newtonian system of the world is at the core, but the absence of matter does not entail a corresponding absence of spiritual substance.

> Earth was not: nor globes of attraction
> The will of the Immortal expanded
> Or contracted his all flexible senses. (*M*, pl. 3, ll. 36–38)

The domain of spiritual substance is a domain of free play and self-renovation. It is not a matter of either expansion or contraction: both are not only possible but operative, the one leading to the other, just as one breathes by inhaling (expanding) and exhaling (contracting) the human breast, where, according to Blake, all deities reside.

The domain of spiritual substance is also apparently a domain of translucence, especially in comparison to what happens in *The Book of Urizen* after "The sound of a trumpet" (*U*, pl. 3, l. 50). The trumpet suggests a satiric characterization of the Creation-as-Last-Judgment or implies the symmetrical fall into materiality at the Creation and emergence from it at the Last Judgment, with both the beginning and end signaled by the trumpet's sound. Another way to view the process is to ask what happens to "The will of the Immortal" if it is constrained by the boundaries of something like a trumpet. That will cannot *both* expand *and* contract, it can *either* expand *or* contract: and it contracts. The corresponding movement is from a domain of translucence to one of opacity. Thus with "the Immortal" entrapped in matter and the sounding of the trumpet to announce that entrapment, "the heavens / Awoke & vast clouds of blood roll'd' / Round the dim rocks of Urizen" (*U*, pl. 3, ll. 50–52).

But a trumpet has two ends: spirit constrained against its nature will out, for there are established limits to "bodying forth," as Blake makes clear in *Milton*: "The Divine hand found the Two Limits: first of Opacity, then of Contraction / Opacity was named Satan, Contraction was named Adam" (*M*, pl. 13 [14], ll. 20–21). Satan is "opaque" in that he is averse to insight: he simply does not think that there is anything more within him than Urizen posits of "Natures wide womb"; accordingly, he deceives himself through the willful refusal to look within and through the resulting projection and denial. Adam is "contracted" in several senses. He is the smallest, most compact embodiment of spirit conceivable—the last refuge, a being created as the repository of the divine spark in this world—and he is also placed under contract, virtually from the moment of his creation, by a God that promulgates terms regarding what may and may not be eaten, the same God that later enters into a seemingly endless number of covenants with Noah, Abraham, Moses, and their descendants.

As Donald D. Ault has argued, Blake is probably criticizing Newton's notion of mathematical limits,[21] much as he also alludes to the Newtonian concept of the moment. But there is also an important biblical sense of "The Divine hand" as agent to consider. "The Divine hand" (H. *yod*) is a metonym for "the Divine person,"[22] and that person is a spiritual being. When it creates Satan and Adam, it creates them in its own image: their physical bodies are no more than the representations of their spiritual beings. However, Satan's willfulness and Adam's naïveté prevent them from understanding the body as the metonym of spirit.

Newton understood the world as the aggregation of opaque, contracted corpuscles; these possessed extension, hardness, impenetrability, mobility, and inertia—five inherent attributes conforming nicely to the five senses—and were acted on by powerful, invisible forces from the outside. To subvert the Newtonian understanding of the world, one must do what Satan refuses to do—to look within rather than without, and do so with the spiritual rather than the bodily eye. This is what Blake has in mind in *A Vision of the Last Judgment*, when he declares that he looks through, rather than with, his "Corporeal or Vegetative Eye" (p. 95). To do so is to recognize the figurality of the "bodied forth" world, as well as to recognize the spiritual cause or origin of that figurality. There is ample precedent for looking within: the prophetic tradition, "inner light" Christianity, and the passage in Milton's *Paradise Lost* (1671) in which the Archangel Michael suggests to the fallen, exiled Adam (Blake's "Limit of Contraction") that "A paradise within thee, happier far" than Eden, awaits the person wise and temperate enough to look within.[23]

The logic of looking within is also motivated by a shift of scale that results from the repetition of "the same dull round" of the "Philosophic & Experimental." If the Newtonian synthesis of force and body ultimately fails because the model, both self-limited and self-limiting, is founded on a metaphor that is derivative rather than primary, it is possible to seek a more nearly primary basis for that metaphor. Looking through the "Corporeal or Vegetative Eye" to this end takes the form in *Milton* of a pilgrimage through the vortex of the material and into the realm of spirit, energy, and the essential humanity that lies inward and beyond.

> The nature of infinity is this: That every thing has its
> Own Vortex; and when once a traveller thro Eternity.
> Has passd that Vortex, he percieves it roll backward behind
> His path, like a globe itself infolding; like a sun:
> . . . .
> Or like a human form, a friend with whom he livd benevolent.
>   (*M*, pl. 15 [17], ll. 21–27)

The vortex is the perfect emblem for looking within. A pilgrimage along the surface of the vortex toward the apex would at first appear to be more or less circular and repetitious, not to mention limited by the apex itself. But the progress toward the apex intensifies along a narrowing spiral. The progress of a scrap of food or soap toward the drain of the kitchen sink illustrates how momentum accelerates in linear terms as the object moves toward the vortex.

There is a sly humor in Blake's choice of this particular emblem. Both the Newtonian model of celestial motion, the circle ("the same dull round"), and the rival model proposed by Descartes, the vortex (which Newton is at pains to argue down),[24] are *figures*: metaphors. Both are rational constructs used by the rational intellect to interrogate the presumedly nonhuman otherness of the universe. And both figures are limited by the failure to recognize and acknowledge creative consciousness as the origin *and end* of the interrogation, at least in the sense that all information systems turn back on themselves, having their origin and end in the speaker who uses them. This is why Blake's "traveller thro Eternity" finds "a human form, a friend with whom he livd benevolent," on the other side of the apex.

The lesson is not lost on the namesake of Blake's *Milton*: for the rest of the poem he keeps his eye and his progress steadily inward in order to pass through to the other side of the vortex and beyond the world of space and time to the place (if it can be called that) of creative consciousness—the origin of metaphor and cognition alike. To accomplish his end Milton, by dint of imaginative power, attains a condition of *ecstasis*. That is, he moves beyond the limits of his own body.

> As when a man dreams, he reflects not that his body sleeps,
> Else he would wake; so seem'd he entering his Shadow: but
> With his the Spirits of the Seven Angels of the Presence
> Entering; they gave him still perceptions of his Sleeping Body;

Which now arose and walk'd with them in Eden, as an Eighth
Image tho' darken'd. (*M*, pl. 15 [17], ll. 1–6)

Milton pursues his end in an exemplary prophetic manner, "By giving up of Selfhood" (17 [19].3). He dispenses with any sort of "bodying forth." From the dualistic perspective of materialism, Milton's renunciation entails divesting himself of both the body and the assumption that it is prior to the mind. From the perspective of materialism, such divestiture—and the metaphoric sense of divestiture as taking off one's clothes is both intentional and fully operative—is tantamount to death. Milton himself is of that mind. Prior to his *ecstasis*, he proclaims, "I go to Eternal Death!" (*M*, pl. 14 [15], l. 14). But as he subsequently discovers, and as the metaphor of divestiture suggests, the "giving up of Selfhood" is more nearly like shucking old clothes than it is like dying—a denial of material priority, but not of life itself as an immanent, immaterial principle. Ridding oneself of the delusion of material priority leads to recognizing the inspired self as the source of all metaphor, of all discourse, of all disciplines, both "scientific" and "poetic." The goal, as Milton states it near the end of the poem, is

To bathe in the Waters of Life; to wash off the Not Human
I come in Self-annihilation and the Grandeur of Inspiration
To cast off Rational Demonstration by Faith in the Saviour
To cast off the rotten rags of Memory by Inspiration
To cast off Bacon, Locke & Newton from Albions covering
To take off his filthy garments, clothe him with Imagination
To cast aside from Poetry, all that is not Inspiration
That it no longer shall dare to mock with the aspersion of Madness
Cast on the Inspired. (*M*, pl. 41 [48], ll. 1–6)

By the close of *Jerusalem*, the task is completed. An inspired "conversation" takes place among the Four Zoas—Blake's four principles, or forces, of life itself. In this conversation, metaphor exists in a condition of free play, to be "bodied forth" as the completion of one creative consciousness, revised by another, and then returned to the originating consciousness without any delusions either of material priority or of exclusivity: there simply is no anxiety or temptation to possess what is neither reified nor ephemeralized as a material object.

And they conversed together in Visionary forms dramatic which bright
Redounded from their Tongues in thunderous majesty, in Visions
In new Expanses, creating exemplars of Memory and Intellect
Creating Space, Creating Time according to the wonders Divine
Of Human Imagination. (*J*, pl. 98, ll. 28–32)

Like the Four Zoas at the end of *Jerusalem*, we have gone forth and returned, describing not the "same dull round" of the Newtonian universe, but rather the spiraling movement of human imagination. We have, in other words, gone forth and returned with the difference that is the principle underlying human creativity, which Blake saw fit to champion against the Newtonian prejudices of his day.

CHAPTER 3

Blake, Freemasonry, and the Builder's Task

In *The Radical Enlightenment: Pantheists, Freemasons, and Republicans*, Margaret C. Jacob, drawing on a large number of previously inaccessible and undiscussed primary materials, has argued convincingly for the place of Freemasonry in Enlightenment Europe, both as a consequence and as a cause of some of the Enlightenment's more radical and influential tendencies: "Men of a variety of political and religious persuasions . . . found meaning in the new science and by the early eighteenth century British Freemasonry gave institutional expression to this new scientific culture. The official Masonic lodges stand as a metaphor for their age. Ruled by grand masters drawn from the peerage, strictly hierarchical in structure yet curiously egalitarian at their meetings and banquets, governed by 'charges' or rules constitutionally enforced, yet indifferent to religious affiliation, the lodges mirrored a larger social and ideological consensus."[1]

By the 1770s, when Blake came to maturity, Freemasonry played a vital role in the artistic and intellectual life of radicals most especially, but of others as well. The influence of Freemasonry was felt both in England and on the continent. In England itself, Freemasonry was virtually an indigenous intellectual force. Modern Freemasonry began with the founding of the Grand Lodge of England in 1717, on the basis of the Old

58

Charges, or pre-1717 Masonic instructions, rites, and catechisms.[2] The Old Charges themselves had a long and noble tradition in England, taking their rise from the Regius Ms. (1390), and continuing down to the founding of the Grand Lodge.[3] Prominent English men of letters who were either Masons outright or wrote from Masonic sympathies included Swift, Pope and Sterne, as well as the somewhat less prominent popularizer of Newtonianism John Theophilus Desaguliers.[4] Internationally, the brotherhood of the Craft included among its members Voltaire, Mozart, Goethe, and Franklin; and its attractiveness as a system of thought is suggested by the fact that Freemasonry continued to flourish in the face of hostility and suspicion on the part of the uninitiated. In its extreme form, this opposition was mounted by the Catholic Church, the Bavarian electorate, and the Austrian monarchy.[5] To a lesser extent, individual clergy and those of class background inimical to Freemasonry's egalitarian leanings kept the hostility and suspicion alive with virulent, though misinformed, anti-Masonic propaganda.[6]

To suggest that Freemasonry was popular among middle- and upper-class men of letters during the Enlightenment is to imply that Blake would have been unsympathetic to the movement and its adherents. Blake's lifelong campaign, from the early confrontation with George Michael Moser, the keeper of the Royal Print Gallery, to the "Preface" to *Milton*, where the invective is directed against the "hirelings" who "depress" art and intellect,[7] was against the established institutions of art and intellect. Moreover, the membership lists of English Freemasonry furnish added cause for assuming that Blake held the movement in low esteem. Bacon, for example, is known for his recognition, under the Old Charges, of the potential importance of Solomon's Temple as a Masonic symbol and article of belief. This Bacon did in *The New Atlantis* (1597).[8] Locke was allegedly a Mason under the Old Charges.[9] The membership of Bacon and Locke, who comprise two-thirds of Blake's unholy trinity, Newton being the third, would have sufficed to alienate Blake from Freemasonry. And even Newton was represented in the Masonic membership, albeit indirectly, in the persons of his popularizers Desaguliers and Pope. Both were powerful apologists for Newtonian thought, whose Lord God Pantokrator displays rather uncanny affinities with the "Almighty Architect" of Masonic prayer and the "Father of all" in Pope's "Universal Prayer."[10] Blake sees his unholy trinity as a collective manifestation of human reasoning power "abstracted" from and denying its origins in the bodily energy of "poetic genius." They are figures that usually appear in the Prophetic Books as Urizen or as one of his numerous, self-denying proliferations.[11]

But Blake's animosity to some practitioners of Freemasonry does not necessarily imply his rejection of Freemasonry itself. Nor would his occasional repudiation of Masonic precept and practice imply a total rejection of Masonic thought. Blake wars against Bacon, Newton, and Locke throughout the Prophetic Books with the goal of redeeming them, not rejecting them. The gang of three appears in the redemptive tableau at the end of *Jerusalem*, along with Chaucer, Shakespeare, and Milton (*J*, pl. 98, l. 9), an appearance indicating that Blake found something of value even in the archprophets of rationalism and materialistic philosophy—two of them presumptive Masons in the bargain—and that even his enemies had something to teach the visionary engaged in unceasing mental warfare. The discussion that follows begins with a brief survey of Blake's verbal and visual allusions to Freemasonry. Then it attempts to make out Blake's case both against and for certain elements of Freemasonry. Finally, it suggests how Blake's intellectual struggle with Freemasonry led to a clarification of that part of the prophetic undertaking here referred to as "the builder's task." It is through "the builder's task" that visionary wrath seeks form, that "ceaseless mental fight" takes place and results, at the end of the prophetic venture, in Blake's having "built Jerusalem,/In Englands green & pleasant Land" (*M*, pl. 3, ll. 15–16).

Blake's references to Freemasonry span a good deal of his mature career—from the time of *The Marriage of Heaven and Hell* to that of *Jerusalem*, in fact (from 1790–93 to 1804–20). The references indicate a wide-ranging familiarity with Masonic matters. Such familiarity does not mean, however, that Blake was necessarily either an initiated Mason or an anti-Masonic "spy." There was a large and highly popular body of Masonic literature in print during Blake's time. Among the titles Blake might have perused are Samuel Prichard's *Masonry Dissected* (1730), the anonymous companion works *Jachin and Boaz* and *Hiram* (1762,

1764), William Hutchinson's *The Spirit of Masonry* (1775), and William Preston's *Pocket Manual* (1790; 1792).[12] Then too, Blake might have gotten his interest in Freemasonry, his information about it, or both from Thomas Paine, whom Blake knew from the circle of the bookseller Joseph Johnson. Although whether he was a Mason is not clear, Paine was sufficiently versed in the Craft to write an essay on *The Origin of Freemasonry*.[13] One could, of course, argue that the references in question are direct references to the Bible, a powerful source for, and influence on, both Freemasonry and Blake. Indeed, Blake might have found the materials in question by consulting the Bible directly. But it should be remembered that most of Masonic lore derived from the Bible is not derived from the most widely read passages of its most popular chapters, such as the Pentateuch, the Prophets, the Gospels, and Revelation. Blake demonstrates clearly enough in his visionary works an acquaintance with not only these passages but also the Bible's more arcane chapters. If Blake did in fact draw directly from the Bible precisely the same arcane material used by Freemasonry, he did so with a fortuitous serendipity that is well-nigh remarkable, given the high correlation that exists between the Blakean and the Masonic taste in, and use for, such arcana.

Whatever the provenance of Blake's references, they begin to appear no later than "A Song of Liberty," the concluding section of *The Marriage*. The final "Chorus" of "A Song" proclaims, "Let the Priests of the Raven of dawn, no longer clad in deadly black with hoarse note curse the sons of joy. Nor his accepted brethren whom, tyrant, he calls free: lay the bound or build the roof" (*MHH*, pl. 27). This reference is a dual one, containing an oblique, anagrammatic rendering of *Free* and *Accepted* Masons ("Brethren"), as well as a recognition of the centrality of architecture as a metaphor, and Solomon's Temple as an icon, in Masonic lore—hence the reference to laying the "bound" and building the "roof" of what is obviously a religious edifice.

Solomon's Temple is the most important symbolic edifice in Masonic teaching, but it is not the first such edifice, chronologically. In modern Freemasonry, the Temple has an important precursor—the Tabernacle built by Moses during the forty years in the desert. Moses was not alone in building the Tabernacle. At God's command, two master craftsmen, Bezaleel (Bezalel) and

Aholiab (Oholiab) were summoned to build the edifice and see to
its ornamentation (Exodus 3:1–11). Their work is accounted impec-
cably wrought and highly beautiful.[14] In one of his satirical notebook poems, Blake recalls the two in the course of complaining
about how inspired art ceases to be inspiring when it is institutionalized and made the authoritative source for the "rules" of art.

And if Bezaleel & Aholiab drew
What the Finger of God pointed to their View
Shall we suffer the Roman & Grecian Rods
To compell us to worship them as Gods
They [the Greeks and Romans] stole them [B. and A.] from the Temple
of the Lord
And Worshippd them that they might make Inspired Art Abhorrd. (*CPP*,
p. 501, ll. 5–10)

The allusion loses a bit of its satiric point because of its com-
plexity. Basically, Blake's complaint seems to be similar to the
one he makes in the "Preface" to *Milton*, albeit in a literary vein,
when the poet complains that "the Stolen and Perverted Writings
of Homer & Ovid: of Plato & Cicero. Which all Men ought to
contemn: are set up by artifice against the Sublime of the Bible."
Later in the same text, Blake makes it clear that the condemnation
he seeks is not to be restricted to literature, when he calls on
"Painters . . . Sculptors! Architects!" to join in the struggle
against the "ignorant Hirelings" of institutionalized art (pl. 1).

Another reference to Freemasonry, also noted by Anne K.
Mellor,[15] appears in *A Vision of the Last Judgment* (1810). Blake
identifies the radiant figure that centers the upper third of his
drawing as "Jesus seated between the Two Pillars Jachin & Boaz
with the Word of Divine Revelation on his knees" (p. 76). The
pillars are those of the porch to Solomon's Temple, named in 2
Chronicles 3:17 and described in several places, including 2
Chronicles 4:11–17, and 1 Kings 7:15–20. Outside the Masonic
circles, the pillars have attracted the commentary of Bede, the
editors of the Geneva Bible, and Samuel Lee. The pillars have a
special significance for Freemasonry, however, both as symbols
of the Masonic ethos and as badges of Masonic office, as is
explained in *Hiram*: "The Senior and Junior Wardens Columns,
which they carry in their Hands, are generally a Foot and an Half
long, and represent the Columns or Portico at the Entrance of the
Temple of Solomon called JACHIN and BOAZ; the Junior's is called

JACHIN, which signifies, *To establish in the Lord*; and the Senior's *BOAZ*, which denotes *STRENGTH*."[16]

Christ, for Blake, is the individual who best symbolizes the indwelling divinity in humanity. In *There Is No Natural Religion [b]*, Blake refers to Christ's role in the intermediation between the human and the divine, saying, "Therefore God becomes as we are, that we may be as he is" (*CPP*, p. 2). This role would account for why Blake places Christ next to Jachin, since the Son of Man is, for Blake, the figure best suited "to establish in the Lord." It is also fitting that Blake would place Christ next to the pillar signifying strength, since the poet views Christ's sacrifice of himself for Albion, recounted in *Jerusalem* (pl. 96, ll. 3–34), as the penultimate act of Christian strength and heroism.

While there is nothing unusual about Blake's collocation of symbols, he makes some interesting and unusual iconographic replacements that are worthy of note and comment. The traditional depiction of Jachin and Boaz—as, for example, on a Masonic Master's apron (fig. 1)—is of a stone edifice situated between two pillars of stone. Instead of the stony edifice of Solomon's Temple, Blake envisions the fleshly, bodily edifice of Christ as the central figure of the tableau. Jachin and Boaz are similarly humanized: instead of stone pillars, they are living beings; instead of possessing abstract virtues, they possess real and tangible ones—they are the bearers of bread and wine, of Eucharist, of larger "incorporation" or "embodiment" for humanity at large (fig. 2). The significance of this iconographic replacement will be dealt with at greater length below.

Concerning the "Word of Divine Revelation" that Blake renders and remarks on the knees of Christ, it should be noted that one of the central quests of Freemasonry is "its age-long quest for the Lost Word, the Ineffable Name; a quest that never tires, never tarries, knowing the while that every name is inadequate, and all words are but symbols of a Truth too great for words."[17] In Blake's rendering, Christ appears to be balancing a linen scroll that is the repository of revelation. Whether the scroll in fact contains that revelation or must be cast off to discover it is not entirely clear. Linen in Blake is a metaphor for the "material" body, identified with the grave clothes that Christ casts off in resurrection. It is also linen or some other closely related "material" that Milton casts off as "the rotten rags of

1. Masonic Master's Apron. © Collection de la Grande Loge de France. Reproduction courtesy of Editions Robert Laffont.

Memory by Inspiration" at the end of his poem (*M*, pl. 41 [48], l. 4). It could be that the linen scroll is an ironic comment on the Masonic quest for the Lost Word: that Word, like the Kingdom of Heaven, is within, in the spiritual realm; the "material" realm, far from containing the Word, only obscures it.

In the third chapter of *Jerusalem*, Albion contemplates the numerous children of the poem's female namesake and has a vision of their essential unity.

> They were as Adam before me: united into One Man,
> They stood in innocence & their skiey tent reached over Asia

1. *A Vision of the Last Judgment*, William Blake. National Gallery of Art, Washington. Rosenwald Collection.

To Nimrods Tower to Ham & Canaan walking with Mizraim
Upon the Egyptian Nile. (*J*, pl. 60, ll. 16–19)

"Nimrod's Tower" is of course the Tower of Babel. "Mizraim" is
Egypt. Blake might have found his references to the two in Genesis
11:1–9 and 10:6, respectively. But the two also have a significance
for Freemasonry that is worth noting in this context. In the Old
Charges—the Regius Ms., for example—Nimrod is accounted the
founder of the Craft, the Tower of Babel being its first edifice. The
Egyptian rite of Memphis-Mizraim, with its prayers to Isis, Osiris,
and a deity referred to as the "Great Architect," was a Masonic
rite of initiation highly popular in Blake's time and current at least
down to the middle of the twentieth century.[18]

The significance of Albion's unitive vision is that it both
embraces and transcends the individual, stony edifices of Babel
and Memphis-Mizraim. The reference to humanity appearing "as
Adam before me: united into One Man" indicates that the unity
Albion envisions is the primal, originary state. At issue in
Albion's vision is the matter of originary authority. The primary
edifice—the model for architecture and the authority for all
succeeding edifices—is not a building, not a piece of Vitruvian
or Palladian architecture,[19] but a man, the first man, Adam.
Therefore the rights accruing to a founder by dint of his primacy,
and the "charges" that proceed from that founder, are not housed
in a tower nor an Egyptian pyramid nor a Phoenician temple, but
in Adam's body.[20] And the person who speaks the "charges" is not
an architect nor a master mason—not someone who uses the stuff
of earth to create works—but the very stuff of earth itself, Adam's
very name meaning "clay."

As the discussion of *The Last Judgment* should have made
clear, Blake borrowed, with alterations, from the vast store of
Masonic iconography for his own ends. None of these borrowings
is more striking in the transformations it works than the last one
to be discussed here—the purely pictorial frontispiece to *Europe*
(1794). As anyone who has ever seen a Masonic ring or auto-
mobile medallion knows, the dividers is one of the principal
symbolic tools of Freemasonry. As now, so in the eighteenth
century: the dividers symbolized the Craft. Blake places dividers
in the hands of his archprophets of reason, as in his color print
of Newton, a figure clearly popular with Freemasonry, though

3. *Newton*, William Blake. The Tate Gallery, London.

not a member himself. The engraving depicts Newton working over a diagram of a circle inscribed in an isosceles right triangle, a gibing reference to Newton's work on the calculus and quadrature of curves, with which Blake was apparently familiar (fig. 3).[21] In the frontispiece to *Europe*, Urizen, who is a Newtonian avatar, wields the dividers, posed in the squatting configuration characteristic of Blake's self-imprisoned exemplars of rationality, with eyes closed or averted in the characteristic pose of the reasoner whose arguments proceed from self-deluding, self-concealed self-interest.[22]

The dividers in Masonic lore is the tool of the "Almighty Architect" of heaven and earth, who divided night from day, heaven from earth, earth from sea, and so on. To show that God is the "Almighty Architect" intended, Masonic iconography often places a flaming, five-pointed star over the dividers to signify His possession of the tool (fig. 4). Often as not the star is inscribed with the letter *G* (fig. 5). A close inspection of Blake's engraving

4. Masonic Ornament.
© Collection de las
Grande Loge de
France. Reproduction
courtesy of Éditions
Robert Laffont.

reveals that the flamelike modeling of Urizen's hair and the batchings that radiate from the celestial orb behind him add up to the impression of a flaming star. An adding up of the number of projecting points that emanate from the figure, including (clockwise) the knee, the feet, the extended arm, the other knee, and the hair, makes it obvious that the impression, if it is of a flaming star, is of a five-pointed one (fig. 6).

What distinguishes Blake's frontispiece from normal Masonic renderings is the decision to portray the flaming five-pointed star as a human being. The decision is thoroughly consistent with the tendency toward humanization glimpsed in the other allusions to, and "corrections" of, Masonic materials. Two texts that help clarify why Blake does what he does are the letter of 2 October

5. Masonic Master's Apron. © Collection Alain Serriere. Reproduction courtesy of Éditions Robert Laffont.

1800 to Butts and "The Everlasting Gospel." The first of these treats of humanization; the second assesses its significance. In the letter, Blake shares an important insight with Butts in the form of a long poem in trimeter doggerel, part of which states,

> Each Grain of Sand
> Every Stone on the Land
> Each rock & each hill
> Each fountain & rill
> Each herb & each tree
> Mountain hill Earth & Sea
> *Cloud Meteor & Star*
> *Are Men Seen Afar* (*CPP*, p. 712, ll. 25–32; emphasis mine)

6. The frontispiece to *Europe*, William Blake. From the Special Collections Department, Auckland Central City Library, Auckland, New Zealand.

The passage from "The Everlasting Gospel" talks of the significance of seeing the world as human: "Thou art a Man God is no more / Thy own humanity learn to adore" (pp. 52–54, ll. 71–72).

Blake's attempt is to show that what Urizen or the Masonic initiate considers "an act of God" is in fact a human action whose origins have been effaced in an effort to heighten the inscriptive and prescriptive force of the act.[23] Giving a definite outline and physiognomy to the flaming star he borrows from Freemasonry is but a small step in Blake's visionary enterprise—one more identification and humanization leading up to, and culminating in, the refrain on which the drama of *Jerusulem* concludes: "All Human Forms identified" (*J*, pl. 99, l. 1). Blake's "corrections" suggest that, for him, the cardinal sin of Freemasonry is its failure, in the midst of much activity that Blake accounted instructive and worthwhile, to identify as human the originary creative act. As Blake saw it, Freemasonry thereby mystified excessively or denied outright a possibility central to the poet's credo: that any of us might have been, and may yet be, that "Almighty Architect," that flaming star.

If Blake undertook to "correct" Freemasonry, he did so only because he believed that in it was something of intrinsic worth that his corrective activities would help to save and enhance. Some aspects of the Craft that Blake might have valued with sympathy and admiration are the rituals of rebirth and fellowship. The former of these involves the symbolic "death" that all Masons, from apprentice to master, must undergo as they advance in their quest for enlightenment. As Jacques Chailley observes, "every cycle of trials presupposes a complete transformation of the personality: the future elect must die in their former life if they are to be born into the new one later. That idea [is one] which Masonry embraces at each advowson of degree (representing a new step toward Knowledge)."[24] The latter ritual of fellowship involves a series of symbolic touchings and claspings that enact the manner in which divine wisdom enters the human body, the manner of all "Masons . . . when they receive the Master's Word."

Ex. How is that?
R. By the Five Points of Fellowship.
Ex. What are they?
[R.] Hand to Hand, Foot to Foot, Cheek to Cheek, Knee to Knee, and Hand in Back, Etc.[25]

A similar symbolic death occurs near the end of *Jerusalem*, where Jesus, whose self-sacrifice is the model for all subsequent "dying," confronts Albion and convinces him that,

> if God dieth not for Man & giveth not himself
> Eternally for Man Man could not exist! for Man is Love:
> As God is Love: every kindness for another is a little Death
> In the Divine Image, nor can Man exist but by Brotherhood.

Albion responds to the lesson by throwing "himself into the Furnaces of affliction" (*J*, pl. 96, ll. 25–28, 35), with the result that he rises to the full fourfold vision characteristic of the end of *Jerusalem*.

The fellowship of the divine and the human is also a characteristic of the end of the poem and is perhaps responsible for the precise posture and nature of the embrace between man and God in the last plate of the poem. Similarly, when Milton goes to do battle with Urizen at Arnon, the "touchings" of the struggle have a stylized quality that leads one to believe they are the visualization of some ritual, probably the Masonic one (figs. 7, 8). The association of the fellowship of the divine and the human with some sort of ritualized embrace, openly expressed, is evident in the following passage from *Jerusalem*, in which the purpose of the embrace described is to transcend the material limits of the body and bring to pass spiritual fellowship. The "disobedient Female" referred to is the material world, which persists in its attempts, or so Blake thinks, to take on an existence independent of its spiritual cause and source.

> Hence the Infernal Veil grows in the disobedient Female:
> Which Jesus rends & the whole Druid Law removes away
> From the Inner Sanctuary: a False Holiness hid within the Center,
> For the Sanctuary of Eden. is in the Camp: in the Outline,
> In the Circumference: & every Minute Particular is Holy:
> Embraces are Cominglings: from the Head even to the Feet;
> And not a pompous High Priest entering by a Secret Place.
> (*J*, pl. 69, ll. 38–44)

Whether he got his notions of rebirth and renewal and fellowship from Masonic sources, or whether those sources merely furnished Blake with support for his own, already articulated beliefs, these notions play an integral part in creating Blake's culminating vision, as it is rendered at the end of *Jerusalem*. There the Four Zoas die the last death and undergo the last rebirth and renewal into the ultimate realm of creative power. It is a process

7. *Milton*, pl. 15 (Huntington Library copy numbering), William Blake. Reproduced by permission of the Huntington Library, San Marino, California.

8. *Jerusalem*, pl. 99 (Harvard copy numbering), William Blake.
By permission of the Department of Printing and Graphic Arts,
The Houghton Library, Harvard University.

Driving outward the Body of Death in an Eternal Death & Resurrection
Awaking it to Life among the Flowers of Beulah rejoicing in Unity
In the Four Senses in the Outline the Circumference & Form, for ever
In Forgiveness of Sins which is Self Annihilation. (*J*, pl. 98, ll. 20–23)

And partly as a result of this death and rebirth, the Zoas are able to enter into a kind of fellowship more powerful than any previously known:

> & they walked
> To & fro in Eternity as One Man reflecting each in each & clearly seen
> And seeing: according to fitness & order. (*J*, pl. 98, ll. 38–40)

But despite Blake's apparent admiration for certain aspects of Masonic belief and ritual, there was a good deal about Freemasonry that he did not like, as several of the allusions discussed in the brief survey above tend to suggest. As Blake saw it, the problem was not so much that Freemasonry and its adherents lacked the basic humanity necessary to become powerfully creative beings, but rather that the movement and its adherents subscribed to beliefs that tended to deny the primacy of that powerful creative drive. In the Masonic dividers, squares, plummets, and other paraphernalia, Blake would have seen evidence for the subjection of the creative act to the disguising cipher of mathematics and technology, with the resultant disowning of human responsibility for, and instrumentality in, the projection of poetic genius in the act of creation. The Masonic icon of perfect wisdom harnessed in the service of creation is Solomon's Temple, depicted in Blake's time as a masterpiece of the Palladian revival, with its Greco-Roman columns, its architraves displaying perfect triangular symmetry, and its imposing dome (fig. 1). The wisdom necessary to build such an edifice is mathematical wisdom, coupled with the ability to use the tools of mathematics. For Blake, no Greco-Roman style of architecture displays the fusion of perfect wisdom and creativity; rather, the Gothic style does, precisely for the same reason that the Gothic later entranced Ruskin. The form of Gothic teems with evidence of the human body expressing itself directly, to the limit of its medium, through the sort of sculptural handwork and detailing that is redolent with the human creative presence. Gothic architecture occupies the same place in relation to the Greco-Roman style that melody does in relation to harmony, and "wirely bounding lines" do to "blots and blurs."[26] Blake makes the distinction with particular reference to styles of architecture in a fragment entitled "On Virgil."

> Rome & Greece swept Art into their maw & destroyed it   a Warlike State never can produce Art. It will Rob & Plunder & accumulate into one place, & Translate & Copy & Buy & Sell & Criticise, but not Make.
>   Mathematic Form is Eternal in the Reasoning Memory. Living Form is Eternal Existence.
>   Grecian is Mathematic Form
>   Gothic is Living Form. (*CPP*, p. 270)

"Living Form," as Blake uses the term, resides not in the object of perception or creation (Blake would make no distinction between perception and creation), but in the subject. Thus the problem with venerating Solomon's Temple or the Tabernacle of Moses is that it tends to draw admiration away from such architects as Hiram Abiff, or Bezaleel and Aholiab, whose genius created these edifices, and to vest the admiration in the edifice itself. This is the basis of the very real objection underlying the lighthearted notebook poem about the last two. Bezaleel and Aholiab exercised poetic genius in building the Tabernacle. In doing so, they paid homage to that element of the divine residing within the human body that prompted the two to draw "What the finger of God pointed to their View." And it is to the extent that they chronicle acts of this sort that "The Old & New Testaments are the Great Code of Art," as Blake says they are in his comments accompanying his engraving of *The Laocoön* (*CPP*, p. 274).

The tyrants of reason, a category in which Blake places the Greeks and Romans and their Enlightenment posterity (including the Masons), fail to realize that the collective example of artist and code alike prescribes the creative act itself, not the embodiment of form the act takes. Blake sees Freemasonry as but one more group victimized by the delusion of material priority—the delusion that the world out there, whether it be composed of Newtonian "corpuscles," Hartleyan "vibratiuncles," or the bodies that house them—or Solomonic temples—somehow exists prior to the perception of the individual whose outer limit of energy that world becomes. With specific reference to Bezaleel and Aholiab, the veneration of Freemasonry is not for their creative spirit, but for the body, or matter of their creation. When Blake complains about being compelled "to worship them as Gods," the meaning he most nearly intends by "Gods" is idols, or graven images, the cold effigies of poetic genius rather than the warm process itself.

One gets a sense of the coercive, prescriptive nature of Free-masonry from the centrality of catechism to its ritual. Catechism is, after all, a formulaic repetition of the letter, not an evocation of the spirit. The extent to which the Masonic catechumen was compelled to worship the created and the letter, rather than the creative and the spirit, may be seen from the following extract from Prichard's *Masonry Dissected*, the very title of which would have enraged the antivivisectionist Blake. The extract is an appropriate one in this context, for it has to do with the interior of the Masonic lodge—in particular, with the floor—the design for which is supposed to have originated with Bezaleel and Aholiab.

Q. Have you any furniture in your Lodge?
A. Yes.
Q. What is it?
A. Mosaic Pavement, the Ground Floor of the Lodge, Blazing Star in the Centre, and Indented Tarsel and Border round about it.[27]

On the basis of those concerns of Blake's elaborated above, it is possible to understand more fully the iconographic replacement in *The Last Judgment* (fig. 2). Creation for Blake is a species of metaphor making, with the poetic genius residing within the individual serving as the intangible but powerful tenor, and the creation "bodied forth," as it were, serving as the tangible vehicle that is the outward form of poetic genius. Jachin and Boaz, the Temple, the Last Judgment, and the drawing depicting them all are alike the outward form of poetic genius, and for this reason Blake's depiction is a proliferation of such "embodiments." For Freemasonry, however, Jachin and Boaz and the Temple have become abstracted from their origins in poetic genius, "abstracted" being the term Blake uses in *The Book of Urizen* (1794) to describe how the archreasoner (and presumptive master Mason) disowns the origins of his own reasoning and distorted genius by disavowing both his own body as a "bodying forth," or "measure" of poetic genius, and the very poetic genius responsible for that body as he perceives it prior to disavowal (*U*, pl. 3, ll. 6ff.). The main problem with such disavowal is that it foists upon humanity a delusory material world that is apparently fixed and unchanging, and for which no single being is willing to acknowledge responsibility. Such a world can be extremely depressing, as Blake himself attests through the actions of his poetic avatar Los, who is "smitten with astonishment" as Urizen's materialist delusion is prescribed upon him, and who ultimately abdicates for a space his creative "task" while immersed "in terrors" (*U*, pl. 8, l. 1, pl. 13, l. 20). But Los prevails and takes up his hammer again, in the service of poetic genius, in order to replace memory with inspiration, to replace the repetitive with the unique, to replace the detritus of "bodies" long since abandoned by their creative genius with the human form, eternally creating and creative. It is the task of Los and his fellow avatars, Blake, Milton, Albion, and others, that is meant by "the builder's task," and it is to that task that the discussion now turns.

The builder's task, as it is set out in the preface to *Milton*, is the building of "Jerusalem / in Englands green & pleasant Land" (pl. 1, ll. 15–16). Jerusalem is several things in Blake's visionary scheme: a city-nation, the bride of Christ/Albion, the locus of redemption, and an exemplar of the form that may be taken by the material "embodiment" of poetic genius. But the metaphor of "building," which is Blake's metaphor ("Till we have built Jerusalem"), identifies Jerusalem also as an edifice, a work of architecture, in a sense that seems rather more strongly rooted in the England of the Restoration and after than in the Jerusalem of the Bible and the Church Fathers. Building Jerusalem becomes Blake's analogue and answer to the Masonic task of building Solomon's Temple, the visionary response to a project hoping to use faith and reason to achieve vision.

The Masonic sense of Solomon's Temple as mystical architecture dates back at least to the time of the Dumfries Ms. (1710), in the Old Charges. Dumfries No. 4 contains the following bit of catechism:

Q. What signifies the temple
A. ye son of god & partly of the church ye son soffered his body to be destroyed & rose again ye 3^d day & raised up to us ye christian church w^c [which] is ye true spiritwal church.
Q. what meant ye golden dore of ye temple Qr [where] they went in to [the] sanctum sanctorum
A. it was another type of Christ who is ye door ye way and the truth & ye life by whome & in whom all ye elect entreth into heaven. Solomon's Temple [which] is ye true spiritwal church.

Q. what meant yᵉ golden dore of yᵉ temple Qr [where] they went in to [the] sanctum sanctorum

A. it was another type of Christ who is yᵉ door yᵉ way and the truth & yᵉ life by whome & in whom all yᵉ elect entreth into heaven.[28]

Solomon's Temple, which was located in Jerusalem, acquires in this catechism the sort of mystical and multiple signification that Jerusalem will later have for Blake.

At this level of generality, however, the analogues between Blake's building of Jerusalem and the Masonic building of Solomon's Temple, while they are interesting, hardly constitute a cogent argument for Blake's use of Masonic lore in formulating his version of the builder's task. Accordingly, this discussion attempts to connect Blake more closely with the Masonic background by looking primarily at *Milton*, in which the builder's task is announced and begins. To be discussed are the role of the poem's titular figure and subject in the builder's task, and the significance of the four "cities" that Los, Blake's visionary builder and the antagonist to his urizenic master Mason, builds on the way to building the fourfold, four-gated city of the Temple itself, Jerusalem.

Blake's decision to draw Milton into a poem about building Jerusalem is hardly coincidental and highly fortuitous. Although he is not associated commonly with Freemasonry in the same way Swift and Pope are, Milton is the "architectural" poet par excellence of the English literary tradition. In the eighteenth century a veritable critical cult, involving such diverse individuals as Addison, Collins, Gray, and Johnson, grew up around the Miltonic legacy. What transcended the diversity of these individuals was their collective agreement that Milton's *Paradise Lost* was "the edifice of art," the paragon that any succeeding poet, to be accounted sublime, truly great, or both, would have to equal or better.[29] Johnson's description of the Miltonic achievement in *Paradise Lost* is to the point. The Great Cham envisions "the fabrick gradually rising, perhaps from small beginnings, till its foundation rests in the centre, and its turrets sparkle in the skies; to trace back the structure, through all of its varieties, to the simplicity of its first plan; to find out what was first projected, whence the scheme was taken . . . by what assistance it was executed, and from what stores the material was collected, whether its founder dug from quarries of nature or demolished other buildings to embellish his own."[30]

If Milton is indeed responsible for the "edifice of art" Johnson credits him with, then the construction of Blake's Jerusalem waits upon the deconstruction of *Paradise Lost*. Blake's interpersonal combat with Milton—or perhaps better, his intrapersonal combat with that Miltonic aspect of himself—is not in this sense the oedipal struggle Harold Bloom makes it out to be.[31] Blake does not want to do away with his poetic precursor/father; rather, he wants to do with Milton exactly what he wants to do with Freemasonry—to demonstrate that what is important about the Miltonic and the Masonic past alike is not the edifices that were erected but the poetic genius that was exercised in erecting them. It is this genius that constitutes the true spiritual past for Blake, not the works that the genius produced, which are the relics of memory rather than the living presence of inspiration. If Blake can show that what is important about the Miltonic "edifice" is not the work of art itself but the genius responsible for it, then he will have at his disposal the genius of Milton as one possibility among many, in what Donald Pease, with specific reference to Blake's Milton, has called "a poetics of pure possibility."[32] Poetic emulation will then be possible and productive.

Blake's undertaking becomes Milton's undertaking in the poem. If, as Los discovers early in the poem, one becomes what one beholds (*M*, pl. 3, l. 29), then the deconstruction of Milton as edifice and his reconstruction as "embodied" poetic genius requires that he constrain someone else to change from edifice to poetic genius and then become what he beholds. This Milton does when he descends into the fallen world through the only access available to the artist in Blake's time, at least as the latter sees it. That access is via architecture cum science.

> But in Eternity the Four Arts: Poetry, Painting, Music,
> And Architecture which is Science: are the Four Faces of man.
> Not so in Time & Space: there Three are shut out, and only Science
> Remains thro Mercy: & by means of Science, the Three
> Become apparent in Time & Space. (*M*, pl. 27, ll. 55–59)

Milton's architectural task is to deconstruct Urizen by causing the latter to own his "body" as the outer form of poetic genius, rather than as the stony seat and edifice of prescriptive authority.

Armed with the red clay of Succoth, Milton strives with Urizen at Arnon. The authority of Milton's poetry is of no avail; only his "naked" poetic genius, in evidence since his earlier ungirding of "the role of the promise" (*M*, pl. 14, l. 13), can serve him in the builder's task.

> Silent Milton stood before
> The darkened Urizen; as the sculptor silent stands before
> His forming image; he walks round it patient labouring.
> Thus Milton stood forming bright Urizen, while his Mortal part
> Sat frozen in the rock of Horeb: and his Redeemed portion
> Thus form'd the Clay of Urizen; but within that portion
> His real Human walkd above in power and majesty
> Tho darkend; and the Seven Angels of the Presence attended him.
> (*M*, pl. 20, ll. 7–14)

The task is successfully consummated. Milton puts off selfhood. Blake, having seen Milton deconstructed, is himself able to put off selfhood and be reconciled with the Miltonic genius in the realm of pure possibility. For Milton, the deconstruction allows for the fusion of his genius, and his reincorporation in, Albion's poetic genius (*M*, pl. 20, ll. 41ff.). Though Milton's heroic tale is retold, with variation, several times subsequently, it is at this point, approximately midway through the poem, that Milton completes his part of the builder's task. That he must repeat the task is a comment on how "encrusted" the world is with the delusion of material priority, not on how effective Milton is in finding the human lineaments that properly take precedence over that "encrustation."

The task of building Jerusalem must wait on the building of the four subsidiary "cities" that are aspects of Jerusalem's fourfold humanity. These are Beulah, Golgonooza, Bowlahoola, and Allamanda. As aspects of person and genius, these four, when held in harmony by poetic genius, are assembled to form the whole person and complete genius. A proverb describing this complete being is to be found in "The Proverbs of Hell": "The head sublime, the heart Pathos, the genitals Beauty, the hands & feet Proportion" (*MHH*, pl. 10, l. 61). The builder's task is to become each of the cities and the traits they represent in the process of himself becoming one with Jerusalem. In building he beholds, and in beholding he becomes.

Beulah is the city of beauty, the city of the genitals. It has already been built at the outset of *Milton*, witness the poet's opening invocation, addressed to "Daughters of Beulah! Muses who inspire the Poets Song" (*M*, pl. 2, l. 1). Moreover, it is a city that bears the stamp of poetic genius rather than that of edifice. Referring to the plight of English soldiers and capital felons, whose putting off of selfhood through death is a chillingly apt symbolizing of the self-transcendence Blake will attempt to effect, the poet shows beauty in control of its sphere, fully self-aware and able to identify its "Mocking Druidical Mathematical Proportion of Length Bredth Highth / Displaying Naked Beauty! with Flute & Harp & Song" (*M*, pl. 4, ll. 27–28).

The first city actually to be built within the poem itself is "Great Golgonooza" (*M*, pl. 3, l. 39). As the anagrammatic reference of its name to Golgotha (New Golgotha) indicates, Golgonooza is the city of the skull—hence, the city of the sublime. Having been fostered by the beauty of Beulah, the poet is then fostered by the fear, or terror of Golgonooza, which is sublime in the period sense of dark, smoky, indistinct, and instinctively terrifying.

> Charles calls on Milton for Atonement. Cromwell is ready
> James calls for fires in Golgonooza. for heaps of smoking ruins
> In the night of prosperity and wantonness which he himself Created.
>   (*M*, pl. 5, ll. 39–41)

If beauty may have terror to it, it is equally likely that terror may move its observer to pity. There is a kind of associative logic—perhaps the logic of the emotions—in the movement from beauty to terror to pity, or what Blake calls pathos. The next part of the builder's task involves the building of Bowlahoola, which is the city of the heart, or pathos. There is admittedly a difficulty in the name, which is usually taken as an anagram on *bowels*. The difficulty may be resolved, however, at lest provisionally, by noting that the two are virtually interchangeable, in the physiology of emotions, as the seat of pity. Blake also calls it the seat of the stomach (*M*, pl. 24 [26], l. 67).

The way that pity is perverted to cruelty in the fallen world is a favorite subject of Blake's, in such poems as "the Human Abstract" and "the Mental Traveller." That perversion occurs as well in Bowlahoola, through the intermediation of law.

Bowlahoola is namd Law. by mortals, Tharmas founded it:
. . . .
In Bowlahoola Los's Anvils stand & his Furnaces rage;
Thundering the Hammers beat & the Bellows blow loud
Living self moving mourning lamenting & howling incessantly.
(*M*, pl. 24 [26], ll. 51–53)

Finally, there is Allamanda, the name of which may refer to one of two German dances (allemandes) making use of the hands and feet in time to the quadrille-like music. Allamanda is the city of hands and feet, of proportion—the sense of calm and balance that follows the cathartic movement from beauty to terror to pity. Allamanda is the last of the lesser cities to be built before the building of Jerusalem itself. It is a resting place of sorts, in the Blakean sense of rest before labor. It marks a period or hiatus between the building of the four individual cities in Jerusalem, which is to be the unitive, corporate "embodiment" of the four. The rest referred to here is not repose but rather routine and order after chaos, the domestication of the terrors wrought in Golgonooza, along with their consolidation for use in the next great building task. Perhaps with a sense that the movement and partner changes of the allemande symbolize the transactions of the business world, Blake observes that "Allamanda calld on Earth Commerce, is the Cultivated land / Around the City of Golgonooza in the Forests of Entuthon" (*M*, pl. 27 [29], ll. 42–43).

With the four cities of Jerusalem's humanity completed, it remains only for the four aspects of the poet's humanity—Milton, Los, Blake, and Albion—to become "reembodied" in such a way that they have the wisdom necessary to make of the four cities a single, visionary one. That reembodiment occurs near the end of the poem, when the renovated Albion rises up and turns "his face . . . toward / The east, toward Jerusalems Gates" (*M*, pl. 39 [44], ll. 33–34). Albion could not have come to this pass without having acquired that craft required to build Jerusalem, and he could not have acquired that craft without having "died" and been "reborn" (or reembodied) into successively higher states of vision and knowledge. Most importantly, Albion could not have become the fourfold individual he is without the fellowship of others.

Craft, rebirth into higher wisdom, fellowship—all three of these are characteristic of the Masonic enterprise and equally of

Blake's visionary one. Blake took Freemasonry as one of the social institutions that were his cultural endowment and transformed it through a visionary poetic critique. The success of this critique resulted in Blake's conception of the builder's task, which provides the means for Blake's transcendence of the constraints of the self and Freemasonry alike, the former being the visionary project of a lifetime.

CHAPTER 4

Blake, Priestley, and the "Gnostic Moment"

One stubborn, deeply latent obstacle to understanding the relationship of literature and science has been the distinction, maintained until recently, between the methods and objects held to be characteristic of the two discourses. Originating with Bacon, ratified for the modern era by the likes of Horkheimer and Adorno, and promulgated in the present age by the likes of Gadamer and Habermas, the distinction, drawn and valorized as essential and fundamental, is between science (*Naturwissenschaft*) and other discourses in general and the human sciences (*Geisteswissenschaft*) in particular. With specific reference to literature and science, Hans Eichner expounds a position very much like the one set down above, distinguishing between a science immune to social and historical contingency, purely objective in its operations, and driven to the end of discovering the timeless laws of external nature, and other discourses (such as philosophy and literature) that are ineluctably dependent upon social and historical contingency, subjective to the point of partial nescience in their operations as the result of such contingency, and driven to the end of discovering the enduring truths of human nature, as

85

those truths are accessible in a given time, in a given place. In his conclusion, Eichner ventures "a brief statement, which admittedly is an oversimplification," distinguishing, after Dilthey, "between *Naturwissenschaft* and *Geisteswissenschaft*. The former studies nature, assumes determinacy, reasons ahistorically, and aims to establish timeless universal laws. The latter studies human creations, assumes free will, takes a basically historicist approach, and focuses on the individual, unique, timebound, and unrepeatable."[1]

To hold a position such as Eichner's is also to propose that the sociology of knowledge applies to the human sciences but not to the natural sciences. The position further implies a belief that the only good history of science is an "internalist" history that views the development of scientific ideas as being somehow removed from the social developments, transitions, and revolutions that serve to shape the rest of the culture and its discourse. The arguments against this position have been around for more than half a century, although extreme examples of the kind such as Boris Hessen's Marxist analysis of the socioeconomic context of Newton's *Principia* have not helped to advance the premise that science is a socially conditioned (and socially constructed) discourse, no different in this regard from all other discourses.[2]

One article of faith that has sustained the *Naturwissenschaft–Geisteswissenschaft* distinction is the belief in the mind's ability to transcend questions of ideology and social contingency, in order to become what Richard Rorty, with a little help from Shakespeare's *Measure for Measure* (2.3.120), terms "the glassy essence" of the object world.[3] However, the very project of epistemology underwritten by this belief—more specifically, the concern, central to philosophy from Plato to Russell and Husserl, "to keep philosophy [and its way of knowing] 'rigorous' and 'scientific' "—has been questioned by Rorty, who argues for the inevitable transition from epistemology to hermeneutics, the "idealistic" way of knowing adopted originally by the human sciences.[4] As a consequence of disenfranchising epistemology, one cannot fail to understand that its motivation is a Platonic or Baconian will to the sort of totalized knowledge that is power. The ideal of such knowledge/power depends for its part on the assumption of a correspondence theory of knowledge (and language) that emphasizes clarity both as an end in itself and as the means of attaining dominion over the life world and its creatures. Such clarity is only possible if one feature of language is an essentialist, totalizing metonymy capable of perfect and complete substitutive "naming" to attain those ends. Cases in point are the superhuman "legislators" who, according to Cratylus, gave things their first and true names and Bacon's unfallen Adam, himself only a little lower than the angels, naming the animals.[5] The person or institution that operates on the assumption that it speaks the language that possesses such metonymic power as its attribute feels empowered in turn to practice a totalizing form of reification to the end of establishing clarity. Moreover, that person or institution privileges clearly defined—one is tempted to say self-evident—structures of authority, be they evil, religious, scientific (or, in an age before "disciplines," some combination of these).

Metonymy is a figural strategy—indeed, a tropological engine— that makes a totalizing form of reification possible. In so doing, however, it supplants metaphor, which is by its nature relational rather than substitutive, leaving both terms and their respective frames of reference intact rather than allowing one term to possess and supplant the other through "naming" its essence. The resultant presence of the metonym testifies to the enactment of a process, described by Fredric Jameson,

> in which "natural" unities, social forms, human relations, cultural events, even religious systems, are systematically broken up to be reconstructed more efficiently, in the form of new post-natural processes or mechanisms; but in which, at the same time, these now isolated broken bits and pieces of the older unities acquire a certain autonomy of their own, a semi-autonomous coherence which . . . serves to compensate for the dehumanization of experience reification brings with it, and to rectify the otherwise intolerable effects of the new process.[6]

As Jameson elsewhere suggests, the process in question betokens class struggle, and the force of the reification is to silence the dialogical discourse of that struggle, in the process reducing what Bakhtin calls "heteroglossia" and Todorov after him calls "heterology" to "a common language" intended to serve the ends of the victorious and dominant ideology.[7]

If the relationship of a figural process such as metonymy and a cultural process such as reification to questions having to do with literature, science, and, as the presence of the concept of gnosticism suggests, religion, is not yet clear, it is now appropriate to attempt a clarification. It is reification, driven by substitutive tropes generally and metonomy in particular, that leads to the creation of literary "truths," scientific "laws," and religious and political "establishments" sanctioned by a dominant ideology.

For example, the authorial subject, seeking a suitable object of contemplation (a "subject," that is), is enjoined to "follow nature," transformed by metonymy into the reified and generally passive, feminized forms—tulips the streaks of which one should refrain from numbering—that constitute the proper object of literary scrutiny. Matter metonymized as "corpuscles" entirely uniform and without immanent potential or interiority leads to Newtonian laws and the ideological construction of a fully reified universe consisting entirely of matter, motion, and force set into being and motion by a transcendent but since absconded first cause. God, metonymized by the creed "I believe in one God, Father Almighty, Maker of heaven and earth," leads within the Church to a reified structure of patriarchal authority.[8] That patriarchy in its turn sanctions the prerogatives of a monarch who, more often than not, is not only God's vice-gerent but a member of a patriarchal succession in his own right. As a logical consequence, the ecclesiastical patriarchy arrogates to itself exclusive license, by dint of the apostolic succession, to dispense *ex cathedra* truths and sacraments alike, including the sacramental viaticum of "daily bread" mentioned in a prayer canonized by the Church Fathers and now held by Catholic and Protestant scholars alike to be the words not of the originally ascribed author but of someone else—perhaps a disciple. The monarchical patriarchy dispenses civil truths and more nearly temporal forms of sustenance—preferments, patents, places at court, and so on. Although it is anachronistic and hopelessly secular and democratic, the common metonym "go fight city hall"[9] does a serviceable job of capturing the sense of frustration, even oppression, that the average person feels in confronting any such avatar of absolute power, the acts of which may well suggest questionable judgment and authority and perhaps a hint of corruption as well.

The examples adduced above in support of the argument about the relationship between metonymy, reification, and the establishment of structures of authority in the name of a dominant ideology have a distinctly late seventeenth- or eighteenth-century resonance that is not coincidental. In the second half of the eighteenth century, the age of Blake, Priestley, and, if the title of the essay is aptly descriptive, somewhere in the midst of a "gnostic moment," the use by those subscribing to the dominant ideology of substitutive tropes—personification, synecdoche, and above all metonymy—rather than tropes demonstrating the relational alternative was in an ascendancy perhaps unequaled before or since.

However, the second half of the eighteenth century was hardly the first historical instance of someone's using the metonymic move as a means of appropriating and sustaining authority "in the name of" an untotalizable totality—God—whose substitutive likeness bears a strikingly close resemblance to an empowered segment of society that wishes, naturally enough, to remain in power.[10] Other instances of note are those of early Christian Rome (from the second century A.D. to the council of Nicea [A.D. 325]), sixteenth- and early seventeenth-century Italy, and early seventeenth-century England.[11]

The gnostic texts themselves demonstrate how early and how astute gnosis in general and gnosticism in particular were in responding to the metonymic move.[12] *Allogenes*, for example, is one of the texts in the Nag Hammmadi Library, which was buried by the gnostic faithful circa A.D. 400, when the post-Nicene intolerance epitomized by the likes of Athanasius was condemning the gnostics and their texts, respectively, as "heretics and . . . 'apocryphal books, to which they attribute antiquity and give the name of saints.'"[13] Commenting on "the Unknown God," "the powers of the Luminaries" speak to the author *of Allogenes*, leaving little doubt that one tropes God by relational rather than substitutive means and must resist the delusion of totalization as a means of self-authorization or empowerment to speak for God or command others in his name.

> Now he [i.e., God] is reified insofar as he exists in that he earlier exists and becomes, or acts and knows, although he lives without Mind or Life or Existence or Non-Existence, incomprehensibly. And he is reified among his attributes. He is not left over in some way, as if he yields something that is assayed or purified or that he receives and gives. And he is not diminished in some way, [whether] by his own desire or whether he gives or receives

through another—it does not affect him. Rather, neither does he give anything by himself lest he become diminished in another way, nor for this reason does he need Mind, or Life, or indeed anything at all. He is indeed better than the Totalities in his privation and unknowability, that is, the non-being Existence, since he is endowed with silence and stillness lest he be diminished by those who are not diminished. (XI, 3: *61*, 24–62, 28)[14]

Seen in historical perspective, the "gnostic moment" is symptomatic of a particular set of circumstances, in its turn the occasion for the production of an exemplar of the genre that Amos Funkenstein calls "counter-history."[15] To return, however, to the "gnostic moment" being played out in the second half of the eighteenth century in England and elsewhere, such as Germany:[16] one of the things that is distinctive about that particular "gnostic moment" is both the discursive breadth of the authority claimed by those basing their empowerment on the dominant ideology and the breadth of the response. Prior to the eighteenth century, claims of authority and the gnostic responses to them were played out almost exclusively in the discourses of ecclesiastical and civil authority, the two discourses more often than not being virtually indistinguishable. Literature, if it had a discursive role in the struggle, assumed that role only as the expression of one of the two contending theological or political positions—here Bruno's *De umbras idearum* (1582) and Campanella's *Citta del Sole* (1623) serve as examples. And scientists, although no strangers to Hermetic lore, did not make that lore the basis of the discourse of science, however else they might have put it to use, the one weakly conjectural possible exception being Galileo.[17]

As the fates of these three Italian "heretics" suggest, the temporal power of church and state, especially the former, was such that there were, up to a certain point, clear winners and losers in the interpretive struggle of the "gnostic moment." Bruno was burned at the stake, Campanella and Galileo recanted their "heresies," and Rome, its Jesuits, and the Inquisition remained in the ascendant. So, too, with the early Christian gnostics, who had to choose either to go underground, in the several senses of that phrase, or to risk persecution for their beliefs. Thus the history of the "gnostic moment" up to the late seventeenth and eighteenth centuries has been, in large measure, obscured, and both the basis and the point of its critique have, for the most part, been lost or obscured. There were winners and losers, that is to say, in a game of winner-take-all.

Another distinction between the "gnostic moment" of the late seventeenth and eighteenth centuries and its predecessors in the context of Western culture, a distinction perhaps owing to the very discursive breadth noted above, is that for the first time there were no clear winners and losers. Thus the "gnostic moment" of that time and all previous "gnostic moments" to which that moment referred, as well as the critique that all of these moments, with some variation, mounted, came to the attention of those seeking alternatives to a hegemonic Western culture and provided them with an alternative cultural position even as the gnostic viewpoint itself began gradually to become assimilated into a pluralized "mainstream" (if not hegemonic) modern Western culture. Whether the "gnostic moment" is responsible for "such movements as progressivism, positivism, Marxism, psycho-analysis, communism, fascism, and national socialism," as Eric Voegelin claims, is debatable.[18] That one particular "gnostic moment" had a good deal to do with establishing a dissenting position from which to mount a powerful critique of the dominant ideology of the moment and the power relations underwritten by that ideology seems certain.

TOWARD BLAKE AND PRIESTLEY'S "GNOSTIC MOMENT"

In assessing the impact of the first "gnostic moment," Elaine Pagels speculates on what Christianity might have become if the gnostic doctrines embodied in the Nag Hammadi codices had not, as it were, gone underground. But their very submersion, as she concludes, underscores the truism that

> it is the winners who write history—their way. No wonder, then, that the viewpoint of the successful majority has dominated all traditional accounts of the origin of Christianity. Ecclesiastical Christians first defined the terms (naming themselves "orthodox" and their opponents "heretics"); then they proceeded to demonstrate—at least to their own satisfaction—that this triumph was historically inevitable, or, in religious terms, "guided by the Holy Spirit."

Nevertheless, as Pagels observes, "the concerns of gnostic Christians survived," if "only as a suppressed current."[19] In the late sixteenth and seventeenth centuries and, more importantly for the present discussion, in the late seventeenth and eighteenth centuries, the current surfaced, giving rise to the "gnostic moment" that is here the subject of discussion. It was a moment in which the history and ideology of the winners were problematized in the attempt recover and reconsider those of the losers. The antiheretical position that originated with such Christian ideologues and propagandists (*propaganda fidei*, "propagation of the faith") as Irenaeus (*Adversus haereses* [ca. 180–92]), Tertullian (*De praescriptione haereticorum* [ca. 200]), Origen (*Contra Celsum* [before 254]), and Epiphanius of Salamis (*Panarion* [374–77]) and was ratified by the Church at the Council of Nicea (325) was no longer conceded to be the last word in the debate. The time had come to reassess the heretical position that originated with gnostics such as Marcion, Valentinus, and Menander and was energized by dissent. This is the nature of the reassessment undertaken by Protestant revisionists such as the Pietist Gottfried Arnold.

Arnold's *Unparteiischen Kirchen- und Ketzerhistorie* (*Impartial History of Churches and Heresies* [1699; 1729]), the product of "the disdain of history and the sharpening of critical faculties" symptomatic of a distinctively Protestant "critical-polemical" approach to history, did not take the winners at their word, arguing forcefully instead "for a new view of church history which could seek the true Christianity among the outlaws and the heretics."[20] To use Funkenstein's term, Arnold's text is, generically speaking, a "counterhistory": "It consists of the systematic exploitation of the adversary's most trusted sources against their own intent: in the fortunate phrase of Walter Benjamin, counterhistories 'comb the sources against the grain,' as Marxist historiography indeed does to reconstruct the history of the victim rather than that of the victors."

Not that Arnold originated the genre: Funkenstein allows that counterhistories had been written "since antiquity."[21] Far more important than the characteristics of the genre itself is its revival at a particular moment in the history of Protestant dissent. Other works in the genre followed closely upon Arnold's—for example, the Reformed theologian Isaac de Beausobre's *Critique de Manichée et Manichéisme* (1734; 1739) and the Lutheran theologian Johann Lorenz von Mosheim's *Ecclesiastical History*

(1739; 1758; trans. 1764). Although "modern research into Gnosis" did not begin until the 1820s, Arnold's counterhistory and the studies of Beausobre and Mosheim after it served notice, in Kurt Rudolph's words, that "the ground was prepared for an independent consideration of the gnostics, and in the first place in particular with the sources relating to them."[22]

If anything, the ground in England was both more fertile and earlier prepared than it was in Germany or France, owing to the vitality of radical English Protestantism and the use to which English commentators put Hermetic thought in defense of that position.[23] Keith Thomas may be correct in characterizing English Hermeticism as "largely a derivative affair, stimulated by continental writings, but adding little of its own," but it soon took on a distinctly English character. Notwithstanding scholarly challenges—for example, "Isaac Casaubon's scholarship [which] deprived the Hermetic books of their claim to be pre-Christian as early as 1614"—(in a "polemic against the Counter Reformation historian Baronius," it should be noted)—"[Robert] Fludd wrote prolifically during the following decades . . . and John Everard's English translation of the hermetic *Pymander* (1649) disseminated the tradition more widely. The preface unrepentantly asserted that the work had been written 'some hundreds of years before Moses.' "[24] Both Fludd and Everard are important to any consideration of the "gnostic moment" in England. As Betty Jo Teeter Dobbs notes, Fludd took Comenian pansophy, which is based on the assumption that immanentist chemical essences are responsible for the full range of intelligible phenomena,[25] and applied it to the account of the Creation in Genesis, fully mindful of the significance of such an application.

> If the act of creation was to be understood chemically, then all of nature was to be understood similarly. In short, chemistry was the key to all nature, the key to all the macrocosmic-microcosmic relationships sought by Robert Fludd and others. A study of chemistry was a study of God as He had Himself written out His word in the Book of Nature. Such a study could only lead one closer to God and was conceived as having moral value as well as contributing to the better grasp of the workings of nature.[26]

Everard was one of the principal importers of gnostic thought into the England of Blake and Priestley, although other possible sources include the Codex Brucianus and the Codex Askewianus, as well as Priestley's own *Disquisitions Relating to Matter and Spirit* (1777). Priestley discusses and quotes at length from Beausobre and Mosheim, especially the latter, who was also available in a 1764 English translation.[27]

But these other possibilities should not cause one to lose sight of the importance of Everard, especially when considered in the context of political and religious radicalism. What Michael Ferber "find[s] interesting" about Everard, in addition to his plausibility as "one source of gnostic ideas in Blake," is both his politics—Everard "was a radical Protestant troublemaker, frequently in jail for heresy (King James said his name should be 'Never-out')"—and, as the religious dimension of those politics suggests, his theology. Everard "preached to the lowest classes that God was immanent in nature, though preeminently in man, and that heaven and hell were in our hearts. The social implications of his teachings, not very different from Gerrard Winstanley's, were clear to the bishops, who continually persecuted him. . . . In 1650, and perhaps again in 1790, the thrust of gnostic speculation seems to have been subversive, radical, and democratic."[28]

A brief glance at Everard's *Divine Pymander* suggests how readily the immanentist metaphysics of the *Corpus Hermeticum* lends itself to a radical program of social reform, even leveling, as well as to an immanentist science of divinely engendered powers and essences. As Ferber's comments on heaven and hell suggest, one of established religion's chief claims to authority is its propounding and interpretation of a doctrine of the afterlife that stipulates rewards for "good" behavior (following the commandments of church and state) and sanctions for "bad" behavior (breaking the commandments of church and state). Any doctrine of the afterlife depends in its turn on the assumption that death is real and irrevocable—at least until the Apocalypse. If death is not real and irrevocable, then there is nothing to be gained by being "good" and nothing to be lost by being "bad," at least not in the senses of "good" and "bad" set forth above. One simply is and acts on the inner "motion" that is his or her vital energy. Such, at least, is one of the implications that might be drawn from the following exchange between Hermes Trismegistus and his son Tat (i.e., Thoth, Theuth):

TAT. Therefore, O Father, do not the living things in the World die, though
      they be parts thereof.
HERM. Be wary in thy Speech, O Son, and do not be deceived by the names
      of things.
      For they do not die, O son, but as compound Bodies they are dissolved.
          But dissolution is not death; and they are dissolved, not that they may
      be destroyed, but that they may be made new.
TAT. What then is the operation of life? Is it not Motion?
HERM. And what is there in the World unmoveable? Nothing at all, O Son.[29]

The vital energy in question is a pervasive form of immanence, and as such it exercises a leveling influence. Acting on the authority of Genesis 2:7 and other texts, the Church sets itself up as the institution best able to deal with the concerns of the soul, that immortal and immaterial entity and emblem of divine afflatus characteristic of human beings alone of all the living creatures in the world. But what if vital energy is everywhere and ensoulment is universal rather than particularly characteristic of humanity alone? As Hermes tells Tat, "the parts of the World are Heaven, and Earth, and Water, and Air, after the same manner the members of God are Life, and Immortality, and Eternity, and Spirit, and Necessity, and Providence, and Nature, and Soul, and Mind, and the Continuance or perseverance of all these which is called Good." These "members" are at work everywhere within the world of matter in which one lives. "If it [i.e., matter] be actuated, by whom is it actuated? for we have said, that Acts and Operations, are the parts of God."[30]

Both Fludd and Everard acted on the gnostic imperative to frame a counterhistory, up to and including a countercosmology, and both endorsed the notion of immanent causation essential to that countercosmology and its revision of orthodox notions of good and evil, although whether they are on the basis of these positions properly regarded as gnostics is neither entirely clear nor necessarily relevant.[31]

BLAKE AND PRIESTLEY'S "GNOSTIC MOMENT"

Blake, for his part, publicly embraced gnosticism—at least on the report of Henry Crabb Robinson. Robinson's *Reminiscences* (1852) includes a report of a discussion with Blake in which the latter reiterates "the doctrine of the Gnostics" that the creation of the material world is a fall into error "with sufficient consistency to silence one so unlearned as myself."[32] Blake's understanding of creation-as-fall comports well with the gnostic understanding of that phenomenon and is discussed at some length below.

Priestley, for his part, repudiated a number of gnostic doctrines—for example, "the doctrine of *pre-existence*, or that of all human souls having been lapsed angels, which was the source of *Gnosticism* and most of the early corruptions of Christianity," and the doctrines that "the Supreme Mind [is] the author of all good, and *matter* [is] the source of all evil, that all inferior intelligences are *emanations from the Supreme Mind*."[33] But this repudiation is partial. Although Priestley rejects the preexistence of souls and particular immanence, it does not follow that he accepts Newtonian materialism as the alternative. He questions its understanding of matter, noting especially "the difficulty which attends the supposition of *the creation of it out of nothing*, and also the continual moving of it by a being which has hitherto been supposed to have no common property with it" (*DMS*, 18). Something more closely akin to such matter than the God of Genesis 1 must preexist it and relate to it as pervasive immanent cause to general effect. Discussing solidity, one of the five irreducible properties of Newtonian matter, Priestley takes a position reminiscent of Comenius and Fludd after him, endorsing the preexistence of powers if not of souls and arguing that this property "is possessed only in consequence of being endued with certain *powers*, and together with this cause, solidity, being no more than an *effect*, must cease, if there be any foundation to the plainest and best established rules of reasoning in philosophy" (*DMS*, 7).

Whatever their particular doctrinal accommodations with "orthodox" gnosticism may have been, Blake and Priestley were critical of and resistant to the metonymic move. Blake, although troubled by the idea of nature—particularly Wordsworthian nature—nevertheless took as his article of faith that the world of natural objects is permeated by an immanent principle that originates with God and is attributable only to him. Blake's view of nature, whether metonymized as feminized and passive by Johnson or by Wordsworth, threatens by its very substitutive presence to preempt and extinguish the imagination's ability to forge the individual's relationship to the life world around him or her by dint of strong metaphor. In the introduction to *Europe* (1794), for example, "a Fairy mocking as he sat on a streak'd Tulip" describes the plight of a reified humanity in a reified world.

> Five windows light the cavern'd Man; thro' one he breathes the air;
> Thro' one, hears music of the spheres; thro' one, the eternal vine
> Flourishes, that he may receive the grapes; thro' one can look.
> And see small portions of the eternal world that groweth;
> Thro' one, himself pass out what time he please, but he will not;
> For stolen joys are sweet, & bread eaten in secret pleasant.[34]

And in His "Annotations to Wordsworth's *Poems*" (1815), Blake writes, "Natural Objects always did & now do Weaken deaden & obliterate Imagination in me[.] Wordsworth must know that what he Writes Valuable is Not to be found in Nature" (*CPP*, p. 665).

The problem with a metonymized nature for Blake is that it locks humanity ineluctably into a solipsistic materialism without the hope or possibility of transcendence. In his first engraved text, *There Is No Natural Religion [a]* (1788), Blake makes the point that if "Man" were "only a natural organ subject to Sense," and if "from a perception of only 3 senses or 3 elements none could deduce a fourth or fifth," humanity would be limited to nothing "other than natural or organic thoughts." However, Blake posits the existence of an immanence that helps to break the circle. "If it were not for the Poetic or Prophetic character the Philosophic & Experimental would soon be at the ratio of all things, & stand still unable to do other than repeat the same dull round over again" (*CPP*, p. 1).

Priestley's lifelong search for underlying, immanent principles, both electrical and chemical, in nature made him leery of the metonymic move and its tendency toward easy reification. In his first scientific text, Priestley suggests by way of preface that Newtonian corpuscles, rather than being the irreducible units of a universe of matter, force, and motion, are themselves the result of a prior, immanent constitutive cause.

> Hitherto philosophy has been chiefly conversant about the more sensible properties of bodies; electricity, together with chemistry, and the doctrine of light and colours, seems to be giving us an inlet into their internal structure, on which their sensible properties depend. By pursuing this new light

97

therefore, the bounds of natural science may possibly be extended, beyond what we can now form an idea of. New worlds may open to our view, and the glory of the great Sir Isaac Newton himself, and all of his contemporaries be eclipsed [*sic*], by a new set of philosophers, in a quite new field of speculation.[35]

The search for immanentist models also helps to explain Priestley's advocacy of the phlogiston theory in opposition to Lavoisier and his admiration for Boscovich, who, according to Priestley's letter of 7 March 1773 to Reverend Joseph Bretland, "seems to suppose that matter consists of *powers* only, without any substance." According to Robert E. Schofield, the "concepts of Boscovich (so influential with Davy, Faraday, Kelvin, and Maxwell in the nineteenth century)" were "introduced to the serious attention of British scientists" by Priestley.[36] As was seen above, Priestley argues in *Disquisitions* not that powers exist without substance, but that powers are a necessary principle prior to substance, a position pointedly at odds with Newton's corpuscular view.

Blake's belief in God as an immanent principle dates from no later than *There Is No Natural Religion [b]*: "He who sees the Infinite in all things sees God" (*CPP*, p. 3).[37] That Blake intends a principle rather than a personification is clear from Isaiah's observation in the second "Memorable Fancy" of *The Marriage of Heaven and Hell* (1790–93): "I saw no God. nor heard any, in a finite organical perception; but my senses discover'd the infinite in every thing, and as I was then perswaded. & remain confirm'd; that the voice of honest indignation is the voice of God, I cared not for consequences but wrote" (*MHH*, pl. 12).

Priestley's belief in God as an immanent principle, apparent no later than 1767, received perhaps its fullest articulation a decade later in *Disquisitions*. Discussing the mechanical philosophy's telling inability to account satisfactorily for consciousness and the relationship of mind to body,[38] Priestley begins by considering perhaps the strongest evidence for the existence of an immanent principle such as *pneuma*: the soul. He argues, contra Newton, that "if we suffer ourselves to be guided in our inquiries by the universally acknowledged *rules of philosophizing*, we shall find ourselves entirely unauthorized to admit anything in man besides that *body* which is the object of our senses." (*DMS*, xiv–xv). To acknowledge such a limitation would be, for Priestley, to beg the question of how one comes to perceive the body itself, let alone to possess the intelligence necessary to posit the existence of a unitive soul that is the ground of the senses. Thus Priestley asserts "that the soul of man cannot be material and divisible, because the *principle of consciousness*, which comprehends the whole of the thinking power, is necessarily simple and indivisible" (*DMS*, 86). As with the principle, so with its origin: "It will be said, that if the principle of thought in *man* may be a property of material substance, the *divine Being* himself may be material also; whereas, it is now almost universally believed to be the Doctrine of Revelation, that the Deity is, in the strictest sense of the word, an *immaterial substance*, incapable of local preference" (*DMS*, 103).

Both Blake and Priestley were aware of the importance of reconsidering the canonical biblical account of the creation in articulating their respective cosmologies. Given the importance of that account for natural as well as ecclesiastical history, the very act of reconsideration cast the two as counterhistorians, although in Blake's case the counterhistorical texts of record were poetic histories, not chronicles. For example, in *The Marriage of Heaven and Hell*, Blake calls into question the "history [that] has been adopted by both parties" (*MHH*, pl. 5), the satanic as well as the messianic, regarding reasons for and significance of the fall. And he questions the delusions arising from the strategies of argument from design and reification employed by orthodoxy, the "system which some took advantage of & enslav'd the vulgar by attempting to realize or abstract the mental deities from their objects: thus began Priesthood." Such an orthodoxy, in using the material world to validate its claims to authority and correctness, denies the primacy of such immanent principles as the gnostic *pneuma*. "Thus men forgot that All deities reside in the human breast" (*MHH*, pl. 11).

The story that Blake tells, like that of Everard's *Pymander*, is supposed to antedate the Mosaic account by a considerable span of time. In fact, Blake's account makes the origin of priesthood connate with the creation of the material world by Urizen, Blake's rendering of the gnostic demiurge.[39] Blake's tale "Of the primeval Priests assum'd power" (*U*, pl. 2, l. 1) in *The Book of Urizen* (1794) begins with Urizen's denial of the primacy of *pneuma* as the manifestation testifying to the existence of the gnostic Protennoia.[40] Prior to Urizen's advent,

1. Earth was not: nor globes of attraction
The will of the Immortal expanded
Or contracted his all flexible senses.
Death was not, but eternal life sprung. (*U*, pl. 3, ll. 46–49)

But when Urizen comes on the scene, he brings with him judgment, death, and above all, matter.

2. The sound of a trumpet the heavens
Awoke & vast clouds of blood roll'd
Round the dim rocks of Urizen, so nam'd
That solitary one in Immensity. (*U*, pl. 3, ll. 50–53)

This is a very different cosmology, or history of the creation, from the "official" reificatory version found in Genesis 1.

Priestley's counterhistory is an attempt to defend the Unitarian view of Christ, which he ascribes to "the ancient Jewish church," against the orthodox view on the one hand and the gnostic view on the other. However, Priestley's disagreements with the gnostic view are actually not so profound as they might at first appear to be. The argument of *An History of the Creation of Christianity* (1782) is "that Christ was simply a *man*, and not either *God Almighty*, or a *super angelic being*."[41] This denial of the orthodox trinitarian doctrine of *homoousia* (consubstantiality) and the gnostic doctrine of Christ's superangelic origins and nature is not a denial of the proposition that God works immanently and miraculously in the world and in at least some of its creatures, however.

Priestley does debunk the belief of "the Carpocratians, Valentinians, and others who were generally termed Gnostics . . . that Christ had a pre-existence and was a human only in appearance" (*History* 1:8). His notion of what a man is and may do when God works in him, however, suggests that the quarrel is less about the efficacy of divine immanence than about whether it is pervasive or particular. Priestley's Unitarian Christ may have been "simply a *man*," but he is the man "whose history answers to the description given of the Messiah by the prophets," the man who "made no other pretensions; referring all his extraordinary power to God, his father, who, he expressly says, spake and acted by him, and who raised him from the dead; and it is most evident that the apostles, and all those who conversed with our Lord, before and after his resurrection, considered him in no other light than simply as *a man approved by God, by signs and wonders which God did by him.* Acts ii. 22" (*History* 1:2).

Priestley's Christ is finally the best of men, but his relationship with God, if it does differ from the relationships of others "approved by God," differs in degree rather than in kind, and the divine immanence that "spake and acted by him" may speak and act by others similarly approved, if not in fact by all. The Church's unwillingness to accept this view, with its disastrously subversive implications for any structure of hierarchy and the consequent need for proprietary control of governance, doctrine, and liturgy,[42] is grounded on a willful misunderstanding of and tendency to reify the doctrine of the *Logos*—a move that Priestley identifies as "the personification of the *Logos*" (*History* 1:30)—by platonizing Jews such as Philo Judaeus and Christians such as Justin Martyr. The former "calls this divine word *a second God*" (ibid.); the latter inaugurates the doctrine of applying the divinity explicitly to Christ (*History* 1:32–35).

The main chance seized by Justin and his successors, according to Priestley, is the beginning of the Gospel According to John ("In the beginning was the word [*Logos*], and the Word was with God, and the word was God" [1:1]).

> The christian philosophers having once got the idea that the *Logos* might be interpreted as Christ, proceeded to explain what John says of the *Logos* in the introduction of his gospel, to mean the same person, in direct opposition to what he really meant, which was that the *Logos* by which all things were made was not a being distinct from God, but God himself, being his attribute, his wisdom and power, dwelling in Christ, speaking and acting by him. (*History* 1:31)

Logos, in other words, is an indwelling or immanent power that originates with God and pervades the world rather than being localized in one person or the church founded upon his life, words, and acts. Priestley refers to the precedent of the Septuagint in his argument for dissevering the concept of *Logos* from the person of Christ: "there is one particular passage in the book of Psalms in which they imagined that the origin of the *Logos*, by way of emanation from the divine mind, is most clearly expressed, which is what we render, *My heart is inditing good matter. Psalm* xlv. 1, this *matter* being *Logos* in the Seventy [Septuagint], and the verb *ereugomenou[,] throwing out*" (*History* 1:30).

Despite their insistence on the superangelic nature of Christ, the gnostics, like Priestley's early Unitarians, likewise believed in at least a partially pervasive rather than a particular immanence. Those "initiates" able to see the creation of the material world for the fall it was were "'released' from the demiurge's power" and from the claims of established ecclesiastical authority by dint of the workings of this pervasive immanence. "Every initiate was assumed to have received, through the initiation ritual, the charismatic gift of direct inspiration [*pneuma*] through the Holy Spirit."[43]

CONCLUSION: THE "GNOSTIC MOMENT" AS CULTURAL SYMPTOM

This discussion of the "gnostic moment"—"gnostic moments," actually, since Rome before the Council of Nicea, with its Valentinians and Marcionites, and the England of circa 1650, with its Hermetics, Anabaptists, Ranters, Muggletonians, and other radical "inner light" sects, are as deserving of the designation as the England of circa 1790, with its dissenting sects—brings one back to the question of whether there are any predisposing conditions for or defining characteristics of each.

The short answer is that there are such conditions and characteristics and that they are evident from the first "gnostic moment" onward. From the beginning of the dispute, in the days of the gnostic "heretic" Marcion and his "orthodox" antagonist Irenaeus (ca. 180–92), orthodoxy has deployed a strategy of metonymic repetition leading to reification, to the end of creating an object world that may be used to demonstrate the presumed originary truth of those reifications, to the exclusion of pluralism, and in celebration of the absolute priority of the status quo of the material universe as that status quo is constructed by the ideology of the empowered as the ground of all meaning and the evidence for any valorization of dogma.

Pagels begins her discussion of "the politics of monotheism" by noting the importance of the beginning of the Christian Creed: "I believe in one God, Father Almighty, Maker of heaven and earth."[44] Learned by rote repetition, often by those too young or otherwise unable to read and reflect, such a creed demonstrates what Shelley, in a discussion of much the same problem, aptly terms "the abuse of a metaphorical expression to a literal purpose"—an abuse, it might be added, that has the precise effect of reducing the "vitally metaphorical" language of the imagination to a condition in which "words . . . become . . . signs for portions or classes of thoughts instead of pictures of integral thoughts,"[45] (metonymy, in other words). The vehicles "Father Almighty" and "Maker of heaven and earth" tend to overwhelm the tenor "one God," with the result that God comes to be understood in terms of earthly authority figures (fathers) and the object world of a "made" heaven and earth and justified with reference to those authority figures and that object world.

Thus a principled objection by "the heretic Marcion," who "was struck by what he saw as the contrast between the creator-God of the Old Testament who demands justice and punishes every violation of the law, and the Father whom Jesus proclaims—the New Testament God of forgiveness and love"[46]—is rejected for its dualistic (and ultimately pluralistic) implications. The process is the perfect illustration of how Bakhtin's "heteroglossia" or Todorov's "heterology" is reduced to ideology when what "arises spontaneously from social diversity" is subjected to "the aspiration, correlative to all power, to institute a common language (or rather a speech)."[47]

The reification in question results from viewing God as—actually, reducing him to—a father and an artisanal maker and from viewing the material world as both the ground and the divinely designed result of God's fatherly and artisanal acts, the culmination of which is the creation of humanity in his own image. If God is the maker of heaven and earth, then the perceived properties *heaven* and *earth* must somehow reveal the mark of divine agency. Thus long before the rise of natural theology in the seventeenth century, some version of the argument from design was being used to justify a particular view of God and the authority structures of an orthodoxy committed to indoctrinating the laity in that particular view. The particular view intended is suggested by the credal phrase "Maker of heaven and earth," which strongly echoes the first verse of Genesis 1 ("In the beginning God created the heaven and the earth"). Implicit in both the credal phrase and its biblical source is the decision to privilege the account of material origins over that of immaterial origins (*pneuma*) that is narrated in Genesis 2,[48] to privilege an externalist metaphysics over the immanentist alternative, and to extend the tyranny of the bodily eye to social control based on the manipulation by the empowered of an ideologically constructed visible world encompassing all that one "sees," from the icons and images of orthodoxy to "nature" itself. Being created in God's image becomes the pretext for speaking for him and ruling in his stead.

The gnostic response of the second century adumbrates what was to follow in the 1650s and 1790s. As Pagels suggests, the gnostics believed neither in the substance of the Christian Creed nor in the metaphysics underwriting it:

> while the Valentinians publicly confessed faith in one God, in their own private meetings they insisted on discriminating between the popular image of God—as master, king, lord, creator, and judge—and what that image represented—God understood as the ultimate source of all being. Valentinus calls that source "the depth"; his followers describe it as an invisible, incomprehensible primal principle. But most Christians, they say, mistake mere images of God for that reality.[49]

To believe in such a principle, whether it is manifested as poetic inspiration up to and including prophetic power, electrical powers of attraction and repulsion, phlogiston, or what-have-you, is to disavow the reification of authority—"God . . . as master, king, lord, creator, and judge"—and those who rule in the name of such reification. To believe in such a principle is the first step toward the "gnostic moment."

CHAPTER 5

Blake on Charters, Weights, and Measures as Forms of Social Control

Commenting on William Blake's "London," first published in *Songs of Innocence and of Experience* (1794), Stewart Crehan notes that "what is exposed is not 'crimes,' 'wickedness,' and 'evil deeds,' but a whole social system."[1] Such a system depends for its perpetuation on powerful social control, acting in the name of ideologically expedient conventions or standards that construct a norm against which the perceptions and actions of the individual are valorized. The conventions or standards themselves are enacted, as Michael Ferber suggests, by a process of repetition leading to both reification and totalization.[2] As Donald Ault argues, there could be no place either in the social fabric of Blake's England or in its system of social control for the anomalous or incommensurable, since incommensurability was viewed as being tantamount to anarchy in the sphere of social relations and illogic in the sphere of an ideologically constructed empirical science.[3] The chartered measures, rights, and duties of Englishmen set forth in the Magna Carta, no less than the five irreducible properties of matter set forth in the "Rules of Reasoning in Philosophy" of Newton's *Principia*, were held to apply universally to the "little bodies" they presumed to describe—Englishmen in the first instance, corpuscular matter in the second.

In Blake's England, chapter 35 of the Magna Carta had the force of incorporating into the English Constitution the system of standardized weights and measures originally much more important for assessing taxes on commodities, stuffs, and manufacturers than for insuring fair value for money paid or facilitating scientific undertakings. Blake's "London," with its focus on the "charter'd" and on the sort of totalization signaled by the repetition of the word *every*, is a trenchant critique of such conventions or standards, but it is by no means his only critique in this vein. With this caveat in mind, I wish to begin by discussing Blake's growing awareness of the role played by the "charter'd" in "London"—specifically, his developing grasp of how the conventional or the standardized results from the imposition of one individual's imagination, figured forth as paradigm, model, or metaphor, upon others. Next, I shall attempt to show the extent to which the status of conventions or standards, mensurative and otherwise, was a hotly debated issue during the 1790s and after. Throughout, I shall attempt to suggest the extent to which Blake's critique permeates his thought and writing. In conclusion, I shall discuss briefly how Blake's critique of the problem of measurement and standardization anticipates, in several important respects, the current wisdom that scientific paradigms (or models, or metaphors) are a necessary precondition for conventions, standards, and measurement, not the other way around.

One of Blake's most frequently discussed emendations is *charter'd*, as it appears in the first two lines of the final version of "London." Between the time that he wrote down the original fair copy of the poem in his Notebook and the time he published the illumination in *Songs*, Blake changed "dirty street" and "dirty Thames" to "charter'd street" and "charter'd Thames," perhaps, as David V. Erdman suggests, after considering the intermediate possibilities of "charter'd streams" and "cheating banks of Thames."[4] Erdman himself sees in the emendation a mocking retort to "Thomson's boast [in 'Rule, Britannia!' (1740)] that 'the charter of the land' [i.e., the Magna Carta] keeps Britons free" as well as an implicit agreement with "the Second Part of *The Rights of Man* [1792], where [Thomas] Paine argues that all charters are purely negative in effect and that city charters, by annulling the rights of the majority, cheat the inhabitants and destroy the town's prosperity—even London being 'capable of bearing up against the political evils of a corporation' only from its advantageous situation on the Thames."[5]

Erdman's reading comports with that of Northrop Frye, who sees Blake using the word in "London" "with the full power of his irony behind it." The same sort of irony characterizes the earlier *King Edward the Third*, a dramatic fragment included in *Poetical Sketches* (1783). The fragment's namesake, who, as it turns out, was instrumental in establishing a system of standardized weights and measures, speaks in praise of "Liberty, the charter'd right of Englishmen" (*KE3*, 1.9).[6]

While the readings of Erdman and Frye convey a general sense of why Blake was mindful of the social and political implications of charters in the early 1790s, neither reading suggests any relationship between Blake's concern and the specific historical developments that provided him with a context of response. Erdman comes close to specifying such a context in his reference to the part 2 of *The Rights of Man*. There, however, Paine is after bigger game than city or corporate charters. Not even the Magna Carta itself is exempt from his critique. In his words,

> If we begin with William of Normandy, we find that the government of England was originally a tyranny, founded on an invasion and conquest of the country. This being admitted, it will then appear, that the exertion of the nation, at different periods, to abate the tyranny, and render it less intolerable, has been credited for a constitution.
>
> Magna Carta, as it was called (it is now like an almanack of the same date), was no more than compelling the government to renounce a part of its assumptions. It did not create and give powers to government in the manner a constitution does; but was, as far as it went, of the nature of a re-conquest, and not a constitution; for could the nation have totally expelled the usurpation, as France has done its despotism, it would have then had a constitution in form.[7]

Paine's critique undoubtedly reinforced Blake's ready sympathies for the French Revolution, which, as he viewed it in 1792, was somewhere between its "dawn" and "fiery noon" and nowhere yet near its "dark night."[8] (The broader significance of the French Revolution for the question of conventions and ideology will be discussed below.) Then, too, the specter of "usurpation" evoked by Paine is a recurrent motif virtually from the beginning for Blake. In *King Edward the Third*, for example, which is a good deal more critical of the "charter'd" than Frye seems to realize, the Minstrel portrays English history at large as a series of such usurpations undertaken to reduce the disorderly diversity of native genius to the orderly uniformity of prescribed thought. He invokes the tradition that Brutus, who fled at the fall of Troy, is the founding father of Britain, declaring it "The sepulchre of ancient Troy," (*KE3*, 6.17), then prophesying, "Our sons shall rise from thrones to joy" (6.49) to conclude successfully the present invasion of France, itself an act of usurpation, albeit one undertaken in retribution.

But such sympathies would not have resulted in the change from "dirty street" and "dirty Thames" to "charter'd street" and "charter'd Thames," had it not been for the direct, relevant, and in the early 1790s, the bitterly debated relationship between the standard rights and privileges conveyed by the Magna Carta and what the radicals of the day viewed as the inherent rights of the inhabitants of London (and "London"). Chapter 13 of the Great Charter ostensibly grants to London the freedom of the street and of the Thames. "And the city of London shall have all its ancient liberties and free customs, as well by land as by water; furthermore, we decree and grant that all other cities, boroughs, towns, and ports shall have all their liberties and free customs."[9] True to the spirit of Paine's analysis, however, the chapter's lack of specificity is "of the nature of a re-conquest." The chapter does not, for example, speak to the issue of London's repeated claims, from 1141 until perhaps as late as 1222, to recognition as "a sworn Commune, presumably of the continental type." Nor does it speak to the claim of the citizens that they had the right to appoint a justiciar of their own choosing, a claim "seen to be inconsistent with the Crown's centralizing policy" when John came to the throne.[10]

In both cases, chapter 13 tacitly denies London's initiatives for freely evolving social structures, prescribing in their stead mechanisms for social control without ever explicitly owning the fact. Paine's comments suggest that only revolution would serve to restore true constitutionality, by setting aside that initial usurpation by William the Conqueror, those subsequent acts of repression by kings and nobles, and the ultimate ratification of the social structures imposed by the promulgation of the Magna Carta. Indeed, as Erdman notes, Thomas Brand Hollis and Horne Tooke in 1791 revived the Society for Constitutional Information "chiefly in connection with the promotion of Paine's *Rights of Man.*"[11] It was Paine, according to Michael Henry Scrivener, who became the ideologue of radical reform in England and the intellectual leader of the London Corresponding Society, "a plebeian organization" comprising "tradesmen, artisans, and laborers" who would not be satisfied with moderate, Whiggish reform.[12]

Chapter 35 of the Magna Carta also bears directly on London (and "London"). The uniformly "marked" faces of the inhabitants of Blake's poetic city are faces showing the effects of a world reduced to a prescribed, irreducible, and "reasonable" common measure, whether of commodities or other matter, down to and including the Newtonian corpuscle. Chapter 35 is at least proximally responsible for this state of affairs, as it establishes a standardized system of weights and measures throughout the kingdom, specifying a London measure in one instance and suggesting it in the others."[13] "Let there be one measure of wine throughout our whole realm; and one measure of ale; and one measure of corn, to wit, 'the London quarter'; and one width of cloth (whether dyed, or russet, or 'lahbergt'), to wit, two ells within the selvedges; of weights also let it be as of measures."[14]

Even though there was initial, widespread noncompliance, London measures became the nation's standards by 1216, a year after the promulgation of the Magna Carta.[15] Nor should the chapter's long-term power be underestimated. In a document that also proclaims the sovereignty of the English Church and defines the rights and duties of the king and barons, chapter 35 not only gives to the central government explicit control of measurement standards but also gives it the power to inspect and verify weights and measures, as well as the power to levy fines for and effect seizures of inaccurate or unauthorized weights and measures and, in the case of alnage (cloth), for goods that are not up to standard.[16]

Blake's most explicit recognition of the implications of chapter 35 in the context of the Magna Carta at large comes in *The Book of Urizen* (1794), written several years after "London," where that archpriest and usurper anticipated by the usurpations recounted in *King Edward the Third* reveals the contents of his brazen book:

> Laws of peace, of love, of unity:
> of pity, compassion, forgiveness.
> . . . .
> One command, one joy, one desire,
> One curse, one weight, one measure
> One King, one God, one Law. (*KE3*, 4.34–40)

To be sure, Urizen in this context is not the double of Edward III, King John, or his successor, Henry III. He is more broadly, as Morton D. Paley observes, a type of "the repressive Reason Blake sees behind all orthodoxies which promulgate 'One King, one God, one Law.'"[17] But there is an awareness, albeit a subtle one, of these implications in "London" as well, where "Palace," "Church," and "Marriage hearse" (ll. 10, 12, 16) are metonyms for "King," "God," and "Law," respectively.

To return to "London": although it is not possible to establish the sequence in which Blake emended the poem, it is possible to read a number of the emendations as following from the change of tone and political awareness implied by the changes from "dirty" to "charter'd." For example, Blake changed "And *see* in every face I meet" to "And *mark* in every face I meet" (l. 3; app. crit., p. 796). In addition to denoting notice, observation, or consideration (cf. *OED* 6:171, definition 3.13–14), *to mark* denotes the imposition of a fixed form or fixed value, at once a type of measurement by convention and a type of reification (*OED* 6:170–71, definition 1.1, 6–7).[18] The verb used in the latter sense also has interesting connotations that bear on property relations. Definition 6, for example, has to do with actions of designation, allotment, apportionment, and the imposition of boundaries.

Moreover, the use of the nominal form of the word in the next line ("Marks of weakness, marks of woe" [l. 4]), part of the poem from the initial fair copy onward, serves to foreground *mark*, causing one to ponder the noun's multiple connotative and denotative senses. In addition to the obvious sense of 3.10—"An appearance, action, or event that indicates something; a sign, token, symptom"—these include definitions 3.12b and c: "*Naut.* A measured notification on a hand leadline, indicated by a piece of white, blue, or red bunting, a piece of leather, or a knot . . . *fig.*, esp. in certain phrases, as *to be above, beneath, near, under, up to, within the mark*: to be above (etc.) a fixed or recognized standard" (*OED* 6:168). The nominal form also has strong implications for the matters of convention, reification, and property relations.

In its monetary sense, *mark* also has to do with standardized measure. Although obsolete except in historiography in Blake's time, *mark* in this sense meant "In England, after the conquest, the ratio of 20 sterling pennies to an ounce [which] was the basis of computation; hence the value of the mark became fixed at 160 pence = 13*s*. 4*d*. or ⅔ of the sterling" (*OED* 6:169). It should come as no surprise that the mark was established by the Composition of Yards and Perches (*Compositio ulnarum et perticarum*), promulgated either by that great standardizer Henry III or his successor, Edward I. That law states in part "that an English Peny, called a sterling, round and without dipping, shall weigh thirty-two wheat corns in the midst of the ear; and twenty pence do make an ounce, and twelve ounces, one pound, and eight pounds do make a gallon wine, and eight gallons of wine do make a London bushel, which is the eighth part of a quarter"—a London quarter, that is.[19] "Clipping" and "coining"—counterfeiting coins either not up to standard weight in the first instance or made of debased or cheapened metals in the second—was a capital crime in Blake's time, as it had been in the time of Newton, who as Warden, then Master of the Mint, was absolute in his insistence on standards of coinage and adherence to the letter of the law—the latter attested to by his vigorous prosecution of counterfeiters and his unwillingness to entertain pleas for the commutation of the death penalty, even under apparently mitigating circumstances.[20]

Before taking up the change from "german forged links" to "mind-forg'd manacles" (ll. 7–8, app. crit,, p. 796)—I wish to suggest that the increasingly stringent legislation and enforcement of standardization in the fourteenth century (especially during the reign of Edward III [1327–77]) may help to provide a context for these two changes in particular and Blake's historical understanding of the period in general.

The effect of the *Compositio* is to prohibit any standard of measurement not in accord with the officially promulgated standard—to ban alternatives, in other words—as well as to enable statutes that address specification and enforcement. According to Ronald Edward Zupko, between the promulgation of the *Compositio* (in the period 1266–1303) and the end of

Edward I's reign (1307), "England witnessed the growth of Parliament and the beginning of statute-making," especially toward the latter part of the period.[21] Edward himself played a part in standardizing both the London bushel and the London quarter. Zupko notes that "in 1296, Edward . . . decreed that the London quarter mentioned in the Magna Carta be fixed at a capacity of eight striked [i.e., level] bushels. . . . His decree of 1296 is unique because hitherto the London quarter had never been defined in terms of its aliquot [i.e., divisible] parts." By making the striked bushel a standard measure, Edward paved the way for nearly universal adoption of the striked measure. During the reign of his successor, Edward II (1304–27), Parliament in 1325 promulgated the Ordinance for Bakers, Brewers, and Other Victuallers, which forbade, with a few explicit exceptions, the use of heaped or shallow measures "and emphasized that all standard measures had to be stamped with the iron seal of the king."[22] By the reign of Edward III, all that was left to do was to enforce the new standards and perfect the previous legislation.

It is worth noting, with respect to the division of the London quarter into its aliquot parts, that in Blake's cosmology the Fall is a measured fall into a presumably aliquot division. In *The Book of Urizen* the activities of that archusurper include the following:

> Times on times he divided, & measur'd
> Space by space in his ninefold darkness
> Unseen, unknown! (*U*, pl. 3, ll. 9–11)

Seen from Blake's visionary perspective, Urizen's actions are anathema. Measurement or any other activity involving comparison, if it is to have any meaning at all, must proceed on the basis of likeness rather than standards. The Second Principle of *All Religions Are One* (1788) states, "As all men are alike in outward form, So (and with the same infinite variety) all are alike in Poetic Genius" (*CPP*, p. 1). Relativism is the rule. "Auguries of Innocence" (between 1787 and 1818) puts the case with epigrammatic wit: "The Emmets Inch & Eagles Mile / Make Lame Philosophy to Smile" (ll. 105–6). Referring at once to the famine in revolutionary France, the fluctuation of good and bad harvests in the England of the 1790s, and the imaginative bankruptcy of an age under the domination of an established orthodoxy, Blake, in one of the "Proverbs of Hell" (from *The Marriage of Heaven and*

Hell [1790–93], envisions standardization as a last, desperate remedy: "Bring out number weight & measure in a year of dearth" (*MHH*, pl. 7, 1. 14). Bring them out from where? From the bastions of the establishment—from the Tower of London or the House of Commons in modern times, and from the temples in ancient times.[23]

As a logical consequence of "charter'd" thought, standardization has two important effects: it serves to create those who live in an ideologically prescribed world in the image of that world's standards. Like Los in *Milton* (1804), the inhabitants of a prescribed world lose (in)sight of their intrinsic creative autonomy and self-worth, then fall into the realm of mere bodily (material) existence: they become what they behold, in other words (see *M*, pl. 3, 1. 29). And standardization causes those so affected to think in terms of standardized (material) units and to equate value with quantity rather than quality—standardization is a necessary precondition to materialism and the mercantile frame of mind, in other words.

In this latter regard, Erdman has written persuasively about how Blake, in *King Edward the Third*, modifies "fourteenth-century matter to suit eighteenth-century issues," one of the latter being what role the merchants should play in supporting the king against the colonists in the American Revolution."[24] But Erdman seems unaware that the materialistic, mercantile frame of mind really did flourish in the 1340s, in large part as the result of standardization. As Clarence, Edward's son and regent, observes them, England's

> merchants [are] buzzing around
> Like summer bees, and all the golden cities
> In his land [are] overflowing with honey. (*KE3*, 2.12–14)

The Mandevillian simile suggests that the private vices of the merchants and their customers resulted in a public virtue of which the crown partook liberally. As Zupko notes, "statutory regulation of alnage duties began in 1328," the year after Edward III ascended the throne. Alnagers, who were especially prevalent in major ports such as London, "measure[d] white and colored cloths with cords of 28 and 26 ells respectively. . . . Fabrics that did not conform to these specifications were seized and turned over to the king." In addition, the king received customs duties for raw stuffs such as wool when these were weighed at port cities. And he received a substantial portion of the "fines, ransoms, issues forfeit and amercements" collected by the commissioners of "the king's standard." When an unscrupulous commissioner such as Thomas de Shirburn attempted to defraud the king of fines collected for violation of that standard, the government made every effort to apprehend him "and to imprison him until he made amends to the Exchequer for the money spent."[25] The merchants' "honey" was the king's as well. No wonder, then, that the Bishop addresses the Prince with "true wisdom [which] drops like honey": "Be England's trade our care; and we, as tradesmen, / Looking to the gain of this our native land" (*KE3*, 2.34–36).

But Clarence's simile has another dimension. To liken the merchants to bees is to reduce them to a common identity—that of little bodies that are in this case apian rather than corpuscular. Indeed, elsewhere in the fragment Blake makes the point that standardization causes a perceived absence of intrinsic individuality. Edward, who claims to support "Liberty, the charter'd right of Englishmen" (*KE3*, 1.9), actually standardizes and reduces his troops in the very act of pronouncing this apparent right. On the battlefield, Edward regards his army, himself included, not as autonomous individuals, but as so many interchangeable parts.

> Our names are written equal
> In fame's wide trophied hall . . .
> . . . .
> whether Third Edward,
> Or the Prince of Wales, or Montacute, or Mortimer,
> Or ev'n the least by birth, shall gain the brightest fame,
> In his hand to whom all men are equal. (*KE3*, 1.26–31)

Earlier, Edward petitions his God, "let Liberty / Blaze in *each* countenance: (*KE3*, 1.11–12; emphasis added); and subsequently, he says of his troops, "*each* man is worthy / Of a triumph" (3.74–75; emphasis added).

This perceived loss of individuality is apparent rather than real, the result of forgetting that human essence as Blake understands it in *All Religions Are One* (1788) inheres in the "Poetic Genius," or soul, rather than the "outward form," or body. But with this perceived loss comes a tendency to equate human and bodily existence—hence the lurking dread, the unreasoning fear of death. Dagworth suspects that "Edward's afraid of [King] Philip" and fights out of fear rather than valor (*KE3*, 3.9–14). Sir Walter Manny alternates between declarations of personal bravery and fearful visions of death, replete with "rotten carcases" and "dismal yells" (5.39–48).

None of Edward's party is exempt from the delusion of bodily priority. In a discussion with his man William, Blake's namesake and double in the fragment, Dagworth reveals himself to be a deluded adherent of an atomism that posits standard, irreducible material (and corpuscular) units as the basis of physical (and phenomenal) reality. His assessment of ambition contradicts the position that Blake makes implicit in *All Religions Are One* and explicit in *The Marriage of Heaven and Hell*—namely, that "All deities reside in the human breast" (*MHH*, pl. 11). From Dagworth's perspective, immanence has about it a sinister aspect. For example, "Ambition," according to Dagworth, "is a root that grows in every breast" (*KE3*, 4.10–13). But Dagworth himself suggests the speciousness of his atomistic model, with its dark view of immanence. William is said to lack ambition; how can he, if it "is a root that grows in every breast"? William, by the by, is, according to Dagworth, "a natural philosopher, and knowest truth by instinct; while reason runs aground" (4.16, 32–33). The implication is that what Dagworth mistakenly views as ambition is in fact an immanent power for the good. Instinctive knowledge of the good depends on a belief in the efficacy of "Poetic Genius." Genius of this sort calls into question the state of ambition: does it grow in every breast as Dagworth says it does, or is it the delusive figment of someone who, like Dagworth, refuses to credit the existence of *pneuma* as a first principle, insisting rather on the delusion of material priority?

To return to "London": in changing the phrase "german forged links" to "mind-forg'd manacles," Blake consolidated his insight as he "undoubtedly improved the line, but he did not abandon social and political meanings in favor of timeless metaphysical ones," as Michael Ferber reminds us. The "manacles" in question are not merely a consequence of the Norman conquest or the Hanoverian monarchy. "Were it only a German or Norman yoke, the task of throwing it off would be an easier one, if more violent, than educating and organizing the entire population."[26] Nor are the "manacles" attributable to "England's alliance with Prussia and Austria against France, or to harboring Hessian and Hanoverian mercenaries."[27] The same frame of mind is evident in the *Compositio*—in the Magna Carta itself, in fact—but as cases in point of a pervasive state of mind rather than as discrete, isolated instances. With specific reference to the *Compositio*, however, the pun sense of "forg'd" comes into play, suggesting that anything fabricated by the mind alone is at best incomplete or "clipped," at worse inauthentic or counterfeit.

In "A Divine Image" Blake offers a gloss on "mind-forg'd" as well as an experienced reprise of the body-soul relationship described in *All Religions Are One* and *The Marriage of Heaven and Hell*:

> The Human Dress, is forged Iron
> The Human Form, a fiery Forge.
> The Human Face, a Furnace seal'd
> The Human' Heart, its hungry Gorge. (ll. 5–8)

The proper "forge" is not the mind alone but "The Human Form," which is the form-giving power entire,"[28] what Blake refers to as "Poetic Genius," with a very prominent emphasis on the Latin root *gignere*, "to beget." If this "forge" has a seat, it is "in the human breast," not in the head. But as the result of a usurpation by the mind, at work on its forgeries behind a "seal'd" and dissembling "Human Face," the body, humanity's variable "outward form," has been fixed as "forged Iron," the standard issue "Human Dress," one size fits all, that all must wear. "The Human Heart," which occupies that breast, starves as the result of having its creative fire usurped by the mind; accordingly, it is the sealed furnace's "hungry Gorge."

The frame of mind that Blake describes in both "London" and "A Divine Image" fashions itself and all it encounters into a type of false currency.[29] In fact, it might be noted that Blake invokes this idea of false coinage in the conclusion of *A Vision of the Last Judgment* (1810), where he distinguishes between the experienced frame of mind described above and his own, freely creative state of mind in the following terms: "What it will be Questiond When the Sun rises do you not see a round Disk of fire somewhat like a Guinea O no no I see an Innumerable company of the Heavenly host crying Holy Holy Holy is the Lord God Almighty" (p. 95).

No less than "forg'd," "manacles" is polysemously suggestive. In addition to the obvious sense of hand fetters or fetters in general (*OED* 6:104), the word has an etymological antecedent in the Latin *manicula*, little hand. Standardization reduces all hands to "little hands," much in the same way that Newton's postulation of corpuscular matter reduces all bodies to corpuscles, or "little bodies," an effect that Blake grapples with in his treatment on the "Gnomes" in *Milton* (pl. 7, ll. 18–38).

Manacles also deprive the hands and arms of freedom, both in the sense of restricting their movement and in the sense of restricting their liberality in the sense discussed in relation to "bans" above—for example, manacles make it impossible to heap a measure—confining any measure based on the hand or arm to norms prescribed by such fetters. It is worth noting in regard to volumetric measurement that "the first units of capacity probably related to the human body; the handful, or the contents of both hands cupped. This would vary according to the size of the hands and the individual doing the measuring."[30] With direct reference to chapter 35 of the Magna Carta, the cloth measure of the ell is, as the Latin original *ulna* (pl. *ulne*) suggests, the length of a forearm, one of the principal bones of which is still known as the ulna.[31] And even certain units of linear measure have Anglo-Germanic origins in the hand rather than the foot.[32]

In the "charter'd" world of "London," there is a place for the dark view of immanence ("ambition"), but not for a belief in the efficacy of immanence ("Poetic Genius"); accordingly, "deities [that] reside in the human breast" in the form of *pneuma* are cast out of the breast—literally, exiled, banned from it, made to appear after the fact of the metonymic "Palace," "Church," and "Marriage hearse."[33] Circumstantially bereft of *pneuma*, humanity reaches what Blake, playing on the nominal sense of contract (i.e., charter) and its verbal sense (i.e., to shrink), calls "Limit[s] . . . of Contraction" (*M*, pl. 13, l. 20). Exiled from its place in the human breast, which as contracted, corpuscular matter no longer possesses the inferiority to house it, *pneuma* serves to reify the very institutions that have been responsible for its exile—at a terrible human cost.

How the Chimney-sweeper's cry
Every blackning Church appalls,
And the hapless Soldiers sigh
Runs in blood down Palace walls

But most thro' midnight streets I hear
How the youthful Harlots curse
Blasts the new-born Infants tear
And blights with plagues the Marriage hearse. (ll. 9–16)

In the background of "London" are the changes rung by the French Revolution during the early 1790s, when the issues not only of duly constituted governance but also of "reasonable" standardized measurement were debated, often in the very same contexts. Not only did France threaten European political stability by replacing a divine-right monarchy with a republic, but the French Revolution also furnished the occasion for the development of new models of standardization in general and of the metric system in particular. In England, spokesmen for the establishment viewed both the new government and the new mensuration with horror, since to adopt either would be to abrogate the Magna Carta, and with it the entire English Constitution that rests on that charter.

Indeed, to adopt the new mensuration would be to do away with Newtonian nature itself. In August 1790 the National Assembly passed legislation introduced the previous April by Talleyrand that instructed the Académie des Sciences to study the feasibility of a system of weights and measures based on "natural" standard (a pendulum beating seconds at latitude forty-five). The legislation also instructed the king to propose that the English Parliament enact similar legislation, and that the Royal Society work jointly on the project with the Académie.[34] But there was no English response. In fact, England did not engage the issue of a "natural" system of measurement until 1814, two years after Napoleon pluralized mensuration in France by allowing the old system of *mesures usuelles* to "be used for retail trade and small business transactions."[35] The 1814 report of a Committee of Parliament repudiated the standard eventually adopted by the French Academy and Assembly (the meter, defined as a "length equal to one ten-millionth part of a terrestrial meridian contained between the north pole and the equator"),[36] reinvented Talleyrand's

118

"natural" standard of the pendulum beating seconds at latitude forty-five, and recommended its adoption.

Even this belated and "safe" recommendation was rejected, however. A blue-ribbon "Commission appointed in 1818 under writ of the Privy Seal" reported no inherent advantage in either a "natural" standard or a decimal scale and raised the specter of widespread confusion as such changes were enacted. Interestingly, the first English approval of the metric system came from a commission convened in 1835, three years after the passage of the first Reform Bill, for the purpose of constructing a new standard yard to replace the standard damaged when the House of Commons burned down.[37] It appears that when reform became an acceptable response to social problems, the concern with standards as a means of social control became less pressing. In the 1790s, however, the most obvious grounds for opposing the metric system was its atheism. The decimalized week in France had ten days, not seven as described in Genesis, and there was no sabbath as ordained in that book and made a holy obligation in Exodus. Even though the ten-day calendar gave way to the restoration of the seven-day original after 1840, the notion "that Anglo-Saxon weights and measures had been Divinely ordained and to tamper with them would be sacrilegious" lingered on.[38]

The English establishment viewed the metric system as a threat to Christianity and indeed to England as underwritten by the English Constitution. One summary of late-eighteenth-century English opposition to the metric system characterizes it as not only "offensive in its religious relations" but also "not in consonance with, and . . . farthest removed from, scriptural and sacred systems of weights and measures, of all known systems," which would include the one standardized by the Magna Carta and subsequent legislation. The summary concludes, "The adoption of the French system . . . would be practically and profoundly oppressive,"[39] the last word carrying with it decisively political implications and suggesting a widespread

"horror at a political movement international in scope, whose moving principle," as Edmund Burke described it, was "a certain intemperance of intellect [which] is the disease of the time, and the source of all its other diseases," sometimes "atheism, the great political evil of the time," and sometimes . . . tyranny, nationalistic imperialism, rebellion of the unpropertied, disaffection of ambitious talents, and, as he stated in the pitch of horror, a truly demonic eruption.[40]

Burke's *Reflections on the Revolution in France* offers a glimpse at his horror of standards anathematic to the English Constitution. Although he does not comment explicitly on the metric system, Burke may have been mindful of its implications in *Reflections*, which appeared in the autumn of 1790, after passage of the legislation enacting the metric system.[41] Whether mindful or not, Burke was keenly aware of the implications of arguments by the French and their English supporters, who sought "natural" and "scientific" standards on which to ground both the French Revolution and the operations of the society which it sponsored, for the notion of standardization.[42]

Against the intellectual basis of the Revolution, Burke supports the historical basis of the English Constitution. "We wished at the period of the Revolution, and do now wish, to derive all we possess as *an inheritance our forefathers*. Upon that body and stock of inheritance we have taken care not to innoculate any cyon alien to the nature of the original plant." The continuity that Burke invokes includes "the antient charter, the Magna Carta of King John, [which] was connected with another positive charter from Henry I. and . . . both the one and the other were nothing more than a re-affirmation of the still more antient standing law of the kingdom."[43]

At its best, the English Constitution is a source of convention, and for Burke it is "convention [that] must limit and modify all the descriptions of constitution which are formed under it. . . . Government is not made in virtue of natural rights, which may and do exist in total independence of it; and exist in much greater clearness, and in a much greater degree of abstract perfection" (*Reflections*, 72). Yet the Constitution may also function as a source of prejudice, as Burke freely admits, offering an argument from custom and usage that equates duration with value.

> Many of our men of speculation, instead of exploding general prejudices, employ their sagacity to discover the latent wisdom which prevails in them. If they find what they seek, and they seldom fail, they think it more wise to continue the prejudice, with the reason involved, than to cast away the coat of prejudice, and to leave nothing but the naked reason; because prejudice, with its reason, has a motive to give action to that reason, and an affection which will give it permanence. (*Reflections*, 100–101)

As the clothing metaphor suggests, prejudices may have to do with the distinctions conferred by rank and indicated by dress. Grounding a constitution on the sort of "natural" or "scientific" basis suggested by the proposition "All men are x" does away with such distinctions, which "are necessary to cover the defects of our naked shivering nature, and to raise it to dignity in our own estimation." Failing these distinctions, "a king is but a man; a queen is but a woman; a woman is but an animal; and an animal not of the highest order. All homage paid to the sex in general as such, and without distinct views, is to be regarded as romance and folly. Regicide, and parricide, and sacrilege, are but fictions of superstition, corrupting jurisprudence by destroying its simplicity" (*Reflections*, 90).

To the extent that such assumptions underwrite the actions of the French National Assembly and its "instructors," such as Rousseau, "their liberty is not liberal. Their science," in the several senses understood of this term in the eighteenth century, "is presumptuous ignorance. Their humanity is savage and brutal" (*Reflections*, 93). Burke is particularly exercised about the new standardized geopolitical division of France, so at odds with the feudal and ecclesiastical bases of division in pre-Reform England (and France before the Revolution).

> They divide the area of their country into eighty-three pieces, regularly square, of eighteen leagues by eighteen. These large divisions are called *Departments*. These they portion, proceeding by square measurement, into seventeen hundred and twenty districts called *Communes*. These again they subdivide, still proceeding by square measurement, into smaller districts called *Cantons*, making in all 6400.

The perpetrators of this scheme, who are referred to disparagingly as "surveyors"—perhaps a gibe also directed at the survey parties that undertook to establish the precise length of a terrestrial meridian (and one ten-millionth therof)[44]—"soon found, that in politics, the most fallacious of all things was geometrical demonstration." Undaunted, "they had then recourse to another basis (or rather buttress) to support the building which tottered on that false foundation" (*Reflections*, 189).

The units of measurement in question are both "modern" and "scientific to the extent that they are wholly quantitative and substantial, without any allowance being made for quality."

Burke is aware of this disposition, and he takes issue with the use of those units precisely because they do not take other considerations into account.

> The troll of their categorical tables might have informed them that there was something in the intellectual world besides substance and quantity. They might learn from the catechism of metaphysics that there were eight heads more [i.e., "quality, relation, place, time, action, affectivity, state or position"] in every complex deliberation, which they have never though of, though these, of all the ten, are the subject on which the skill of man can operate any thing at all. (*Reflections*, 201)[46]

Although, as D. G. Gillham notes, Blake's "London" demonstrates an awareness of Burke's position in *Reflections*, Blake is not at all sympathetic to that position. The new French standardization, operating on the premise that all comparable units are and ought to be equal, strips away uniqueness and distinction—the uniqueness and distinction of a king, for example. But Burke's mistake is to equate the individual with the office, and the speaker of "London" is aware of this mistake, according to Gillham.

> He sees that administration, good or bad, does not involve the administrator as human individual, but as officer. Institutions engage men impersonally, and this is true, even of an institution like the Church, which provides spiritual guidance. Under the control of proper institutions man is prevented from doing much harm and from coming to much hurt, but he is also prevented from being much more than a machine, prevented from doing "good" in any sense of the word that implies personal choice or a sensitive consideration of others.[47]

Administration, in Gillham's sense of it, involves a prescribed and standardized notion of what human beings are, when viewed impersonally, as well as a prescribed sense of the "laws of motion" by which they are governed impersonally. Blake characterizes the administrative frame of mind aptly in a letter of 11 September 1801 to Thomas Butts, suggesting in the process that those in such a frame of mind may know, be able to predict, and perhaps even be able to control the motion of bodies, but that those in such a frame of mind have little control over the minds (or souls) of others. "Bacon & Newton would prescribe ways of making the world heavier to me & Pitt would prescribe distress for a medicinal potion. but as none on Earth can give me Mental Distress, & I know that all Distress inflicted by Heaven is a

Mercy, a Fig for all Corporeal Such Distress in My mock & scorn" (*CPP*, p. 716).[48]

But if Blake repudiates Burke, it does not follow that he embraces the Revolution or the philosophy of "natural" standards on which it rests. The Notebook poem "Mock on Mock on Voltaire Rousseau" suggests that the "All men are x" approach, no less than the "charter'd" approach, has the potential of reducing human beings to (hu)manacles, atomistic standard units that deny the powerful efficacy of *pneuma* rather than bodily matter as a first principle. In "Mock on Mock on," Voltaire and Rousseau, two "reasonable" men, propose (place before) the true first principle of *pneuma* ("wind"), the false first principle of atomistic matter ("sand"), and the pneumatic wind, the origins of which are connate with what Blake, in *Jerusalem* (1804–20), identifies as "The Breath Divine" (*J*, pl. 95, l. 5), disposes in its turn. It shows that matter, like the Tabernacle situated amid "Israels tents," is the dwelling place of a divine immanence that is prior to matter and "shine[s] so bright" through it, much as the breath of life (*ruach*) had to exist prior to humanity in order to transform "the dust of the ground" into "a living soul" (Genesis 2:7).

> Mock on Mock on Voltaire Rousseau
> Mock on Mock on! tis all in vain!
> You throw the sand against the wind
> And the wind blows it back again
> . . . .
> The Atoms of Democritus
> And Newtons Particles of light
> Are sands upon the Red sea shore
> Where Israels tents do shine so bright. (ll. 1–12)

The allusion to "Newtons Particles of light" suggests some concluding remarks concerning Blake's views of the problems to measurement and standardization in relation to treatments of this problem in the philosophy and history of science. Blake anticipates the current understanding that paradigms, models, or metaphors on which scientific laws are based retain heuristic value only insofar as they are figuratively fresh. When these constructs are generalized as standards, corpuscular or otherwise—that is, when their imaginative uniqueness is at once denied and "naturalized" in the service of mensuration—all heuristic value is lost. Thomas S. Kuhn notes that Newton's corpuscular model of light and color, bolstered by a host of measurements allegedly attributable to light's corpuscular nature, worked well enough to explain phenomena such as reflection and refraction. But neither the corpuscular model nor the type of measurements that apparently validated it in the cases of reflection and refraction served to explain phenomena such as interference, diffraction, and double refraction, later explained by Young and Fresnel. Moreover, no amount of measuring these last three phenomena made them amenable to explanation in terms of the corpuscular model. "The road from scientific law to scientific measurement can rarely be traveled in the reverse direction."[49]

Newton's corpuscular model used as a mensurative standard could not account for these phenomena because the model has no place for the incommensurable (and immanent) model proposed by Young and validated by Fresnel, despite Newton's attempt to consider phenomena such as those explained by Young and Fresnel as special cases of his corpuscular model.[50] In particular, Newton shows a disdain for the possibility of immanent causation in the thirty-first "Query," where it is reduced to the status of Aristotelian "occult qualities."[51] Young's first Bakerian Lecture (1801) and Fresnel's experiments (1814–18) begin with the hypothesis—and hypothesis itself is anathema to Newton—that the structure of light is undular (wavelike) rather than emissive (corpuscular),[52] and undular light, from the time of Huygens onward, has been explained on the basis of an immanentist model. It is not possible to hold that the corpuscle is the irreducible standardized unit of light and to record meaningful measurements of the full range of optical phenomena, nor is it possible to record meaningful measurements of the full range of optical phenomena by postulating the wave as the irreducible standardized unit. With the work of Young and Fresnel, optics began to move beyond "the one-sided application of quantitative methods and purely empirically-oriented measurements"[53] and toward owning the very real possibility that incommensurability, far from being anomalous, might be an essential condition of at least some if not all sciences. The pluralistic mode of accommodation at present is quantum theory. Allowing that in some instances light appears to behave as a particle, while in others it appears to behave like a wave, quantum theory simultaneously allows for the existence of the incommensurable and sets limits on the applicability of either standardized unit, wave or corpuscle.

In contemporary physics, contraries may, under certain circumstances, be equally, if partially, true. So, too, in Blake's realm of Beulah, the place of married oppositions, "where Contraries are equally true" (*M*, pl. 30 [33], 1. 1). Beulah is the first visionary step beyond the conception of "Nature" (and the human social organization said to arise out of it) as entities founded on irreducible principles or units—a "Nature" that is the delusive "Vision of the Science of the Elohim" (*M*, pl. 29 [31], 1. 65), the same God who, in the thirty-first "Query," "in the Beginning form'd Matter in solid, massy, hard, impenetrable, moveable Particles, of such Sizes and Figures, and with such other Properties, and in such Proportion to Space, as most conduced to the End for which he form'd them."[54] Indeed, if nature were as Newton says it is, we could not aspire to know more than the sum of its material parts, much less know anything about the creative power that makes the mind the locus of coherence through poetic genius. The Fourth Principle of *All Religions Are One* states, "As none by traveling over known lands can find out the unknown. So from already acquired knowledge Man could not acquire more. therefore an universal Poetic Genius exists" (*CPP*, p. 1). The authority of charters, measurement, and standardization must be resisted whenever that authority denies the efficacy of such genius, whether in the service of literature or of science, when these discourses "find out the unknown."

CHAPTER 6

Power Tropes:
"The Tyger" as Enacted Critique
of Newtonian Metonymic Logic
and Natural Theology

Without question, the single most striking rhetorical feature of Blake's "The Tyger," which first appeared in *Songs of Innocence and of Experience* (1794), is its questions—"thirteen unanswered questions, bound by the six hammered stanzas, [which] give the poem its peculiarly compressed verbal power," according to Stewart Crehan.[1] Numerous commentators have addressed the "tiger-questioner issue." For E. D. Hirsch and Roderick Huang, the questions posed by the speaker are essentially unanswerable.[2] For Morton D. Paley, the rhetoric of the poem and the speaker's questions are "sublime"—comparable to the questions asked in the Book of Job and therefore probably beyond the ken of human knowledge.[3] Paul Miner and Kathleen Raine both argue that Blake suggests or infers answers, while Larry Swingle wonders whether there is even a need to enter into conflict over the perplexities raised by these questions—whether, indeed, Blake was even mindful of such perplexities when he wrote the poem.[4] More recently, Crehan has argued that the questions underscore Blake's "response to the terrible, new-born beauty of violent revolution"

126

(*Blake in Context*, 125). And Harold Pagliaro has stated that the speaker's "questioning reveals an intense interest in an unclarified element of God's design. How can it be that the Creator of this world ordained hostility and death as the means of sustaining physical life at the same time he ordained love?"[5]

Perhaps Pagliaro's is the most apt of the preceding assessments of the ontological status of the poem's repetitive, even obsessive questioning. But neither he nor the others cited take account of the logical and rhetorical—more precisely, the figural—status of those questions. They are metonymic, attempting to mobilize the logic of *effectus pro causa* to reason back from the tiger as created effect to an understanding of his creative first cause. In their repetitions, the questions enact a critique of the Newtonian version of metonymic logic as well as of the applications of that logic by natural theology. Briefly summarized, the point of the critique is that the logic of the questions is circular, referring back to the cause of the questions—the speaker—rather than to the creative cause of the tiger. The long-term effect of the questions is to create the illusion that the speaker is empowered to speak in place of the tiger's creator by insisting on the tiger as a reified, naturalized effect of that first cause, and as a mechanism about which the speaker has some expert knowledge, when in fact the speaker has no such knowledge, mistakenly creating the tiger—and all of the delusory material universe, one might add—in his fallen image, not any version of God's. Another way of making this point is to say that figures such as metonymy do not hold open the possibility of transference, only the possibility of substitution.

To be sure, the speaker seeks to gain some sense of what "the Creator of the world" is like, but not by means of simile or metaphor. The latter of these may be, as Jonathan Culler argues, "the figure of figures, a figure for figurality," but it is not a figure employed by those aspiring to certain knowledge nor, more important, is it a figure used by those aspiring to empowerment through the attainment of certain knowledge.[6] Granted, metaphor comes into play tangentially in the implied comparison of the tiger's creator to an inspired (and implicitly divine) artisan who, with "immortal hand or eye, / Could frame thy fearful symmetry."[7] But the point of the metaphor is to propose a metonymic relationship of effect-for-cause—a relationship that is reified and naturalized by the speaker's unremittingly repetitive questioning—in which the tiger-as-effect testifies to the existence of an artificer-as-cause that is the ultimate object of the speaker's knowledge.[8] The tiger, in other words, is the metonym for its creator (and all of his creation), the "literal term for one thing applied to another with which it has become closely associated," just as "Milton" is the metonym for "the writings of Milton [and their author]."[9]

The same logic frames book 3 of Newton's *Principia* (1687; 1729), his "System of the World." The axioms, or "Rules of Reasoning in Philosophy," that frame his discourse begin with an apparent statement of the law of parsimony, namely, that *"We are to admit no more causes of natural things than such as are both true and sufficient to explain their appearances."* The attribution of the causes of natural effects should save the phenomena while explaining them satisfactorily, with the corollary implication that effects (or *"appearances"*) are metonyms of their causes. But what sort of effects—and, by extension, what sort of causes—are we talking about? Newton's second axiom—*"Therefore to the same natural effects we must, as far as possible, assign the same causes"*—offers the following as examples: "As to respiration in a man and in a beast; the descent of stones in Europe and in America; the light of our culinary fire and of the sun; the reflection of light in the earth, and in the planets."[10]

The cause of all of these effects as Newton understands them is God—specifically Elohim, the creator-God of the *P*-account of the creation (Genesis 1:1–2:4a).[11] He creates "the fish of the sea, and . . . the fowl of the air, and . . . every living thing that moveth upon the earth," as well as the man and women that "have dominion" over these (1:28) and, by implication, is the final cause of their respiration, markedly without the distinction of the ensoulment wrought by "the breath of life" (*ruach*) in Adam in the *J*-account (2:7).[12] He creates the celestial bodies, earth among these, out of void formlessness (1:2), and imbues them with gravity.[13] The cause of light—by *fiat*, as it were—is God (1:3). So, too, is he the cause of reflected celestial light, at least as Newton reads the account of the "two great lights," the stars, and "the firmament of the heaven to give light upon the earth" (1:16–17), which make possible "the reflection of light in the earth, and in the planets."[14] Thus framed by a metonymic logic that attributes the *"causes of natural things"* to a divine first and final cause, no less fundamental a constituent of the Newtonian universe than corpuscular matter itself, the subject of the third of the "Rules" is attributable to that cause (*Mathematical Principles*, 399). Newton does not say as much in the "Rules," but he does in the thirty-first query of the *Opticks* (1704; 1730). That "the least particles of all bodies [are] also all extended, and hard and impenetrable, and movable, and endowed with their proper inertia" is directly attributable to a God who "in the Beginning form'd Matter in solid, massy, hard, impenetrable, moveable particles . . . as most conduced to the End for which he form'd them."[15]

The addition of the notion of ends to that of causes suggests that the function of metonymic logic in Newtonian thought is justificational as well as explanatory, theological as well as scientific.[16] And indeed, it is metonymic logic that furnishes a basis for natural theology no less than for Newtonian science. For Newton's contemporary Robert Boyle, the Newtonian universe is, "as it were, a great piece of clockwork, [and] the naturalist, as such, is but a mechanician," or engineer charged with understanding the mechanism that is a metonym for its transcendent (and absconded) maker, appreciating its design, and celebrating the obvious skills of that maker.[17] So, too, for Blake's contemporary William Paley, writing in *Natural Theology* (1802): "This mechanism being observed . . . the inference, we think is inevitable, that the watch must have had a maker: that there must have existed, at some time . . . an artificer or artificers who formed it for the purpose which we find it actually to answer; who comprehended its construction and designed its use."[18]

Repeated with sufficient frequency, the metonym of the clockwork universe becomes reified as clockwork *tout court*, its creator as clockmaker (and winder), and the Newtonian scientist (and natural theologian) the person who speaks in the place (and name) of clockmaker and clockwork alike.[19] As such, that scientist or theologian operates on the assumption that he (and it is, most emphatically, *he*) has God's charter to utter pronouncements on a wide range of subjects, the civil and the social as well as the scientific and the theological, were such distinctions to be maintained as operative.[20]

As the title of this essay suggests, "The Tyger" is Blake's *enacted* critique of Newtonian metonymic logic and natural theology, but it is not his only critique. Before turning to consider the implications of the critique's enactment in "The Tyger," one ought to consider the most overt and perhaps earliest of Blake's critiques—the one found in *All Religions Are One* and *There Is No Natural Religion* (1788), Blake's earliest engraved texts.

The critique is in evidence virtually from the first word of *All Religions Are One*. Its "Argument," or thesis, engages the issue of what the true nature of experiment and experience is, holding that "the true faculty of knowing must be the faculty which experiences" (*CPP*, p. 1). Aware that the reified clockwork universe is a world of objects that presupposes transcendently created objects—corpuscles, "mechanism[s]," or what-have-you—but cannot account for the subjects that experience these objects, Blake, much as Joseph Priestley had done in his discussion of a possible electrical basis for matter, argues for an immanent creative principle rather than a transcendent first cause.[21] That principle is what he calls "Poetic Genius," and it is the immanent informing principle of all bodies, human or otherwise. "Principle Ist" of *All Religions* states "That the Poetic Genius is the true Man. and that the body or outward form of Man is derived from the Poetic Genius. Likewise that the forms of all things are derived from their Genius which by the Ancients was call'd an Angel & Spirit & Demon" (p. 1).[22]

Without acknowledging the existence of this creative principle, one can never reason back to God, metonymically or otherwise; rather, one can only reason solipsistically. Blake's fourth principle reads, "As none by travelling over known lands can find out the unknown. So from already acquired knowledge Man could not acquire more. therefore an universal Poetic Genius exists" (*CPP*, p. 1). The source of this genius, as Blake tells the reader of his "Principle 7th," is not simply God, but God incarnated as Christ. "The true man is the source, he being the Poetic Genius" (p. 2).

The principle of Christ's inspired incarnational exemplarity is as unquestionably fundamental to Blake's trinitarian metaphysics as it is repugnant to Newton's unitarian variant.[23] The "Conclusion" that follows upon the seven principles of *There Is No Natural Religion [b]* asserts that "If it were not for the Poetic or Prophetic character. the Philosophic & Experimental would soon be at the ratio of all things & stand still, unable to do other than repeat the same dull round over again" (*CPP*, p. 3). We would, in other words, be locked in precisely the sort of solipsism implicated in metonymic logic, replete with the Newtonian clockwork imagery that Blake's fourth principle evokes with its unflattering reference to "a univer[s]e [that] would soon become a mill with complicated wheels" (p. 2), were it not for the exemplarity in question. "Therefore God becomes as we are, that we may be as he is" (p. 3).

Not coincidentally, both of the texts cited above are grounded on seven principles, seven being in Biblical numerology the number of greatest (and divine) completeness—for example, the seven days of the Hexameron, during which the plenitude of this world was created. By way of contrast, *There Is No Natural Religion [a]* sets forth six principles, six being in Biblical numerology the number of greatest (and worldly) incompleteness—for example, the insignia 666 on the forehead of Leviathan (Revelations 13:18). The seven-six distinction is a doubling of the metaphor-metonymy distinction, the former being characterized by full relationality and free (although not unmediated) transference, the latter being characterized by occulted relationality and impeded transference. With its uncanny echoing of Boyle's description of the task of the "naturalist," this brief tract demonstrates what is wrong with "natural" man. Rather than bearing witness to God's love manifested in his assumption of human form—Blake's understanding of what it means ultimately for God to create humanity in his image—"natural" man creates God in his image, "naturalizing" and reducing him accordingly. Without "Poetic Genius" to transcend the limits of sense (and common sense)—without the mutuality of transference that allows "God [to] become as we are, that we may be as he is," in other words—everything, including godhead, is reduced to terms of sense and defined in terms of what Blake calls "selfhood." As the fourth principle of this critique of natural theology states, "None could have other than natural or organic thoughts if he had none but organic perception" (*CPP*, p. 2).

As the conditionality with which the preceding principle is stated suggests, having "organic perception" that leads to "natural or organic thoughts" is a matter of choice or circumstance rather than of the human condition or unalterable fate. The alternative vision is strongly suggested by the second principle of *No Natural*

Religion [b]. "Reason or the ratio of all we have already known. is not the same that it shall be when we know more" (*CPP*, p. 2). Whether choice or circumstance, "natural or organic perception" results from per-versity—literally, a strong swerving from the inspired alternative.[24] This swerving, given one of the Greek roots of *trope* (*trepein*, "to turn"), may be viewed as the enactment of troping, of figuration. It is a willed turning away from the radiantly emanative source of "Poetic Genius," not a spontaneous turning to that source. It is a turning to look downward, not a turning to look upward, as the concluding lines of Night One of *The Four Zoas*, which portray aspects of Urizen and Luvah taking the form of the downward emanating gnostic demiurge, suggest: "But perverse rolld the wheels of Urizen & Luvah back reversd / Downwards & outwards consuming in the wars of Eternal Death" (*FZ*, p. 19, ll. 14–15).

Moreover, it is the swerving remarked by the bard-speaker of the "Introduction" to *Songs of Experience* in the lines

> Turn away no more:
> Why wilt thou turn away
> The starry floor
> The watry shore
> Is giv'n thee till the break of day. (*SE*, 30.16–20)

If the world of *Experience*, with its topsy-turvy geography of the stars below and watery (rather than rocky or sandy) shores, is a world turned upside down, it is so largely as a function of "turn[ing] away." Matters will be, in several senses of the term, righted with "the break of day"—that is, in John of Patmos's terms, the dawning of "a new heaven and a new earth: for the first heaven and the first earth were passed away; and there was no more sea" (Revelations 21:1). Such is Blake's article of faith, realized—artistically, at least—in the vision of Albion's announcement near the end of *Jerusalem* (1804–20), "For lo! the Night of Death is past and the Eternal Day / Appears upon our Hills" (*J*, pl. 97, l. 34). But for the present time figured forth throughout *Experience*, in "The Tyger" as elsewhere, the perversity that arises from "natural or organic thoughts" is in the ascendant.[25] "The starry floor / The watry shore" anticipates narration of "natural" events offered by the speaker of "The Tyger."

> When the stars threw down their spears
> And water'd heaven with their tears:
> Did he smile his work to see? (*SE*, 42.17–19)

What the Bard sees as a "starry floor" (and what "the wheels of Urizen & Luvah" perversely project downward) is, for the speaker of "The Tyger," a starry ceiling, a point of view suggestive that he is one of the creatures who resulted from that downward projection. The speaker's point of view also causes him to get the surrendering of arms precisely backward. If the stars in fact did what the speaker said they did, they would have set in place exactly those conditions necessary for another downward-tending gnostic genesis, the sort in which "the Spirit of God moved upon the face of the waters" (Genesis 1:2). From the perspective of dialectical visionary struggle, as it is presented in *The Four Zoas*, "The stars threw down their spears & fled naked away" (*FZ*, p. 64, l. 27).[26] That is, the stars relinquish the phallic symbol of hegemonic authority wielded by all male-dominated eighteenth-century establishments.[27] And when they do, the stars are relieved of both their oppressive duties of enforcement and their garments, characterized elsewhere (in *Milton* [1804]) as the metonymic (and potentially gendered) "rotten rags of Memory by Inspiration / . . . Bacon, Locke & Newton" (*M*, pl. 41 [48], ll. 4–5), and allowed to return to their emanative source.[28] Finally, the very idea that the stars are "naturally" supposed to water heaven suggests that the speaker of "The Tyger" projects upon heaven the aura of physical (and spiritual) dryness characteristic of rationalistic Deism, when in fact "the break of day" will reveal it as a powerful, divine emanative source more usually associated with the evangelical sects—a pentecostal fountain, or "The Four Rivers of Paradise" (*J*, pl. 98, l. 25), among others.

Like his demiurgic original, Urizen has a considerable ability to create the landscape that, according to Blake, we mistakenly take to be the "natural" world. In fact, like Elohim in the *P*-account, he creates his world by *fiat*, in the very act of exploring the delusory Newtonian space that it occupies.[29] Thus the act that occurs at the very beginning of Night Six of *The Four Zoas*, where "Urizen arose & leaning on his Spear explord his dens" (p. 67, l. 1), gives rise to the landscape glimpsed near the beginning of Night Seven.[30]

> . . . fierce his lions
> Howl in burning dens his tygers roam in the redounding smoke
> In forests of affliction. (*FZ*, p. 77, ll. 8–10)

This is the landscape of "The Tyger" viewed from the Urizenic perspective, which is the opposite of the speaker's perspective, just as the bard's view of a "starry floor" is the opposite of the speaker's view of starry skies. For example, where Urizen sees "tygers roam in redounding smoke," the speaker of "The Tyger" sees the "Tyger, burning bright, / In the forests of the night" (*SE*, 42.1–2). As the image of tigers roaming in "redounding smoke" suggests, the tiger that the speaker encounters is ultimately without telos or theodical purpose—the truth of the matter is that it "roam[s]"—it is insubstantial, and it is a solipsistic if necessary material excrescence, no matter whether it be a material effect attributed to a divine cause, witness the "redounding smoke."

The speaker, however, buys into the Newtonian metonymic logic of natural theology and reifies the tiger in the very act of questioning it, his operative assumption being that the tiger is akin to Boyle's clocklike mechanism, and that he, as a "naturalist" playing the "mechanician," can gain some understanding of the Great Transcendent Clockmaker and Clockwinder himself. By the terms of such logic, the "fire" of the tiger's "eyes" is an effect that implies as its cause a (blacksmith's? lamplighter's?) "hand [that] dare sieze the fire." The striated musculature of "the sinews of th[e] heart" is an effect that implies as its cause a cordwainer's "shoulder, & . . . art." The bilateral symmetry and involutions of the "brain" are effects that imply as their cause an extremely skillful blacksmith, equipped with "hammer . . . chain . . . furnace . . . [and] anvil" sufficient to have wrought that brain much as iron is wrought (*SE*, 42, passim).

I stated near the outset of this essay that the speaker creates the tiger in his fallen image, and indeed he does, with this important qualification: that the speaker's image is also Urizen's image, albeit inverted or reversed, suggesting perhaps that Blake slyly insinuates the optics of the convex lens or mirror into his topsy-turvy of the created world. I make the point as a way of making a start toward resolving the oft-remarked problem of resolving the fit of the poem to its illumination. The illumination is, as John E. Grant argues, something of a *jeu d'esprit*.[31] But the humor incidental to such a play should not be allowed to obscure its point: that the tiger is the misbegotten product of Urizen's deluded acts of creation and the speaker's correspondingly deluded acts alike.

As Pagliaro notes, the illumination is not so much of a tiger as it is of "a cat with human features" (*Selfhood and Redemption*, 87). In the Rosenwald Collection copy of *Songs* that served as the original of the Oxford University Press facsimile, these features include a rather prominent, possibly Semitic nose; beady eyes, if one can infer the character of the eye not seen from that of the eye that is seen; a rather grimly set mouth and distinctly human jaw; and forelegs and forepaws that look more like arms and hands than like the animal homologs of these.[32] These very same features, rotated ninety degrees on the vertical axis to give a frontal rather than a profile view, and augmented by the addition of a markedly Urizenic beard, are seen in the human head depicted in the finis picture of plate 24 of *The Marriage of Heaven and Hell* (1790–93). The figure, moreover, is posed in precisely the same four-footed stance as the tiger. This human figure, identified by David V. Erdman as "the oppressor (King Nebuchadnezzar)," rests above the motto "One Law for the Lion & Ox is Oppression."[33]

Identifying the speaker of "The Tyger" as Nebuchadnezzar—or, at the very least, as someone with Nebuchadnezzar's literalistic, materialistic, authoritarian, idolatrous frame of mind—makes a good deal more sense than may at first be apparent.[34] To begin with, Nebuchadnezzar was king of Babylon, a state (and state of mind) that Blake equates with natural theology throughout his poetry. For example, at the conclusion of Night Eight of *The Four Zoas*,

> The Ashes of Mystery began to animate they calld it Deism
> And Natural Religion as of old so now anew began
> Babylon again in Infancy Calld Natural Religion. (*FZ*, p. 111, ll. 22–25)

As one of the kings of Babylon, Nebuchadnezzar was, for a time, his nation's principal natural theologian.

Identifying the speaker as Nebuchadnezzar also gives an interesting spin to the images of fire and furnaces in the poem—images the awe of which is tempered by the speaker's literalistic insistence on identifying the mode of the tiger's production. For their failure to pay worship a sixty-cubit-high golden idol that he has caused to be built, Nebuchadnezzar condemns the Jews Shadrach, Meshach, and Abednego to death in "the burning fiery furnace." The flames are so lethally hot that they kill the warders who toss the three in, but Shadrach, Meshach, and Abednego emerge unscathed. Nebuchadnezzar himself suspects that the miracle has been divinely caused—in effect, that it is the result of the action of divine transference in which a metaphor for God ("Son of God") provides the sustaining presence that enables mortals to transcend the material limits of their existence. As he says, "Lo, I see four men loose, walking in the midst of the fire, and . . . the fourth is like the Son of God" (Daniel 3:22-25).

Nebuchadnezzar is sufficiently impressed with the deliverance of the three by their God to decree "that every people, nation, and language, which speak any thing amiss against the God of Shadrach, Meshach, and Abednego, shall be cut in pieces, and their houses shall be made a dunghill: because there is no other God that can deliver after this sort" (3:29). But he is not sufficiently impressed to change his ways or convert. His own stiff-necked literalism results in a figural distancing suggested by Nebuchadnezzar's unwillingness to admit that he has seen the actual Son of God, but to admit only that he has seen something "like the Son of God." If anything, he grows ever more prideful than he had become when Daniel prophesied Nebuchadnezzar's reign as "a [but not *the*] king of kings" (2:37), an event that caused the king mistakenly to "worship Daniel and command that they should offer an oblation of sweet odours unto him" (2:46), not to mention causing the huge golden idol to be built.

Until the end, Nebuchadnezzar just does not get the point. He regards Daniel, whose name in Hebrew means "God is my judge," not as a divinely inspired prophet (maker of metaphors), but as "Belteshazzar, master of the magicians" (manipulator of metonyms; 4:9). His prideful ways cause him to refuse worship to Daniel's God, even if Nebuchadnezzar does honor him with lip service, as it were. Finally, after dreaming a dream that he sees as portending his end, in terms highly reminiscent of those associated with the Tower of Babel (see Daniel 4:22; Genesis 11:1-9, esp. 4-6), Nebuchadnezzar calls upon Daniel to learn that his fate is to be "driven from men" and to become, for a time, a mindless beast that "did eat grass as oxen, and his body was wet with the dew of heaven, till his hairs were grown like eagles' feathers, and his nails like birds' claws" (Daniel 4:33). But this is not Nebuchadnezzar's ultimate fate: he has a conversion experience. "Now I Nebuchadnezzar praise and extol and honour the King of heaven, all whose works are truth, and his ways judgment: and those who walk in pride he is able to abase" (4:37).

As in the implied answer to the tiger-lamb question discussed in conclusion below, it all comes to one for Nebuchadnezzar once the prideful and deluded natural theologian in him is able to see the error of his ways and repent. But before that moment comes to pass, distinctions of the sort that Blake engages—the distinction between memory and inspiration, the distinction between reason and inspired vision, the distinction between making-as-fabrication and making-as-poiesis, and the distinction between art as metonymic and metaphoric representation—are being played out in the Book of Daniel. And while such distinctions are operative, "One Law for the Lion," which is subsequently associated with Daniel, "& the Ox," which is clearly associated with Nebuchadnezzar in his grass-eating phase, "is Oppression."[35]

Only two issues remain to be dealt with: the significance of the incremental repetition that sees the last line of the first stanza ("Could frame thy fearful symmetry") transformed to the last line of the sixth and last stanza ("Dare frame thy fearful symmetry"; *SE*, 42.4, 241), and the status of the question "Did he who made the Lamb make thee?" (l. 20). In the first instance, the lack of any satisfying results from the metonymic interrogation that occurs throughout the poem may begin to suggest that his questioning— and, by extension, the supposed acts of the object of his questioning—constitute illicit usurpations and applications of creative force. What appears to be the result of the mere capability of a powerful, transcendent creator in the first stanza arguably appears, by the last stanza, to be a transgression, not in the least because the speaker is finally not persuaded by the very argumentative logic he mobilizes.

In the second instance, the answer is yes, the sacramentality of the Lamb of God is meant to heal the division of material body and immaterial soul that occurred when the unified gnostic entity Pistis Sophia (Faith Wisdom), in the throes of a failure of imaginative nerve, allowed the demiurge to emanate downward into the material sphere thinking that he was the creator of the universe. This creator made both the material lamb and the material tiger, the former of which is raised from metonymic to metaphoric status in the capacity of the Lamb of God, whose free gift is meant to redeem an otherwise fallen and deluded humanity. In Blake's cosmology, the same forces that conspire to enact the rationalized and rationalistic divisions of the universe also participate unwittingly in the healing of those divisions. To return, in closing, to Urizen's spear, it is the type of the spear that "the Sons of Urizen" use when

> They vote the death of Luvah & they naild him to the tree
> They piercd him with a spear & laid him in a sepulcher
> To die the death of Six thousand years bound round with desolation.
> (*FZ*, p. 92, ll. 13–15)

In this account Luvah is clearly the type of Jesus, who is similarly pierced with a spear after his crucifixion. In commenting both on that action and the decision not to break his legs, John says that "these things were done, that the scripture should be fulfilled" (John 19:36). The Logos was "in the beginning . . . the Word," God ineffable. Then "the Word was with God," Jesus as transferent, co-present, metaphoric extension of God. Finally, once again, "the Word was God" (1:1). Even that spearing, a cause which generates the effect of blood and water, is part of the movement from radiant unity to a diminished, dimmer multeity, and once again to radiant unity that constitutes the fulfillment of scripture, with its resurrection, judgment of the living and the dead, and everlasting life. The tiger, the lamb, and our imperfect understanding of these are but faltering steps along what, for John and for Blake alike, is a certain way.

CHAPTER 7

Blake and the Ideology
of the Natural

BLAKE'S CASE AGAINST NATURE
AS METONYMIC EFFECT

William Blake's view of nature as commonly understood in his lifetime was all but unquestionably negative. He concludes his annotations to Dr. Robert John Thornton's *The Lord's Prayer, Newly Translated* (1827), pubished in the last year of his life, with an acidly ironic dismissal of Thornton's argument for the natural fitness of orthodox Christianity. The argument, heavily indebted to the argument from design characteristic of Natural Theology, is taken by Blake to imply that there is little to choose between the tyranny of the bodily eye and political tyranny, between empiricism and imperialism, between the materialist philosophy that furnishes an empirical basis for the argument from design and the materialism of politically absolutist regimes such as that of imperial Rome: "Thus we see that the Real God is the Goddess Nature & that God Creates nothing but what can be Touchd & Weighed & Taxed & Measured all else is Heresy & Rebellion against Caesar Virgils only God See Eclogues i & for all this we thank Dr Thornton."[1]

This same view is as evident in Blake's later poetry as it is in his polemics. Near the end of *Jerusalem* (1804–20), Los argues that the denial, by the likes of Francis Bacon,[2] John Locke, and Isaac Newton, of the sacred or secret, the innate, and the immanent is a sign that the return of an inward-working spirit, which Los calls "The Breath Divine," must soon take place.

> if Bacon, Newton, Locke,
> Deny a Conscience in Man & the Communion of Saints & Angels
> Contemning the Divine Vision & Fruition, Worshiping the Deus
> Of the Heathen, The God of This World, & the Goddess Nature
> Mystery Babylon the Great, The Druid Dragon & hidden Harlot
> Is it not that Signal of the Morning which was told us in the Beginning.
>   (*J*, pl. 93, ll. 21–26, pl. 95, l. 5)

From the time of *All Religions Are One* and *There Is No Natural Religion* (1788), Blake criticizes the positing of a sensorily apprehended material nature as the ground of all being and all meaning. He begins the A-text of *No Natural Religions* as follows: "Man has no notion of moral fitness but from Education. Naturally he is only a natural organ subject to Sense" (*CPP*, p. 2). After he has articulated it fully in the A-text to show its failings, Blake subjects this proposition to the critique of the B-text. "Mans perceptions are not bounded by organs of perception," the speaker argues: "he percieves more than sense (tho' ever so acute) can discover." The individual able to transcend organic bounds and "see the Infinite in all things sees God." Such transcendence occurs by means of "the Poetic or Prophetic character," that spark of divinity instilled in humanity as "the breath of life" (Genesis 2:7), not by the Elohim-God[s] of the *P*-account of the creation, who directs the completed subject to look outward and see her/himself in God's image and the natural world as a private domain made to his/her measure, but by the Jehovah-God of the *J*-account.[3] Jehovah, whose name as Tetragrammaton hints at the fourfold perfection of the Hebrew verb *hayyah*, "to be,"' directs the desiring subject to look inward beyond the finite repetitions of "the Philosophic and Experimental" toward the infinite.

As Leopold Damrosch Jr., suggests, "A compromise is possible, however. Natural beauty need not be rejected so long as its 'vegetative' impermanence is clearly understood. . . . [Blake] perceived the forms of beauty through the glass or shadows of matter."[4] Blake, in fact, says in *Milton* (1807),

Blake and the Ideology of the Natural

And every Natural Effect has a Spiritual Cause, and Not
A Natural: for a Natural Cause only seems, it is a Delusion
Of Ulro: & a ratio of the perishing Vegetable Memory.
    (*M*, pl. 26 [28], ll. 44–46)

This distinction between a "Spiritual Cause" and "A Natural," which will be discussed at some length below, is crucial for understanding Blake's reaction to the construct of assumptions and procedures responsible for what I am here calling "the ideology of the natural." For now, suffice it to say that Blake reacts to this ideology as a construct founded on the choice of one tropological strategy over another. A natural cause ordains a substitutive and metonymic relationship between causal subject and caused object, thus reifying subject and object alike, whereas a spiritual cause ordains a transferential and metaphorical relationship between causal subject and caused object, thus reifying neither and maintaining both in a state of (re)constitutive play.

Given Damrosch's comments above, the moral of Blake's conclusion—"Therefore God becomes as we are, that we may be as he is" (*CPP*, pp. 2–3)—is worthy of some consideration. *To be* as God is, is *to become* the other. God's ontological status, as well as the ontological status of the individual who completes him/her, in other words, is that of an endless, immanent, metaphorical transference, of becoming the other, who does not totalize God but completes him/her, and in so doing becomes an origination in need of completion, who is both self and other, who is that God and who is not that God in something like an oxymoronic oscillation.[5] The same process is deployed in the Bible in two typologically parallel places: Genesis 2:7 and John 1:1–3. The former describes how Jehovah uses the "breath of life" to create Adam "a living soul"; the latter, how "In the beginning was the Word, and the Word was with God, and the Word was God. . . . All things were made by him; and without him was not any thing made that was made."[6]

Logos, "the Word" to which John refers, is of course Christ, who is both consubstantial with God and God's causal link with the created world, by means of which that fallen place may be recuperated at the end of time. Such recuperation involves recognizing that the word *metaphor* is itself a metaphor—"a metalepsis, the metaphor of a metaphor"[7]—likening a cognitive and linguistic

141

process to one of spatiotemporal displacement or deferral in which one moves out of one term of the likening into the other, and does so endlessly. Another way to make the point is to propose metalepsis as metaphor understood from a visionary perspective. This proposition would seem to underwrite the visionary conversation that takes place at the end of *Jerusalem*. Metaphor is there refigured as unending metalepsis that is itself metaphorized as a versing or walking or flowing together, or conversation. Even a supposed absolute such as

> the all tremendous unfathomable Non Ens
> Of Death was seen in regenerations terrific or complacent varying
> According to the subject of discourse & every Word & Every Character
> Was Human according to the Expansion or Contraction, the Translucence or
> Opakeness of Nervous fibres such was the variation of Time & Space
> Which vary according as the Organs of Perception vary & they walked
> To & fro in Eternity as One Man reflecting each in each & clearly seen
> And seeing: according to fitness & order. (*J*, pl. 98, ll. 33–40)[8]

In both the Greek term *metapherein* and the Latin term *transferre*, which are commonly taken as the bounds or foundational terms of figuration, there is, as Blake understands, a deeply latent metaleptic potential that neither language clearly reveals. Obfuscation of this sort in the Greek and Latin cognates is, for Blake, emblematic of how, as he argues in the preface to *Milton*, "The Stolen and Perverted Writings of Homer & Ovid: of Plato & Cicero. which all Men ought to contemn: are set up by artifice against the Sublime of the Bible" (*M*, pl. 1). In a more "primitive" language such as Hebrew or English, the tropaic status of the verb itself would be more nearly obvious.[9] The English cognate, for example, would be "to bear, or to carry across."

Metaphor, then, is for Blake the enactment, through the medium of language, of the sacramental—in bearing or carrying divinity across from God to humanity, it bears, or carries a cross, in virtue of the redemptive potential symbolized in the act of becoming. Furthermore, all of nature that is created by "the Word" is endowed with the sacramental potential that it conveys in the act of becoming. As Blake puts it in *The Marriage of Heaven and Hell* (1790–93), "every thing that lives is Holy" (pl. 27). Full recognition of this sacramental potential allows the unmediated merger of becoming and being, in which what has been carried across to humanity works in humanity the miracle of being carried back from the natural world to a consubstantiality with God. Humanity in Blake's Beulah, the married land, exists on the verge of such translation,[10] which is also emblemized by the prophet Elijah, who is "translated" by a whirlwind directly to heaven (2 Kings 2:11), a typological anticipation of the coming of Christ (Malachi 4:5).

The ontological status of an individual in a transferential relationship with God is both that of originating or desiring subject and completing and desired object.[11] To become the other, it should be added, is not merely to become human in a species-specific sense. Blake makes a similar qualification in his comments on "Poetic Genius" in *All Religions*. His first principle is "That the Poetic Genius is the True Man. and that the body or outward form of Man is derived from the Poetic Genius. Likewise the forms of all things are derived from their Genius. which by the Ancients was call'd an Angel & Spirit & Demon" (*CPP*, p. 1).[12]

The ontological alternative to endless, immanent, metaphorical transference is a condition of alienation characterized by repetitive attempts at the deduction, from the presumably natural effects that surround the subject, of a transcendent first cause—a situation in which the subject attempts to reason from the apparent harmony, order, and design of nature to the existence, however inconceivable, of the absconded deity presumably responsible for that harmony, order, and design. Such is Newton's reasoning in the "General Scholium" of the *Principia*, where he posits, on the basis of his observation of the regularity and his formulation of the laws governing the mechanics of celestial motion, the existence of a "*Lord God Pantokrator*, or *Universal Ruler*," who "is eternal and infinite, omnipotent and omniscient," and in whom "are all things contained and moved; yet neither affects the other."[13] This reasoning leads to the rise of a science that views nature as something instrumental rather than sacramental and puts it on the Baconian rack of experiment to wring secrets from it.[14] Such reasoning also leads to the rise of a Natural Theology that probes the clockwork universe relentlessly for its "contrivances" and concealed (but not inaccessible) secrets, which, when found, are used to argue for the existence of a clockmaker and clockwinder God who placed those secrets there for the natural philosopher and natural theologian to discover.[15] It is this sort of reasoning that Blake criticizes in *No Natural Religion*. The assumption, made in the A-text, that a subject's thoughts are limited by what is "out there" in the object world— that "None could have other than natural or organic thoughts if he had none but organic perception"—leads to a state of boundedness and loathing for one's puny and constrained situation in a clockwork universe. Thus, as the speaker of the B-text observes, "The bounded is loathed by its possessor. The same dull round even of a univer[s]e would soon become a mill with complicated wheels" (*CPP*, p. 2).

A subject-object relationship in which an a posteriori subject attempts to deduce from the natural order in the object-world the existence and identity of an a priori first cause is informed by every bit as much figurality as is a subject-object relationship in which the individual, through the process of metaphoric transference, experiences the eternal becomingness of godhead. As Umberto Eco notes, the relationship between cause and effect, possessor and possessed (compare "the bounded is loathed by its possessor"), inventor and invention, container and contained, is a relationship figured forth by metonymy.[16] Moreover, it is precisely the metonymic figuration of the object world—what Robert N. Essick refers to as "literalization of figuration," as the result of which a speaker "grants substantial being to what we would usually take to be only a figure of speech"[17]—that is responsible for constructing, both socially and intellectually, the reified articulations of what is in this discussion being characterized as "the ideology of the natural."

While Blake's insights concerning the falling off from metaphor to metonymy are not original with him, his insights concerning the tropics of the imagination are.[18] He synopsizes the process by which one moves from perceiving a universe of endless, immanently originated metaphorical transference to perceiving a universe of constrained, transcendently originated metonymic substitution in *The Marriage*. Themselves divinely ensouled (L. *anima*, "soul"), "The ancient Poets animated all sensible objects with Gods or Geniuses, calling them by their proper names" (*MHH*, pl. 11). The moment of naming, a seemingly innocent human echoing or reminiscence of divine animation, contains in itself the potential for the fall into the conception of

144

the natural world that Blake criticizes in *No Natural Religion [a]*. The potential for a fall is there because every such act of naming is an echo or reminiscence of Adam naming the animals, which is for Blake a profoundly conflicted event. In keeping with the epistemological conundrum of the Fall (presence cannot be known in the absence of the very absence that negates it, or "You cannot know what you have until you lose it"), the act of naming sets in motion parallel processes of ontological and figural decline—from a condition of plenitude to a condition of nescience in the former instance, and from a condition of transferentiality to a condition of substitution in the latter.[19]

After animation and naming comes naturalization. "The forms of all things are derived from their Genius," as Blake argues in *All Religions* (*CPP*, p. 1). Thus the poets continue in *The Marriage* by "adorning them [all sensible objects] with the properties of woods, rivers, mountains, lakes, cities, nations, and whatever their enlarged and numerous senses could percieve." With naturalization comes the reification that results in subject and object, creator and created, cause and effect, appearing as distinct and, ultimately, separated in a hierarchical relationship, without the possibility of transference. Once cities and nations have been named and adorned—made materially present and articulate as effects by the figural power of language[20]—the next step is to assume they exist as the effects of an absent and silent (that is, transcendent) cause that oversees, literally, these effects. Of "The ancient Poets" Blake says, "particularly they studied the genius of each city & country. placing it under its mental deity" (*MHH*, pl. 11).

The adverb *particularly* sheds some light on how one moves toward the situation glimpsed in *Jerusalem*, where Los

> saw every minute particular, the jewels of Algion, running down
> The kennels of the streets & lanes as if they were abhorr'd
> Every Universal Form, was become barren mountains of Moral
> Virtue: and every Minute Particular hardend into grains of sand.
> (*J*, pl. 45, ll. 17–20)

It is this "study" that creates "Poets" and "sensible objects," subject and object alike, as "minute particular[s]," material effects, cases in point to be exploited by a "Priesthood" that interceded in the matter of cause, which it mystifies to its own ends while purporting to explain it. What "study" does—and what "Priesthood" ratifies—is to posit form as existing before desire; accordingly, "study" causes one to forget, to lose sight of the alternative that Blake holds to be true—that form exists after the fact of desire, as its completion. In *All Religions* Blake argues "That the Poetic Genius is the true Man. and that the body or outward form on Man is derived from the Poetic Genius" (*CPP*, pl. 1). Or as he ways in *The Marriage*, "Thus men forgot that All deities reside in the human breast" (*MHH*, pl. 11). Blake accuses "Priesthood," itself a metonym of ecclesiastical authority on the order of "Canterbury," of "Choosing *forms* of worship from poetic tales" (*MHH*, pl. 11; my emphasis), with the result that the "forms" appear to come before the "poetic tales." Implicit in the accusation is an analogy—immaterial, spiritual cause: material, natural effect:: (prophetic) poetry: (natural) religion. Blake makes this analogy explicit in plate 27 of *Jerusalem*, discussed below.

Desire that is repressed or neglected as an originating force or source of a sense of living belatedly in an always already created world manifests as the perverted variant reason, which has the subject seeking rather to contemplate from a distance the presumed cause of surrounding natural effects than to exist in transferential intimacy with the derivative "sensible objects" that are its true "outward form." Elsewhere in *The Marriage* Blake suggests that the "historical" account rendered in plate 11 is, or may be, recapitulated in the life of the individual. "Those who restrain desire," he argues, "do so because theirs is weak enough to be restrained; and the restrainer or reason usurps its place & governs the unwilling." Desire restrained "becomes passive" and takes the form of its restrainer, reason, which is "only the shadow of desire" (*MHH*, pl. 5). The Spectres in Blake's system are just so: shadows of desire projected and denied by desiring Zoas ontologically or "historically" disposed toward repression. The Emanations are also an outcome of such repression, and by a nice turn of events, the very same Zoas who project and deny their own Emanations also project and deny their projection and denial on these Emanations, who appear always to be in the act of denying the Zoas. The dynamic that gives rise to Emanations is captured finely by Oothoon's analysis of desire acted upon versus desire denied in *Visions of the Daughters of Albion* (1793). Oothoon argues that acting upon one's desires brings about an

146

awakening that is a harbinger of heaven, whereas repressing, projecting, and denying one's desires creates an enfolded and materialized simulacrum of a love object.

> The moment of desire! the moment of desire! The virgin
> That pines for man; shall awaken her womb to enormous joys
> In the secret shadows of her chamber; the youth shut up from
> The lustful joy. shall forget to generate. & create an amorous image
> In the shadows of his curtains and in the folds of his silent pillow.
> Are these not the places of religion? the rewards of continence?
> The self enjoyings of self denial? Why dost thou seek religion?
> Is it because acts are not lovely, that thou seekest solitude
> Where the horrible darkness is impressed with reflections of desire.
> (*VDA*, pl. 7, ll. 3–11)

The most striking of the Emanations is Milton's—Ololon, who to the very end of *Milton* insists on the importance of her wholeness, intactness, sacrosanctity as a being separate and distinct from Milton. Her name says it all: as a result of this dynamic of repression, projection, and denial, Ololon, who ultimately becomes "as a Garment dipped in blood" (*M*, pl. 42, l. 12)— Christ's prophetic garment (and his bride),[21] that is—exists before that transformation in the same condition as her name, which is from the Latin *ululare*, "to wail, to howl." Ololon's condition provides a key to understanding the wailing, howling, shrieking, and general auditory din that Blake takes as the ground of his prophetic meaning. That sound is the noise of prophecy repressed, projected, and denied. Instead of being prophets as Blake, with a little help from Numbers 11:29, enjoins them to be, "all the Lords people" (*M*, pl. 1, l. 17), including the silent Milton at the outset of the poem, let their repressions, projections, and denials speak for them. Blake, then, seeks to do more than expose the ideological underpinnings of his age's apparently (but only apparently) self-contradictory discipleship of rational inquiry while harboring gloomy thoughts about the insufficiency of rational inquiry and a lurking fear of being cut off from higher truth, godhead, or both of these. He undertakes to show how the failure to acknowledge openly the artistic or prophetic impulse gives rise to such self-contradictions. They are the currency of a psychic economy unable to see and fix imagination as its standard.

Before turning to Blake's discovery of and prophetic response to the ideology of the natural, I wish to deal with two other matters—first to offer a working definition of *ideology*, and then to historicize that definition to show that the ideology of the natural, privileged if not created by the rise of modern science, was very much a force to be reckoned with in Blake's time.

Michael Ferber, who has written very well on Blake and ideology, provides a useful starting point for a definition of terms. *Ideology*, according to Ferber, means

> a set of related ideas, images, and values more or less distorted from the "truth" (which presumes some grasp of the way social totality really works) through the impact on it of the material interests, conscious or unconscious, of those who believe and propagate it, insofar as they are divided from one another in classes with conflicting interests.

This definition, which Ferber characterizes as Marxist, is certainly not without its problems—most notably the besetting problem of Marxist essentialism. Ferber's decision to place the noun *truth* in quotes suggests his awareness of this problem, although one wishes that he had done the same for the adverb *really*. But Ferber's definition is important and useful for its characterization of ideology as interested distortion arising from a perceived conflict, actual or potential, of "material interests."

How does ideology make good on its bid to be taken as the truth? According to Ferber, "The pretensions of ideology are usually two: first, a claim to universality . . . which typically depends on the 'naturalization' of something social and the exaltation of a part into the whole, and secondly, the very claim to be autonomous or *audessus de la mêlée* that a theory of ideology must assume to be impossible."[22] Michael Ryan echoes Ferber here, noting, after the precedent of "British thinkers like Stuart Hall, Annette Kuhn, Stephen Heath, Catherine Belsey, and Tony Bennett," that ideology makes the social world seem natural and endowed with a selfevident truth value. Ideology depends on a kind of transparent intelligibility that seems unmediated, that seems not to be constructed by relations, codes, conventions, signifying practices, and strategies of representation. Social reality is simply there, a fact whose being is self-identical and unmediated, luminous and true, prior to all representation.

By raising the issue of representation, Ryan adds a useful deconstructionist perspective. "Deconstruction suggests," as he observes,

> that the intelligible presence of being that ideology ascribes to social reality may itself be the product of strategies of representation. What supposedly comes second may in fact determine what is supposedly primary. Perhaps women would not be what they supposedly already are—passive social beings—if they were not represented in a certain way in our culture, if they did not adopt or wear certain symbolic representations that actively constitute them from a seemingly derivative, non-constituting position, as what they supposedly already are. Dresses make one feel vulnerable, after all, as chains make one weak.[23]

Ryan's excursion into social semiology causes him to lose sight momentarly of a key element in the process of social construction—the linguistic. A dress may make a woman feel weak because it leaves her vulnerable to an aggressive and physically powerful man—a point not lost on Blake's contemporary Mary Wollstonecraft in her animadversions against Dr. John Gregory's *A Father's Legacy to His Daughters* (1774).[24] But the ideology of strength versus weakness represented by that article of clothing is not only enforced but created outright by the operation of metonymy, which serves as the crucial agent in constructing an ideology of dress as a subcode of the ideology of gender. M. H. Abrams illustrates metonymy in the act of constructing an ideology of gender with an example drawn from Shakespeare's *As You Like It* (2.4.6): "Doublet and hose ought to show itself courageous to petticoat." Most likely, Shakespeare's all-male troupe of players and his mostly male audience, seduced by the self-concealing, naturalizing operation of metonymy, accepted the preceding statement as a self-evident truth, even though it was uttered by the character of Rosalind and further complicated by the fact that she was disguised as the bisexual (or homosexual) Ganymede. By analogy, the contemporary slang representation of a woman as a "skirt" both fetishizes the skirt (and what it conceals), and dehumanizes and reifies the object of address.[25]

The use of metonymy to deny the intrinsic equality of the other interdicts transference even as it ordains gendered power relations. Yet neither Ferber nor Ryan discusses the role of metonymy in constituting ideologies and concealing their figurality as they operate. At least two characteristics of metonymy seem to bear on its efficacy. The first of these is the apparently self-evident logic of its operation. Another way to make this point is to say that the logic of cause and effect, which is essentially the logic of metonymy, is also the logic of symbolic logic and natural science. Newton's *System of the World*, for example, is founded on an apparent statement of the Law of Parsimony that is in fact the metonymic basis for making the natural synonymous with the Mosaic cosmogony.[26] The second of these characteristics is metonymy's ability to become, to use Ryan's term, "transparent," denying even the existence of the moment of desire (or the operation of the will) that gives rise to metonymy, while at the same time privileging, reifying, or fetishizing the very object that metonymy figures forth.

IDEOLOGY HISTORICIZED

The example of Newton, along with the previous examples of Bacon, Newton, and Locke, begins to suggest the specific historical situation of "the ideology of the natural." In historicizing my definition of this ideology, I begin by making explicit one obvious inference to be drawn from the preceding discussion: that there is an important relationship to be observed between the tropes that one uses and the gender and power relations informing the subject-object relationships that result. Moreover, the choice of tropes is historically conditioned, if not determined outright, by historical context.

To suggest how this relationship operates as a function of history, one might begin by considering the tropes employed by Boethius and Bacon, then compare how subject-object relationships play out in the two. *The Consolation of Philosophy* (ca. 524) is allegorical, that is, for Boethius (and for Aristotle, Cicero, and Quintilian before him), metaphorical; *De augmentis* (1623) and most other Baconian texts, metonymic.[27] Hardly Bacon's inquisitor "entering and penetrating into . . . holes and corners when, the inquisition of truth is his whole object" (4:296), Boethius, for his part, suggests a higher mutuality and transferentiality, even a reverence, for the female object, although in his case it is Dame Philosophy and her muses rather than Dame Nature. Rather than probing, Boethius keeps his chaste distance and prepares to learn from a woman standing overhead "whose countenance was full of

150

majesty, whose gleaming eyes surpassed in power of insight those of ordinary mortals, whose color was full of life, and whose strength was still intact though she was so full of years that by no means would it be believed that she was of our times."

Dame Philosophy in fact reclaims Boethius from the pastime of profligate probing, even if his pastime has left him in a situation much different from that of Bacon's natural philosopher.

> When she saw that the Muses of poetry were present by my couch . . . she was stirred a while; her eyes flashed fiercely as she said: "who has suffered these seducing mummers to approach this sick man? . . . I would think it less grievous if your allurements drew away from me some common man like those of the vulgar herd, seeing that in such a one my labors would be harmed not at all. But this man has been nurtured in the lore of Eleatics and Academics. Away with you, sirens, seductive sirens even to perdition, and leave him to my muses to be cared for and healed![28]

As the rejection of seduction for nurturance suggests, the relationship between Dame Philosophy herself and Boethius is of the order of mother and son. But as she herself makes clear, she has muses of her own to command, and the relationship that is to obtain between these muses and Boethius will be one of Platonic mutuality, under the sway of which there will be a free and unremitting exchange of intellectual (but not sexual) favors. Or perhaps the word *exchange* is misapplied in the sexual context as Boethius understands it: it seems clear that "the Muses of poetry" are being held accountable for the depleting illness that afflicts Boethius at the outset. And it seems clear that Dame Philosophy offers Boethius a binary choice: either mingle with the world and leave philosophical essence (and salvation) behind, or mingle with philosophical essence, attain salvation, and leave the world behind.

Although the Catholicism of the Middle Ages sustained this binary choice, the Protestantism of the Reformation and English Puritanism above all did not. Charles Taylor characterizes the Puritan stance thusly:

> So to take their proper place in God's order, human beings had to avoid two opposite deviations. They must spurn the monkish error of renouncing the things of this world—possessions, marriage—for this amounts to scorning God's gifts, which they should instead be bringing back to him through worshipful use. . . . The other error was to become absorbed in things and take them for their own end.[29]

151

One of the two binary choices is still available. Mingling with the world as an end in itself is as sure a pathway to hell for Bunyan as it is for Boethius. But it is no longer possible, in a world gone beyond miraculous intercession and real eucharistic presence, to gain direct, transferential access to godhead. What lies between God and humanity is "God's gifts"—metonymic effects of the First Cause—of which one makes "worshipful use" in the hope of detecting the workings of Providence in the natural world or, far more important to the individual, evidence of election.

But one should not lose sight of the fact that "worshipful use" is, in an important sense, proprietary use. Possessions are chattels—as were wives in the seventeenth-century context. The natural philosopher of the seventeenth century "owns" those of "God's gifts" that he interrogates, discovers, or presents to others. Like Browning's Duke of Este in "My Last Duchess," none but Bacon—or someone else who has likemindedly dedicated his life and talents to probing nature's womb for valuable lore—puts by the veils that conceal "God's gifts." Figuration, whether for Bacon or for Newton and Locke and the numerous line that comes after, is prescription.

"Worshipful use," scientific or otherwise, is, in another important sense, a hermeneutical praxis. As an interpretive activity, it has its original in the practice of reading first the Bible and then the Book of Nature for the truths the two contain.[30] Indeed, "the Deist picture . . . of the universe as a vast interlocking order of beings," metaphorized from no later than the time of Robert Boyle onward as a clock,[31] was as likely to be metaphorized as a syntagmatic interlock as a mechanical one—as a text, in other words. Locke, the figure that Taylor is discussing in the preceding brief citation, closes *An Essay Concerning Human Understanding* with a "Division of the Sciences," the third and last of which is "*semeiotike*, or *the Doctrine of Signs*, the most usual whereof being Words." Mastery of *semeiotike* can lead to mastery of all knowledge included in the other two divisions as well, both "*Praktike*, The Skill of Right," and "The Knowledge of Things, as they are in their own proper Beings, their Constitutions, Properties, and Operations." "The Consideration then of *Ideas* and *Words*, as the great Instruments of Knowledge, makes no despicable part of their Contemplation, who would take a view of humane Knowledge in the whole Extent of it" (4.21.2–4 [720–21]).

Locke's semiotic enterprise is of the order of a decoding of a very particular kind, not to be completed until the events prophesied in Revelations transpire and Christ and his Bride, the Logos and the world, are again one and unmediated. An unrolling or unfolding must precede this stage in order that one reach it. In the case of the last things foretold by John of Patmos, this prelude takes the form of unsealing seven scrolls, unrolling them, and reading from them the world's ultimate and progressively unmediated fate. In the interim, the decoding takes the form of removing what Bacon terms "infoldment." Of the "use of Poetry Parabolical for an infoldment," Bacon comments, "The dignity whereof requires that they should be seen as through a veil; that is when the secrets and mysteries of religion, poetry, and philosophy are involved as fables and parables" (4:316). The task of natural philosophy, as Bacon views it, is to unfold the "infoldment," to find out what lies behind the "veil." On one level, the task involves flattening out and reducing the parable (Gr. *parabole*, "placing beside, comparison"), removing the turn from the trope (Gr. *trepein*, "to turn"). But in positing the veil, Bacon fetishizes both it and the object it presumably conceals: the enfolded vagina, and beyond that, the womb itself. Bacon is not content to see Dame Nature through a veil. Notwithstanding a modicum of dread as to the outcome of his enterprise, he wants to get into her knickers—lawfully, of course, since she is his chattel.[32] As the result "of entering and penetrating into these holes and corners" (4:296), Bacon finds "much ground for hoping that there are still laid up in the womb of nature many secrets of excellent use having no affinity or parallelism with anything that is now known."[33]

For seventeenth-century writers such as Bacon, Newton, and Locke, the enfolded, whether Bacon's "womb of nature" or Newton's corpuscle in the *Opticks* (1706; 1730), was the site of potentially apocalyptic knowledge of its cause.[34] By the late eighteenth century, however, the apocalyptic potential latent in the revealed design of nature no longer existed. Hume, writing in *Dialogues Concerning Natural Religion* (1779) in the persona of the skeptic Philo, argues that

> *the cause or causes of order in the universe probably bear some remote analogy to human intelligence. . . . If this really be the case, what can the*

most inquisitive contemplative, and religious man do more than give a plain, philosophical assent to the proposition, as often as it occurs, and believe that the arguments on which it is established exceed the objections which lie against it?

Hume's skeptical probabilism does not allow him to credit arguments such as those of the Deist Cleanthes, who argues that "the comparison of the universe to a machine of human contrivance is so obvious and natural, and is justified by so many instances of order and design in nature, that it must immediately strike all unprejudiced apprehensions, and procure universal approbation."[35]

Despite its demystification, the ideology of the natural, often manifesting as variant of Natural Theology, survived throughout the eighteenth century and well into the nineteenth, continuing to exist, as it always had, as a vehicle of proprietary interest. Although it could no longer hold out the promise of transcendent knowledge, the ideology could provide a locus for consensus in the age of Hume and Johnson, even if that consensus built on fictions *"felt to be true* by most people all of the time, and by philosophers most of the time." Sometimes, the ideological content of the position was so blatantly proprietary that it all but overwhelmed the presumably scientific content. Speaking of the naturalist Gilbert White, Leopold Damrosch assesses his position as follows: "And even if social and scientific ideology have more in common than they want to admit, they are still far from identical. There remains a significant difference between asserting that the Church of England ought to be established by law and that harvest mice build spherical nests."[36]

BLAKE: PROPHET AGAINST IDEOLOGY

Blake understands the ideology of the natural, both in terms of its historical origins (including the excesses that follow from these), and in terms of how rhetorical or tropaic strategies are used to form such an ideology.[37] His quarrel of long duration with Bacon, Newton, and Locke is both about the way that their prescriptive textualization preempts original perception and about the way in which their figural strategies diminish both the created universe and humanity's place in it.

In a letter of 11 September 1801 to Thomas Butts, Blake claims that although "Bacon & Newton would prescribe ways of making the world heavier" to him, Blake himself is "so far from being bound down" that the "world," which he takes along on his "flights . . . often seems lighter than a ball of wool rolled by the wind" (*CPP*, p. 716). "The wind" to which Blake refers is not the west wind bringing autumn to England, but the same wind that blows in "Mock on Mock on Voltaire Rousseau," the same wind that has a part in transforming "The Atoms of Democritus / And Newtons Particles of Light" to "Sands upon the Red sea shore / Where Israels tents do shine so bright" (ll. 9–12).

Here and elsewhere, Blake articulates the idea of language—especially in its originary spoken form—as a boundary phenomenon that empowers the speaker to draw a full range of distinctions, up to and including the distinction between the mortal and immortal. Language takes its rise out of the mortal and immortal as these are combined in the form of desire, but language is all too susceptible to a fall into the sphere of the mortal and, consequently, into reification. When it functions in the manner that, for Blake, it ought to, language, one form that desire takes, functions in much the same manner in the auditory medium as line functions in the visual. As Morris Eaves notes, "the line in art . . . is the ultimate artistic act, an act with overtones of seeking truth and making final judgments." Like line, language carries out this function by enacting "sharp distinctions." The only difference between line and language in this instance is that line is "part of a family with members in history, philosophy, and science, such as metaphors of precision," whereas language, owing to its basis in metaphor, is a metalepsis of precision.[38]

Language in Blake's notebook poem exists and is uttered in the context of human desire. Desire, in its turn, is situated between humanity's recognition of mortality—with the inevitable consequence that the physical body will perish in the sea of space and time (Red Sea)—and humanity's hope for transcendence or salvation as part of a prophetic or visionary line (Israel's tents). The Bard of the introduction to *Songs of Experience* has got it right, albeit not in a manner calculated to instill comfort in himself or in his audience, when he concludes,

> The starry floor
> The watry shore
> Is giv'n thee till the break of day" (ll. 18–20).

The materialist's reified, regularized universe of celestial mechanics ("starry floor") and tide tables ("watry shore") itself takes form out of the language of desire, albeit repressed or deflected desire. This language mediates between the certainty of perishability and the hope of transcendence.

A reprise of this notion of language as a boundary condition is found at the end of *Milton*. There Ololon relieves herself of her delusions of wholeness, intactness, or sacrosanctity when she allows the sixfold virgin form that she thought she was to flee, thus leaving her mortal part to perish "into the depths / Of Miltons Shadow as a Dove upon the stormy Sea" (*M*, pl. 42 [49], ll. 5–6). Then Ololon ceases her wailing and howling and, as a character who defines the boundary condition of articulate language, becomes Christ's garment, and his bride:

> round his limbs
> The Clouds of Ololon folded as a garment dipped in blood
> Written within & without in woven letters: & the Writing
> Is a Divine Revelation in the Litteral expression.
> (*M*, pl. 42 [49], ll. 11–14)

"Litteral" is an intentional (and effective) pun, here meaning both "literal" and "littoral"[39] Even the literal has the figural potential to turn into something else, and that transformation attests once again to the fact that language—even prophetic language that has attained the condition of materiality (cf. "woven letters")—exists as a boundary between meanings that are at best antithetical, at worst incommensurable.

In its full, unmediated manifestation at the end of *Jerusalem*, this wind is "The Breath Divine [that] Breathed over Albion," revived him, and "went forth over the morning hills" (*J*, pl. 94, l. 18, pl. 95, l. 5).

The fact that the wind rolls a ball of wool is also important. Wool is the coat of the lamb. It suggests the Lamb's garment, and in doing so comments on the objectification of the material world as a gauge of how far everyday lived experience has become estranged from a lived experience that is fundamentally sacramental. Wool, knitted or woven, is the basis for the material and a metonym for all that exists materially, just as the wind is the basis for the immaterial and a metaphor for all that exists spiritually. That the wind is able to roll the ball of wool so easily suggests the lightness or insubstantiality of the material. What persists through change—substance, in other words—is the wind, not the wool, to which Blake implicitly likens himself in describing how he is, on occasion, hurried away from the proper visionary object by "Abstract folly" (*CPP*, p. 716). Visual perception and causality are at odds in Blake's account of his "flights." An observer sees the material ball of wool first, but who would claim that the ball of wool "causes" the wind—that the material "causes" the spiritual? Without the wind blowing as a prior causative force, that observer sees nothing. And yet the tendency is to confuse the sequence of observation.

The letter enacts a little parable concerning the relationship of the basis of the spiritual to the basis of the material. Living belatedly in the natural world, both after the Fall as historical event and after the Fall recapitulated as personal loss of innocence, human beings see the material first, just as Adam and Eve see each other's bodies first (Genesis 3:7)—especially when what we see is "prescribed" by the likes of Bacon or Newton as a fetishized female nature or body (corpuscle). If one makes an unchallenged start out of such a prescriptively rendered "natural" possession or effect, which presupposes a "natural" possessor or cause, one can never arrive at a clear understanding of the spiritual basis for the existence of something rather than nothing, and why that something is good, if only in a theodical and not an immediate context.[40]

No later than *The Book of Urizen* (1794), Blake engages the Enlightenment legacy of science according to Bacon, Newton, and Locke. Bacon proposes that "there is therefore much ground for hoping that there are still laid up in the womb of nature many secrets of excellent use having no affinity or parallelism with anything now known."[41] The statement begs the question of what or who encrypted the "secrets" in that enfolded and fetishized place. In *The Book of Urizen*, Blake gives his answer. Urizen recounts his first act after separating himself from the other Zoas as follows:

> First I fought with the fire; consum'd
> Inwards, into a deep world within:
> A void immense, wild dark & deep,
> Where nothing was: Natures wide womb. (*U*, pl. 4, ll. 14–17)[42]

As one follows along with Urizen's account, it becomes clear that the "secrets" to be found in "Natures wide womb" are of Urizen's making and not God's. As the former confides,

> Here alone I in books formd of metals
> Have written the secrets of wisdom
> The secrets of dark contemplation. (*U*, pl. 4, ll. 24–26)

Urizen completes his metonymic account of cause and effect and emerges from the darkness of the womb, which gives birth not to nature or secrets but to Urizen and laws. He reveals "the Book / Of eternal brass, written in my solitude" (*U*, pl. 4, ll. 32–33). The containing monism of this book—and its existence as the invention of Urizen the inventor, the possession of Urizen the possessor—all signal Blake's awareness that "nature's womb" is a metonym, a fictive contruct in Urizen's head and the heads of all who would follow him. It is, to borrow from *Milton*, "a Vision of the Science of the Elohim" (*M*, pl. 29 [31], l. 65). Urizen's brass books, like the Mosaic tablets they resemble, are the laws of the Elohim. The Ten Commandments, it should be recalled, are spoken by God (Elohim), not the Lord (Jehovah [Exodus 20:1–17]).

Blake engages Newton and Locke in a manner slightly different from the one he uses to engage Bacon. In each instance, he takes a salient scientific or philosophical metonym—the moment in Newton's case and the globule in Locke's—and views it from the transferential perspective of the infinite. In both instances, Blake's article of faith seems to be that "words contain revolutionary powers never entirely effaced by the paradigmatic and syntagmatic manacles used to control them." To turn to Newton: we have known for some time, thanks to F. B. Curtis, that Blake got his concept of the "moment of time" from Newton's theory of fluxions.[43] The moment, like the corpuscle, is an irreducible, indivisible unit—the infinitesimal straight line that is the differential of the curve, and which may be summed by the integral to recreate the curve. As a mathematical construct, it is presented as existing somehow in a space outside of time, in the timeless Platonic realm of the ideal. Blake sees the moment as a metonym from Newton's fallen perspective, but as a figure that may be revitalized as metaphor from the perspective of the infinite. The first thing to realize is that the moment of time is the contingent historical form of transferential desire.

> Every Time less than a pulsation of the artery
> Is equal in its period & value to Six Thousand Years.
> For in this Period the Poets Work is Done: and all the Great
> Events of Time start forth & are concievd in such a Period
> Within a Moment: a Pulsation of the Artery.
> (*M*, pl. 28 [30], l. 62–pl. 29 [31], l. 3)

Blake's position, with a little help from Bishop Ussher, is that the historical duration of the material world—from the beginning chronicled in Genesis to the end prefigured by Revelation—is six thousand years. But this span is as infinitesimal in relation to eternity as the Newtonian moment is to the curve of which it is the differential. Moreover, both are metonyms that mask the workings of transferentiality. Newton is, for Blake, a poet who denies his poetic inclinations—as are Bacon and Locke, both of whom are brought back in that guise, along with Chaucer, Shakespeare, and Milton, at the end of *Jerusalem* (pl. 98, l. 9). Through the mediation of the body privileged by Blakean "pity," the pulse is made to appear the cause of the moment as effect— and it is true that the sixty-second minute bears striking similarities to the resting pulse rate of a healthy adult. What is responsible for the pulse—what completes it—is "the breath of life." Newton's mistake, as Blake sees it, is to reify the pulsebeat and make it the cause of the moment, denying the existence of anything anterior or interior to it. Although Satan, who is "Newton's Pantocrator" in *Milton* (pl. 4, l. 11), can create the metonym of the moment and use it as a mathematical operator, he cannot repress or suppress all of its immanent potential. This is Oothoon's "moment of desire" with a difference.

> There is a Moment in each Day that Satan cannot find
> Nor can his Watch Fiends find it, but the Industrious find
> This Moment & it multiply & when it once is found
> It renovates every Moment of the Day if rightly placed.
> (*M*, pl. 35 [39], ll. 42–45)

The renovation is of a kind with that which occurs in *Jerusalem*, when "All things acted on Earth are seen in the bright Sculptures of / Los's Halls & every Age renews its powers from these Works" (*J*, pl. 16, ll. 61–62).[44] It involves seeing the underlying genius of the trope, stripping away its reified detritus, and wondering at the immanence that gives rise to such genius.

Blake takes his idea of the globule from Locke's *Essay Concerning Human Understanding*. In the fourth book, Locke discusses the causes of ideas.

> For those other simple *Ideas* being appearances or sensations, produced in us, by the Size, Figure, Number, and Motion of minute Corpuscles singly insensible, their different degrees also depend on some, or all of these Causes; which since it cannot be observed by us in Particles of Matter, whereof each is too subtile to be perceived, it is impossible for us to have any exact Measures of the different degrees of these simple ideas. For supposing the Sensation of Idea we name Whiteness, be produced in us by a certain number of Globules, each having a certain verticity about their Centres, strike upon the Retina of the Eye, with a certain degree of Rotation, as well as progressive Swiftness; it will hence easily follow, that the more the superficial parts of the body are so ordered, as to reflect the number of Globules of light, and to give them that proper Rotation . . . the more white will that Body appear.[45]

Here the globule becomes to epistemology what the corpuscle is to mechanics. The globule of light, taken directly by Locke from Newtonian optics, is the cause of simple ideas. What Locke has here constructed is a metonymic chain. Light, which Locke, after Newton, holds to be the metonymic effect of divine *fiat*, in its turn becomes the cause of ideas in human beings, twice removed from their transcendent God.

Just as Blake temporalizes and embodies Newton's moment in *Milton*, he temporalizes and embodies Locke's globule.

> For every Space larger than a red Globule of Mans blood.
> Is Visionary: and is created by the Hammer of Los
> And every Space smaller than a Globule of Mans blood. opens
> Into Eternity of which this vegetable Earth is but a shadow:
> The red Globule is the unwearied Sun by Los created
> To measure Time and Space to mortal Men. (*M*, pl. 29 [31], ll. 19–24)

Blake makes the red globule, the completed form that Los's creative desire takes, the basis of perception. Light is created for Blake not by transcendent fiat, but by immanent, transferential desire, of which it is the completing form, just as Jehovah took red dirt and created "a living soul"(Genesis 2:7) as his/her completed form. The sun/son pun is fully operative in Blake's description of Los's daily activity. That Blake chooses to see the sun as red rather than white light has something to do with his choice of cosmogonies, but also has to do with the fact that white light is differentially refrangible, while red light is not. White light can be decomposed into "minute particulars," that is; red light cannot. Seen from the perspective of the infinite, Locke's globule, then, is a denial and distancing of immanent potential. The sun is not an effect further reducible as the cause of a simple idea. For Blake, the sun/son acts as exemplar of how to temporalize space beyond the globule and render it visionary, while at the same time the sun/son is powerfully immanent as the eternity, or kingdom of heaven, that lies within the globule.

For Blake, the goal of prophecy as a historically situated activity is the transformation of an alienated speech that posits an unbridgeable distance between cause and effect, possessor and (to-be-)possessed, inventor and invention, container and contained, subject and object, speaker and spoken, to full speech that overcomes such a positing. In a poem such as *Milton*, such speech has as its goal the re-membering and re-presenting of the prophetic line, activities often metaphorized by the strapping on of sandals and walking forward on newly renovated members—powerful feet[46]—through the present and toward the apocalyptic future. Such re-membering and re-presenting have the force of enacting the transference of the object from past to future—enacting metaphoricity, in other words—thus rehabilitating the object from its prior condition of metonymic cause (e.g., Milton as regicide or as "influence"), effect (e.g., Milton as deluded Puritan or as poet of the English Revolution), or some combination of these. The "Great Harvest & Vintage of the Nations" (*M*, pl. 43 [50], l. 1), toward which Milton, and Blake, and Los, and all the other "States" of the "Individual" (see *M*, pl. 32 [35], ll. 22–29) known as Urthona move, is a condition of pure and unmediated transferentiality, of eucharistic all in all, of "breath of life," or mind in matter and matter in "breath of life," or mind, in which there are no spatial or temporal categories by means of which to distinguish cause from effect.

While Damrosch is right to qualify Blake's hermeticism by noting that he "has no use for arcane secrets reserved for the adept," Blake's dilemma—and the goal he sets by way of resolving the dilemma, not to mention the unmistakable presence of hermetic lore in his work—points squarely back to the dilemma that hermetic thinkers faced at the dawn of the Scientific Revolution: how to maintain what Frances Yates, speaking precisely of this historical moment, terms "this internalisation, this intimate connection of the *mens* with the world," at the very moment when "mechanics and mathematics" claimed that such a connection "had to be avoided at all costs."[47]

Blake's solution to the "dilemma," full speech[48]—and speech here is a metaphor, as it also is elsewhere in Blake's poetry, for other types of artistic endeavor—probably cannot come to pass in the fallen world. Such speech must transcend the temporality that prefigures its decline from fullness, and it must transcend the spatiality of "inner" and "outer" and thus take place in a context in which the immanence of "Genius" and the resultant potential for full transferentiality is readily evident. The future state that Blake calls "Eternity" is what the end of *Jerusalem* verges on: the marriage of Albion and Jerusalem is the marriage of time and "Eternity," at which instant "Time was Finished!" and "All Human Forms [are] identified even Tree Metal Earth & Stone" (*J*, pl. 94, l. 18, pl. 99, l. 1)—known, that is, for the presence of the immanent, transferential "Genius" within.

However impossible it may be to participate in full speech in this life, it is nevertheless possible to discern signs that it may yet come to pass in "Eternity," where and when the Four Zoas converse visionarily in "the Four Arts."

> in Eternity the Four Arts: Poetry, Painting, Music,
> And Architecture which is Science: are the Four Faces of Man.
> Not so in Time & Space: there Three are shut out, and only
> Science remains thro Mercy: & by means of Science, the Three
> Become apparent in Time & Space, in the Three Professions
>
> Poetry in Religion: Music, Law: Painting, in Physic & Surgery:
> That Man may live upon Earth till the time of his awaking.
>   (*M*, pl. 27 [29], ll. 55–61)

The relationship of these professions to these arts is that of Blake's Emanations to his Zoas. Art forms suspend spatiotemporal categories by teasing us out of thought, as Keats's urn does—and by so doing create the very transferential "Eternity" in which they are situated. Thus a causal chain: art forms give rise to historically situated discourses, the scientific among them, each of which deals in its turn with and rationalizes matters of cause and effect. The realization that the fixity of this relationship is delusory—that transferentiality can begin to replace causality, and that the full speech of metaphor can begin to replace the alienated speech of metonymy—is a precondition to being translated, as Elijah was, to what Blake calls "eternity."

The relationship between Zoa as desiring (or willing, in both senses of the term) subject and Emanation as desired object in Blake's mythic system depends, both for its coming into existence and for its etiology, on the operation of metonymic logic and metonymic transparency. As Damrosch observes,

> (a) The Emanation is the female aspect of the androgynous self, which would never exist at all in separation. (b) It is that which is desired and/or that which is created. (c) It is the body as opposed to soul, garment as opposed to body, space as opposed to time. The conception comes close to the Neoplatonic conception of emanation, colored by Blake's Gnostic suspicion of birth into the body.[49]

Just as an Emanation "would never exist at all in separation," so a metonym, "the literal term for one thing applied to another with which it has become closely associated,"[50] would never exist at all in separation from the original literal term. Neither second term has any meaning without the first. The Emanation as desired and/or created completion—body as completion of soul, garment as completion of body, space as completion of time—recapitulates the relationship of terms laid out by Umberto Eco in his discussion of metonymy, namely, the relationship of cause to effect, possessor to possessed, inventor to invention, container and contained.[51]

Furthermore, the Emanation is every bit as privileged, reified, and fetishized as any other object similarly constructed by metonymy. Not only is it impossible for an Emanation to exist in isolation from its causal source, but it is also impossible for that Emanation to diminish or change that source, as the Neoplatonic sources that Damrosch recommends would seem to confirm.[52] As completion, the Emanation is secondary and derivative rather than coeval and transferential. Reunited androgynous Zoas, who "converse" as the four at the end of *Jerusalem* do, on the other hand, are fully transferential, "Creating Space, Creating Time, according to the wonders Divine / Of Human Imagination" (*J*, pl. 98, ll. 31–32).

But despite the utter secondariness of the Emanation, she is privileged, reified, and fetishized as the object of the newly divided Zoa's desire. In fact, she becomes the object of value in a perverse economy of desire that has important affinities with Derrida's "economy of pity." Indeed, pity is Blake's operative term for describing the establishment of this economy. For example, in *The Book of Urizen*,

> Los saw the Female & pitied
> He embraced her, she wept, she refus'd
> In perverse and cruel delight
> She fled from his arms, yet he followd. (*U*, pl. 19, ll. 10–13)

Pity is a way of knowing the object by granting it autonomous existence as the materially other. To allow this autonomy to come to pass is to suffer a lapse, a moment of forgetfulness, in which the subject loses sight of the fact that the "breath of life" precedes the embodied, "living soul" (Genesis 2:7) dependent upon that "breath," and sees the embodied object as something independent and materially other. In *Milton* Los suffers such a lapse when he allows Satan to manage Palamabron's harrow. Palamabron's job is to harrow the hell of appearances that is this world, metaphorized as "breathing fields" (*M*, pl. 5, l. 2), in order to demonstrate repeatedly the priority of "the breath of life" to the material "dust of the earth" (Genesis 2:7).

Whatever it is that Satan does when he takes over for a day from Palamabron, he does the job wrong, creating the delusion, through "mildness and . . . self-imposition" (*M*, pl. 7, l. 21), of material priority—the delusion that the dirt that Palamabron has been harrowing is somehow the material effect of an immaterial and divine cause rather than an excrescence inseparable in this world from the immanent potential it encloses, the delusion that the dirt serves as the basis for a materially grounded, transcendently created nature rather than as the by-product of a spiritually grounded, immanently created nature. Los has Satan dead to rights earlier in the poem when the former asks, "Art

thou not Newtons Pantocrator weaving the Woof of Locke[?]"
(*M*, pl. 4, l. 11).

Why does Los suffer such a lapse? There is no brief answer,
other than "it is a necessary part of the theodicy." It would be
no easier to answer the preceding question than it would be to
answer why it is that the Word of God suffers the lapse that
allowed the Demiurge of the Gnostic cosmogony to split off and
turn "round as a wheel his own Workmanships."[53] But while the
answer to the question is not apparent, the effect is this: pity
divides the real soul from the apparent body and the real male
from the apparent female, creating sexual difference. "Mine is
the fault!" Los declares. "I should have remember'd that pity
divides the soul / And man, unmans" (*M*, pl. 8, ll. 19–20).

Once granted this autonomy, the object perpetuates its existence by means of something like a law of conservation. Newtonian matter cannot be created or destroyed—at least not within the
context of the Judeo-Christian theodicy.[54] The discourse of that
matter, as mastered by the arch-Newtonian Satan, is natural
philosophy or natural science—what Blake calls "the science of
pity." The discourse of the first and last things comprehending
the delusory existence of the material world and its discourse is
prophetic poetry—what Blake calls "the science of wrath." The
division of soulless matter from immanent potential, the body
from the soul and the female sex from the male occurs, through
the agency of Satan, along with the division of these discourses.
"And Satan not having the Science of Wrath, but only of Pity: /
Rent them asunder, and wrath was left to wrath, & pity to pity"
(*M*, pl. 9, ll. 46–47). The divisor of these two "sciences,"
glimpsed reunited at the end of *The Four Zoas* (1797), where
"sweet Science reigns" (*FZ*, p. 139, l. 10 [9:855]), is also the
division between a "Nature," in *Milton*, that "is a Vision of the
Science of the Elohim" (*M*, pl. 29 [31], l. 65) and a mind or soul
that is, by logical extension, "a vision of the science of Jehovah."

In *The Four Zoas* Enion, Emanation to Tharmas's Zoa, says
more than she knows, declaring,

> In Eden Females sleep the winter in soft silken veils
> Woven by their own hands to hide them in the darksom grave
> But Males immortal live renewd by female deaths.
> (*FZ*, p. 5, ll. 1–3 [1:65–67])

The Emanations would preserve the illusion of their palpable desirability (and of their power over the Zoas, who are their male subjects) by concealing themselves in "soft silken veils." Yet "Males immortal" do not fear castration, as Diane Hoeveler's Freudian male does;[55] neither do they make the mistake of considering the erotic and the thanatic as oppositional terms, displaying instead the sort of polymorphous perversity that amalgamates the erotic and the thanatic, as is suggested by the undecidable phrase "female deaths," meaning both thanatos and eros, *death* being a standard eighteenth-century euphemism for *orgasm*.

Form, whether it be natural, literary, artistic, or of some other kind, is the shape that desire takes, and the reassimilation of form and desire is a matter of resisting the tendency to allow desire to be mediated by the form of something ontologically anterior to it—first resisting the tendency to perceive one's surroundings as somehow "naturally" pregiven, then resisting the impulse to allow what is inscribed or prescribed in the name of the "natural" to remain as it is unchallenged by other instances of form-seeking desire. The "soft silken veils" of the Emanations are of a type of the natural landscape, given the veils/vales pun, and they are also, as silk, a type of the material world, an artifice that assumes the existence of an artificer.

They are also a type of textualization. As Tilottama Rajan reminds us, "the word 'text,' meaning something that is woven together, designates a collection of signs with grammatological but not pneumatological status."[56] No less than the sky itself is a textualized object. In *Milton* it is referred to as "an immortal Tent built by the Sons of Los" (pl. 29 [31], l. 4). And if the sky is such a tabernacle, then it is we who are the "pneumatological" within the "grammatological," the breathing Holy of Holies within the tent. Blake's purpose, then, in combatting the ideology of the natural is to recognize the immanent basis of the life world in general and of humanity in particular for what they are—the creative basis of all that has ever existed and all that will ever exist. He has many metaphors for this act of recognition—circumcision, sexual intercourse, and the casting off of old and rotten clothes, among others.

In employing the last of these variant metaphors, Blake makes startlingly apt and ironic use of Locke—not only to deconstruct

Locke, but to deconstruct the whole project of empiricism as it proposes the study of the fixed, externally situated reality intended by the concept of nature. In discussing habits of thought that are responsible for "Wrong Assent, or Error," as it is characterized in book 4, chapter 20, of *Concerning Human Understanding*, Locke implicates received hypotheses as having a large part to play in the perpetuation of error. Yet Locke is not sanguine about the likelihood of overturning such received hypotheses. "And who ever, by the most cogent Arguments will be prevailed with, to disrobe himself at once of all his old Opinions, and Pretences to Knowledge and Learning, which with hard Study, he hath all this Time been labouring for; and turn himself out stark naked, in quest afresh for new Notions?" (4.20.11 [714]), he asks. As Blake fully understands, the argument is as readily turned against Locke as it is against Locke's opponents. In *Milton* the poem's namesake comes, he tells his emanation Ololon,

> To cast off Rational Demonstration by Faith in the Saviour
> To cast off the rotten rags of Memory by Inspiration
> To cast off Bacon, Locke & Newton from Albions covering
> To take off his filthy garments, & clothe him with Imagination.
>   (*M*, pl. 41 [48], ll. 3–6)

Whether it is Milton returning from heaven to reclaim his true identity as metaphor for poetic inspiration rather than metonym for his textualized collected works, Los "Striving with Systems" in *Jerusalem* "to deliver Individuals from those Systems" (*J*, pl. 11, l. 5), or the reader who finds her/himself surrounded by Blake's etched text and the illuminations of what is presumably "out there," the message is, "cast it off as prescriptive cause or prescribed effect and respond transferentially as to a visionary conversation." All deities do exist within the human breast, as Blake says in *The Marriage of Heaven and Hell*, and in visionary conversation they become one God. As Los says in *Jerusalem*, "Why stand we here trembling around / Calling on God for help; and not ourselves in whom God dwells" (pl. 38, ll. 12–13). In *Milton* the poem's namesake "took the outside course, among the graves of the dead" (pl. 14 [15], l. 34), just as Blake did throughout his artistic career, for the purpose of showing that there is no such place, and none of its presumed perils, for one who is able to distinguish metonymy from metaphor, ideology from inspiration. Seen from the perspective of eternity in *Jerusalem*, "the outside course" is the inside course, and one is able to converse at journey's end if one is able to respond to the Blakean text and illumination as creation "according to the wonders Divine / Of Human Imagination" (*J*, pl. 98, ll. 31–32) rather than prescriptive redaction of God's truth. At the fold of the book, or at the fold of the visual and the verbal, one sees either divinely inflected trope or humanly inflected mystery.

At the beginning of *Milton*, Blake misquotes Numbers 11:29 slightly. "Would to God that all the Lords people were Prophets" (pl. 1), he writes, adding a gratuitous *to* to the original as it appears in the King James Version. Perhaps more important, however, is that part of the verse which Blake omits: "and that the Lord would put his spirit upon them!" (Numbers 11:29). At issue in this chapter of Numbers is whether true nourishment occurs by dint of lust of the flesh or desire of the spirit. Eldad and Medad, who "prophesied in the camp" (11:26), are nourished by desire of the spirit and preserved. Those who gather up quails and batten on them are smitten "by Jehovah with a very great plague" (11:33). "And he called the name of that place Kibroth-hattaavah: because there they buried the people that lusted" (11:34). Embodied humanity does not live by matter alone; spirit, not by matter at all.

CHAPTER 8

The Din of the City
in Blake's Prophetic Books

The urban landscape of the Prophetic Books—most pointedly, that of *Milton* (1804) and *Jerusalem* (1804–20) presents an utterly appalling tableau of holocaust and cacophony. This fiery, smoky, high-decibel assault is compounded of howling, shrieking, wailing, and other human sounds verging on the merely animal, and the sounds of industrial processes, particularly those having to do with the fabrication of metals and the manufacture of textiles. The following passages from chapter 1 of *Jerusalem* are but two of numerous possible cases in point:

> Prepare the furniture O Lambeth in thy pitying looms!
> The curtains, woven tears & sighs, wrought into lovely forms
> For comfort. there the secret furniture of Jerusalems chamber
> Is wrought.
> . . . .
> Hertfordshire glows with fierce Vegetation! in the Forests
> The Oak frowns terrible, the Beech & Ash & Elm enroot
> Among the Spiritual fires; loud the Corn fields thunder along
> The Soldiers fife; the Harlots shriek; the Virgins dismal groan
> The Parents Fear: the Brothers jealousy: the Sisters curse
> Beneath the Storms of Theotormon & the thundring Bellows
> Heaves in the hand of Palamabron who in Londons darkness
> Before the Anvil, watches the bellowing flames: thundering
> The Hammer loud rages in Rintrahs strong grasp swinging loud

Round from heaven to earth down falling with heavy blow
Dead on the Anvil, where the red hot wedge groans in pain.[1]

There is a sense in which the cacophony in the Prophetic Books may be said to be mimetically or naturalistically motivated. Blake's London was an ecologically disastrous place to live. From 1750 to 1801, the year in which the first census was taken, the city's population increased by an estimated third, from 675,000 to 900,000.[2] Many of those flocking to the city and swelling its population were the rootless poor, turned out of common grazing and farming lands by the Enclosure Acts and bereft of parish aid; factory laborers and their families, forced to work ever harder in an ever-inflating economy to meet subsistence needs; and émigrés fleeing the political turmoil of the French Revolution and its aftermath.[3] Wordsworth's observation, in his letter of 1801 to James Charles Fox, that "the rapid decay of the domestic affections among the lower orders of society"[4] was taking place in the Lake District as the result of the industrialization of the North might well have been extended to include the South Midlands and London as well.

Moreover, this uncontrolled growth was not restricted to London proper. With increasing frequency, the open countryside surrounding London and Westminster was transformed into suburbs subject to same ever-growing din and pall that characterized those older cities.[5] And here demographics can only begin to suggest what the quality of life must have been like. London's 900,000 and their suburban counterparts cooked and heated with coal, which also powered local industry. Accompanying the incessant din, the smoke from household and factory flues fouled the air with a smog that was to become, by the end of the nineteenth century, the "yellow fog" that seemed perpetually to pervade the damp air of London. Another disincentive to breathing the air, let along drinking the water, was the sewage that ran in open gutters and into the Thames in such magnitude as to make the hyperbolic description of the Thames found in Swift's "A Description of a City Shower" (1710) into an everyday lived reality.[6]

In addition to an unhealthy ecology, London and environs increasingly became the site of violent social unrest and cruel spectacle. For example, for several days in June 1780 mobs of rioters of the lower orders, motivated by strong anti-Catholic sentiment and dissatisfaction with England's management of the war against the American colonies, took part in what have come to be known as the Gordon Riots. As David V. Erdman notes, "the *Annual Register* describing the flames ascending from the prisons, from the hated ha'penny tollhouses on Blackfriars Bridge, from the alcohol blazing in a demolished distillery, mentioned 'the tremendous roar of the authors of these horrible scenes' continuing all the night (the fifth day)."[7]

There is also a sense in which, underwritten by, and in reaction to, the unrest and cruel spectacle of his social milieu, passages from Blake's Prophetic Books such as the ones cited above may also be said to allegorize, through multilingual punning and other means,[8] their own difficult production as articulate texts. The very word *text* is the Englishing of the Latin *textus*, woven, the past participle of *tessere*, to weave, nor was Blake the only English romantic to understand this etymology.[9] Lambeth's "woven sighs & tears, wrought into lovely forms / For comfort," accordingly allegorize the textualization of affect as "forms" of consolation.

The second passage allegorizes its production as an articulate text with a difference. The "fierce Vegetation," save for the "Corn fields," which will be discussed below, is all trees, above all, "The Oak," with its warlike and Druidic associations.[10] But the oak is not the only tree named in this passage. "Beech & Ash & Elm" also threaten Hertfordshire's "Spiritual fires." The paradox here is that fire usually threatens trees. But that paradox may be resolved by recalling that the Latin word for tree, *caudex*—a variant form is *codex*—also means *book*, and is what Blake intends when he refers to "All Bibles or sacred codes," as these "have been the causes" of spurious dichotomies, such as those between soul and body, reason and energy, and good and evil (*MHH*, pl. 4)[11] In this instance, preexisting, lettered texts of English civil and religious law create such spirit-killing dichotomies, thereby prescribing and subverting the speech of soldiers, harlots, virgins, parents, brothers, and sisters, rendering it inarticulate because it is no longer susceptible to authentic inspiration.[12]

The second passage also allegorizes textualization as the means of transmitting knowledge. In *The Marriage of Heaven and Hell* Blake describes the process of textualization "in a Printing house in Hell"—that is, under nearly ideal conditions that allow the imagination to function without impediment. "Hell" is a landscape of "gold silver and precious stones," in the fourth "chamber" of which are "Lions of flaming fire raging round & melting the metals into living fluids." These are "cast . . . into the expanse" of space and time by "Unnam'd forms. . . . There they were reciev'd by Men who occupied the sixth chamber, and took the forms of books & were arranged in libraries" (*MHH*, pl. 15). The "casting" process in question is ambiguous—deliberately so, most likely—referring either to using molds to create textual form, or simply to throwing the "living fluids" out "into the expanse" and letting them assume their own form, which would be spherical,[13] or, to use a term nearer to Blake's lexicon, globular.[14]

But under the less-than-ideal conditions of the fallen world, knowledge does not take textual form without impediments and the creative struggle necessary to overcome these, however imperfectly. Hence the imperative to forge, in the several senses of that verb, rather than merely to cast.[15] Moreover, the relationship between who is at the forge and what is being forged is highly significant.

Under the best of circumstances, Los, Blake's poetic-prophetic avatar, true to the model set down in *The Marriage*, forges globules.

> The red Globule is the unwearied Sun by Los created
> To measure Time and Space to mortal men. every morning.
> Bowlahoola & Allamanda are placed on each side
> Of that Pulsation [of the artery] & that Globule, terrible their power.
>
> But Rintrah & Palamabron govern over Day & Night
> In Allamanda & Entuthon Benython where souls wail.
> (*M*, pl. 29 [31], ll. 23–28)

The last two lines say it all. Rintrah and Palamabron—Blake's figures for Pitt and Parliament[16]—govern the fallen world of time and space that Los's globe marks or remarks from a distance. And as they govern, so they forge. The "red hot wedge [that] groans in pain" does so because it is to be forged into a sword, knife, or battle-ax for use in the continuation of a war that Rintrah/Pitt and Palamabron/Parliament, under the guise of the

the prescriptive laws of England (the trees) and a climate of hypocritical self-righteousness ("the Storms of Theotormon"), declared in 1793.

Given the noisy, smoky, distinctly unhealthy quality of life in London and environs and other English urban areas at the turn of the nineteenth century, given the attendant social unrest and spectacle, and given the difficulties that English urban ecology and the English social milieu pose for the production of articulate texts, it would stand to reason that many of Blake's renderings of the urban landscape are decidedly unpleasant and pointedly noisy. But it is an oversimplification to reduce Blake's renderings to merely mimetic or naturalistic responses to the urban landscape of his time and place. Nor are his renderings reducible to allegorizations of their own coming into being. To attempt either sort of reduction—or to attempt both sorts—is to lose sight of the larger sociohistorical and socioeconomic situatedness of those renderings and the very profound social and political issues that inform them, An English landscape in which "loud the Corn fields thunder along / The Soldiers fife" is an English landscape in the throes of an ongoing war with France and food crisis compounded of bad harvests, profiteering, and government intervention in ways ranging from unfair regulation to the repression of dissent by the military.[17]

Perhaps more importantly, an urban landscape filled with "woven tears & sighs"; "the Harlots shriek; the Virgins dismal groan"; "thundering Bellows"; and a "thundering . . . Hammer" is a landscape that bespeaks the all but total alienation of language and the means of artisanal or artistic production (or destruction), let alone self-expression, from the human subject whose labor is ultimately responsible for both alike.[18] The scene of the Prophetic Books is one in which language and the means of artisanal or artistic production as a form of self-expression threatened to become finally and irrevocably separate from the productive, languaged subject, to take on a fiendish life of their own about which neither the prescribed subject nor that subject's intended audience has any say.[19]

The drama of the alienation of language-as-labor from the human subject underwrites much of Blake's poetry leading up to the Prophetic Books. The narrative of the alienation of language and its restoration to the productive, languaged subject, moreover, is heavily underwritten by the Old and New Testaments, and as such, the narrative constitutes a theodicy in its own right. Although considerations of space prevent a full elaboration of this drama, I wish at least to suggest where and how its operations may be observed. Already in *Poetical Sketches* (1783) one repeatedly encounters poetic speakers who either lack the artistic nerve to say something original or find that the impulse to originality is overwhelmed by the preexistent utterances, repetitions, and conventions of a classically ordained and stylized canon.[20]

Much of the drama of the passage through the state of innocence in *Songs of Innocence* (1789) has to do with the ever-present threat that established forms of order and their "official" language(s) pose for the labor of the authentically inspired but naïve poetic speaker. In fact, because one cannot know any better in the state of innocence, such a speaker participates in the very process of the alienation of language-as-labor. In the "Introduction," for example, the Piper reports, "On a cloud I saw a Child" (*SI*, 1.3), not knowing that he sees, in John of Patmos's words, "Jesus Christ, who is the faithful witness," the same whom John announces as follows: "Behold, he cometh with clouds; and every eye shall see him" (Revelation 1:5, 7). In fulfilling the child's commandments to "Pipe a song about a Lamb," then to "Sing thy songs of merry cheer" (ll. 5, 10), the Piper does well.

But this failure to recognize the child as Christ, and thereby to recognize the imminence of apocalpyse that his appearance signals, leads the Piper to misunderstand the child's commandment to "sit thee down and write / In a book that all may read" (ll. 13–14)—or if not to misunderstand the commandment, at least to fall victim to the dilemma that the commandment occasions. The Christ Child echoes Paul in 2 Corinthians, where he characterizes Christ as "our epistle written in our hearts, known and read of all men: For as much as ye are manifestly declared to be the epistle of Christ ministered by us, written not in ink, but with the Spirit of the living God; not on tables of stone, but in the fleshy tables of the heart" (3:2–3). That is, the Christ Child intends for the Piper to internalize the encounter and thereby to become one with Christ, creating in this process the highest possible degree of intimacy between subject, language-as-labor, and the God-as-Logos that underwrites both.[21]

Paul elects to labor with ink and script, to substitute medium and message of the particular letter for those of the universal spirit, in order to advert to the higher scriptural truth of that spirit.[22] The result is not universalization but generalization. The Piper, who tellingly loses sight of the Christ Child before beginning his labors, must do much the same—must make use of "a rural pen" and "staind . . . water" (ll. 17–18) to record what in his case is an unacknowledgedly numinous encounter. The result, not surprisingly, is generalization—in the Piper's words, "happy songs [that] / Every child may joy to hear" (ll. 19–20).

And just as generalization gives way to precept—and, ultimately, to dogma—in Paul's discourse, so generalization does in a number of the *Songs of Innocence*—for example, in "The Little Black Boy," "The Chimney Sweeper," and "Holy Thursday." The tension between the potential for personal revelation and the intrusion of dogma in the second of these is particularly acute. Much as the Christ Child appears to the Piper, "little Tom Dacre" appears to the speaker of "The Chimney Sweeper," who also fails to recognize the imminence of apocalpyse that the child's appearance signals. Tom, whose "white hair" is reported to have "curl'd like a lambs back" (ll. 6, 8), has his original in John of Patmos's "Son of man," whose "head and his hairs were white like wool, as white as snow" (Revelation 1:14).

One key to the speaker's failure of recognition is the failure of language—Tom's and the speaker's—to register the imminence of apocalypse that Tom's curly white hair betokens. John characterizes Christ's "voice as the sound of many waters" (1:15). Tom's voice is certainly associated with water. He "cried when his head . . . was shaved" (ll. 5–6), and he dreams that he and his mates "run / And wash in a river and shine in the Sun" (ll. 15–16). But neither the speaker nor Tom realizes that the "Sun" [Son] shines in him. The reason is that the language of both is alienated from them virtually from birth. This alienation is symbolized by the shaving of Tom's head, which weakens him expressively, much as the shaving of Samson's head (Judges 16:19) weakens him physically. Tom cries while his head is being shaved, but thereafter, the speaker reports, "he was quiet" (l. 9).

Once alienated, language-as-labor becomes not the way of personal revelation for Tom or the speaker, but the way of profit for their master and the way of coercive social control for the established power of church and state. Virtually the speaker's first articulate sounds, "weep weep weep weep" (l. 3), take the form of the street cry with which he hawks his services. And his last words, the platitudinous "So if all do their duty, they need not fear harm" (l. 24), bear witness to the impact of that coercive social control on his language. Tellingly, the Christ of the white woolly hair and the powerful voice that appears to John of Patmos must be heard before he is seen, as though to inform John of the imperative for a revelatory hermeneutic. It is a hermeneutic that accounts for all things, both in this life and after it, metaphorized as linguistic possibilities—insofar as these possibilities are contained in the alphabet summed by its first and last letters. In fact, Christ appears in part for the purpose of instructing John in the hermeneutic's operation, "Saying, I am Alpha and Omega, the first and the last: and, what thou seest, write in a book, and send it unto the seven churches which are in Asia" (Revelation 1:11). The first and last speeches of the speaker of "The Chimney Sweeper" stand in ironic contrast to the last-cited statement in Revelation, bearing witness to a process of prescription and alienation that subverts the power of authentic voice for the purposes of thriving commerce and an orderly church and state.

Songs of Experience (1794) begins on such a note of prescription, alienation, and subversion, although the subversion in question is circumstantially prescribed rather than willed. In the "Introduction," the bardic speaker tells his literally benighted audience not what to see, but what to hear, reserving the role of seer to himself. "Hear the voice of the Bard! / Who Present, Past, & Future sees" (ll. 1–2), he proclaims. But the Bard's claim to visionary authority is gainsaid by his unwitting admission that the encounter with God-as-Logos on which he bases his authority has been merely auditory rather than visionary. That is, the Bard's fallen "ears have heard / The Holy Word" (ll. 3–4), but that word has not instructed the Bard in what to see in the same sense that the Christ of the white woolly hair and the powerful voice tells John of Patmos what to see. The Bard's fallen eyes have not seen God-as-Logos, in other words.

That the Bard represents himself as being able only to hear, not to see, God-as-Logos suggests his sense of distance and alienation from that God, not to mention the alienation of his own language from him, suggests his sense of living in a world in which

God-as-Logos has already had the last word and all of earthly existence is foreordained. The Bard's situation, in other words, is that of Adam and Eve (and all other lapsed souls) after the Fall, and before learning that the alienation that occurs in consequence of the Fall is not irreversible. The serpent tells Adam and Eve half truthfully, "your eyes shall be opened, and ye shall be as gods, knowing good and evil" (Genesis 3:5)[23] In fact, what Adam and Eve come to see and know is their own fallenness, metaphorized as their vulnerable nakedness (3:7), which is what God knows—interestingly enough, not by seeing Adam and Eve, but by hearing Adam's account of his nakedness (3:9–10)—and God's account of their past, present, and future.

They no longer see good in the form of the companionably intimate Jehovah, the "LORD God," before whom and before each other they "were both naked . . . and were not ashamed" (2:25), and who brought the animals to Adam for naming and brought Eve to Adam to be "an help meet" (2:19–22), in large part because they no longer wish to see that good—or Jehovah himself. In fact, Adam and Eve also take on some of the serpent's slyness, hiding from him when "they hear[d] the voice of the LORD God walking in the garden in the cool of the day" (3:8).[24] When he learns that Adam and Eve have eaten the forbidden fruit, God characterizes the transgressive nature of their past actions ("Hast thou eaten of the tree, whereof I commanded thee that thou shouldst not eat?" [3:11]); specifies the fallen condition of their present state ("cursed is the ground for thy sake. . . . dust thou art, and unto dust shalt thou return" [3:17, 19]); and offers a glimpse of their wretched future ("in sorrow shalt thou bring forth children. . . . In the sweat of thy face shalt thou eat bread" [3:16, 19]). All of the fallen and cyclically repetitive futurity of the Old Testament waits to "the east of the garden of Eden" (3:24).

To return to the Bard: he both plays God as he understands God and fears God as he understands God. The Bard has "heard / The Holy Word" much as Adam heard God, and as God, having heard Adam, proclaims the past, present, and future of the human race. Because the Bard has not, in his fallen state, seen God-as-Logos, and because the Bard fears such an encounter, he wishes in his nescience and confusion not for the sort of companionable intimacy with God-as-Logos that preceded the Fall, but for an entirely different Genesis cosmogony—that of the *P*-account, the state of affairs that preceded the moment of ensoulment (2:7) on which the *J*-account begins. The wish arises in part from the creative efficacy of the Elohim, the God of the *P*-account, and as the result of the notions of material permanence and dominion that that creative efficacy serves to foster. The references to "the evening dew" and "the dewy grass" (ll.7, 12) allude to the conclusion of the *P*-account—specifically, to the "mist" that "went up . . . from the earth, and watered the whole face of the ground" (Genesis 2:6). Thus, while it is arguably appropriate for Jehovah, "The Holy Word" in question, to walk "among the ancient trees. / Calling the lapsed Soul" (*SE*, 30.4–6), it is highly inappropriate for this God even speculatively to

> controll
> The starry pole;
> And fallen fallen light renew! (ll. 8–10)

Renewing light would fall to the Elohim, its original creator, who said "Let there be light" (Genesis 1:3), and who named the very "Earth" (1:10) that the Bard calls upon to "return!" (l. 11).

The Bard's confusion about the identity of God-as-Logos opens onto two very different views of the operation of language in the world—views that the Bard has unwittingly conflated. *Elohim* means *Judges*, and the collective God of the *P*-account acts prescriptively and judicially insofar as it issues declarations, names the material results of those declarations, and assigns legal dominion over those results. *Jehovah* is from the Hebrew *hyyah*, *to be*, and in its acts of ensoulment and companionable intimacy before the Fall, it approaches the condition of pure spontaneous possibility, existing simultaneously as pure being and pure being-with. Blake's views on which of these two is more nearly conformable with God-as-Logos is clear enough. In *There Is No Natural Religion [b]* he observes, "Therefore God becomes as we are, that we may be as he is (*CPP*, p. 3).

But the Bard's conflation of judging, being, and being-with also suggests that, for Blake, without the third term of the New Testament, in which the "Son of man" exposes Mosaic priest-craft for the delusory systematization by the conflation of self-contradictory accounts that it is, the *P*- and *J*-accounts and the notions of language underwriting them are inadequate. Jehovah, for example, is made to appear at odds with his name, becoming prescriptive and punitive when he sees fit to do so. Jehovah is, it should be noted, credited by Moses as the author of the Ten Commandments (Exodus 20:1–17). His observation that "the man has become as one of us, to know good and evil" (Genesis 3:22) suggests that Jehovah both possesses the ability to wax judgmental and the willingness to do so for what he sees as just cause. Moreover, the observation suggests that Jehovah is uneasy with the process of becoming-as-being when it originates with humanity rather than God.

In "Earth's Answer," the poem's namesake, previously urged to return by the Bard, characterizes the speaker as "the Father of the ancient men / Selfish father of men" (*SE*, 31.10–11). This characterization suggests the need for that third term and implies a full typological deployment: "ancient" (old), new; "father of men," "Son of man"; plurality or division, unity. The way to "Break this heavy chain" (l. 21)—the chain of command(ments) "That free Love with bondage bound" (l. 25)—is to undo the alienated language of command(ments). But there is apparently no one present in "Earth's Answer" to follow her imperative to break the chain. Apparently: the alienation that has transpired has resulted in a failure of imaginative nerve, a failure to attain the realization that the kingdom of heaven lies within, that, in Paul's words "the head of every man is Christ . . . and the head of Christ is God" (1 Corinthians 11:3).

That failure pervades the scene of *Songs of Experience*. In such poems as "The Garden of Love," "The Poison Tree," and above all, "London," the reader encounters the grim consequences of the alienation of language in the absence of any hero or heroic initiative to take it back from those responsible in the first place for the alienation—or, to use the legal metaphor of appropriation for exclusive use that I have analyzed elsewhere, chartering.[25] In fact, the soundscape of "London" is very much the soundscape of the passage from *Jerusalem* quoted at the outset of this discussion. In the former, one encounters "the Chimney-sweepers cry," "the hapless Soldiers sigh," "the youthful Harlots curse," and arguably, "the new-born Infants tear" (*SE*, 46.9, 11, 13, 15). In the latter, one encounters "The Soldiers fife; the Harlots shriek; the Virgins dismal groan / The Parents Fear: the Brothers jealousy: the Sisters curse" (*J*, pl. 16, ll. 6–7). Alienated from the language of being and being-with, the speakers of "London" and this passage from *Jerusalem* have available to them no better than a guttural antilanguage that can neither express their desires nor create in accord with those desires.

The scenario thus far poses a clear imperative to take back language thus alienated. And that taking back is what Blake announces in *The Marriage of Heaven and Hell* (1790–93). In a coda to his "Argument," the speaker of *The Marriage* proclaims,

> As a new heaven is begun, and it is now thirty-three years since its advent:
> the Eternal Hell revives. And lo! Swedenborg is the Angel sitting at the tomb;
> his writings are the linen clothes folded up. Now is the dominion of Edom,
> & the return of Adam into Paradise; see Isaiah xxxiv & XXXV Chap.
> (*MHH*, pl. 3)

Blake proclaims his own rise, in the several senses of the term, to prophetic preeminence—like Jesus, thirty-three years after his "advent." In a nice conflation, Blake's announcement of his rise, which overthrows the authority of Swedenborg in matters touching on heaven and hell,[26] figures "his writings" as "the linen clothes folded up," recalling both John 20 and Isaiah 34–35. In the former text, Mary Magdalene and Peter run to the tomb, where he "seeth the linen clothes lie," and she, looking "into the sepulchre," sees "two angels in white sitting, the one at the head, and the other at the feet, where the body of Jesus had lain" (12:5, 12). Before ascending to heaven, Jesus, the living Word, about to become the Word with God (see John 1:1), meets with his assembled disciples and confers upon them the power of inspired language, reenacting typologically the ensoulment of Adam by Jehovah in the process. "Then Jesus said to them again, Peace be unto you: as my Father hath sent me, even so send I you. And when he said this he breathed on them, and saith unto them, Receive ye the Holy Ghost" (20:22–23).

The latter text envisions God's wrath against Israel, as the result of which "all the host of heaven shall be dissolved, and the heavens rolled together as a scroll" (34:4). In that day of reckoning, the mighty will fall and "The wild beasts of the desert shall also meet with the wild beasts of the island, and the satyr shall cry to his fellow; the screech owl also shall rest there, and find for herself a place of rest." In the midst of such unlanguaged cacophany, Isaiah counsels, "Seek ye out the book of the LORD, and read: no one of these shall fail, none shall want her mate: for my mouth it hath commanded, and his spirit it hath gathered them" (34:15-16). The power of Isaiah's God is such that "the eyes of the blind shall be opened, and the ears of the deaf shall be unstopped. Then shall the lame man leap as an hart, and the tongue of the dumb sing: for in wilderness shall waters break out, and streams in the desert." Ultimately, "the ransomed of the LORD shall return, and come to Zion with songs and everlasting joy upon their heads: they shall obtain joy and gladness, and sorrow and sighing shall flee away" (35:5-6, 10). Old man or new: the taking back of inspired language is the necessary precondition for "the return of Adam into paradise."

To return to the scene of the Prophetic Books: the only stay against such effects as inarticulateness and separation is the individual who mobilizes language and the visual arts to oppose the alienation of his or her labor and the resultant effects: the artist. In the context of the Prophetic Books, that artist, of course, is Los, the figure of the poet and and artisan, and the avatar of "the Divine Family"—the Four Zoas acting on the example of Jesus-as-self-sacrifice and accordingly made "One in Him" (*J*, pl. 36 [40], ll. 45-46). It is Los who reestablishes the fundamental interchangeability between—indeed, the identity of—inspired language as a form of inspired labor and inspired labor as a form of inspired language.[27]

The identification of work and language may not be self-evident, and it would therefore seem worthwhile to digress briefly for the purpose of establishing a basis for that identification. In the Judeo-Christian tradition, the creator-God of the *P*-account in Genesis creates by means of Logos-made-fiat, which takes the form in English of the command "let there be." When this God has completed his creation of "the heavens and the earth . . . and all the host of them," he rests. The narrator announces that "on the seventh day God ended his work which he had made" (2:1-2). The tradition that this passage gives rise to, if not the passage outright, is recalled at the opening of the Gospel According to John: "In the beginning was the Word, and the Word was with God, and the Word was God. The same was in the beginning with God. All things were made by him; and without him was not any thing made that was made" (1:1-3).

The same tradition is picked up in the patristic motto *laborare est orare* ("to work is to pray"), which implies that one worships

God by imitating his example—and that of his son—of working in the world. Nor is the tradition restricted to the Judeo-Christian world. In Plato's *Republic*, as John Sallis notes, Socrates undertakes to found "the fourth city, the city of the philosopher. He will found this city, not just in *logos* [language, experience], but in *ergon* [the labor of dialectic], by educating Glaucon" to *he tou agathon* (the idea of the good).[28]

In England, the tradition of regarding language—especially inspired language—as a form of work takes on political overtones virtually from the start. "Pains and Gains," included in T. Bedingfield's *Cardanus's Comfort* (1576), focuses on the misappropriation of the work product of imaginative language by the wealthy and powerful. The poem takes the form of an extended analogy between other workers, such as "The labouring man, that tills the fertile soil / And reaps the harvest fruit," but "for all his toil . . . gets the straw, the lord will have his seed," and "he that takes the pain to pen the book." The latter

> Reaps not the gifts of goodly golden Muse
> But those gain that, who on the work shall look
> And from the sour the sweet by skill cloth choose.[29]

That the poem produced by "he that takes the pain to pen the book" results in gain for another who, by the analogy of the previous stanzas, is a landowner if not in fact a noble makes it clear that the political overtones in question are those resulting from class struggle.[30] If not in 1576, then no more than a generation or two thereafter, the class struggle in question was a credal struggle as well, in which the party of the Monarchy and the Church of England sought, through the licensing of the press, to control language-as-labor and the thought that is its product, while the party of Dissent sought freedom from such control. Speaking out in his *Areopagitica* (1644) against Parliament's ordinance of 14 June 1643, which provided for the licensing of the press, John Milton both invokes the metaphor of language-as-labor and speaks to the magnitude of the offense that licensing poses in imposing an extraneous and questionable system of value on such labor. In the commentary that follows the oft-quoted statement that "who kills a man kills a reasonable creature, God's image; but he who destroys a good book, kills reason itself, kills the image of God, as it were, in the eye," Milton cautions,

We should be wary, therefore, what persecution we raise against the living labors of public men, how we spill that seasoned life of man preserved and stored up in books; since we see a kind of homicide may be thus committed, sometimes a martyrdom; and if it extend to the whole impression, a kind of massacre, whereof the execution ends not in the slaying of an elemental life, but strikes at that ethereal and fifth essence, the breath of reason itself, slays an immortality rather than a life.[31]

As a member of the party of Dissent, Milton is at once representative of its position and, as a university-trained poet and thinker, unrepresentative of the party's class affiliations. E. P. Thompson reminds one usefully that "in cultural or intellectual terms it is significant that antinomianism is an artisan or tradesman stance" that serves to reaffirm "the basic polarity of the gentry and 'the industrious sort' or 'the labouring poor.' " As this "polarity" of class and creed comes down through the eighteenth century, it engrosses a wide range of distinctions, including those having to do with language.

Everything in the age of "reason" and "elegance" served to emphasise the sharp distinctions between a polite and a demotic culture. Dress, style, gesture, proprieties of speech, grammar and even punctuation were resonant with signs of class; the polite culture was an elaborated code of social inclusion and exclusion. Classical learning and an accomplishment in the law stood like difficult gates-of-entry into this culture: the grammarian must show his expertise in derivations and constructions, the politician a familiarity with the models of Rome, the poet and artist a fluency in classical mythology. These accomplishments both legitimated and masked the actualities of brute property and power, interest and patronage. A grammatical or mythological solecism marked the intruder down as an outsider.[32]

The operations of the party of "brute property and power, interest and patronage" in the area of language-as-labor are worthy of a note in passing. Those in power refused to accord any efficacy to speakers and writers of the lower classes, while simultaneously representing those classes as owning their own language as a means of production and being happy with that circumstance. As Olivia Smith observes, "Between 1793 and 1818 (and later as well), Parliament dismissively refused to admit petitions ['favouring extended or universal male suffrage'] because of the language in which they were written."[33]

It is hardly coincidental that in 1793, when the suffrage petitions began to pour in and the Reign of Terror began in

France, the English ruling class, in the attempt to deny that it feared the English masses all the more as a result, flocked to purchase what Robert N. Essick characterizes as "Francis Wheatley's immensely popular *Cries of London*, published by Colnaghi as a series of fashionable stipple prints beginning in 1793."[34] Perhaps more remarkable than the appearance of the series in the first place is transformations wrought by Wheatley on his source, Paul Sandby's *The Cries of London* (1760), which Essick characterizes as "a group of twelve etchings depicting the wandering tradesmen and hawkers of London." In translating "those 'cries' into visual representations, Sandby's prints do not shy from the rough and tumble nature of life in the streets." That is, Sandby's prints comment on the hard lot of, and the relative paucity of the power and value produced by, language-as-labor in the mouths of these "wandering tradesmen and hawkers." By way of contrast to Sandby's series (and Blake's "London" [1794], concurrently under discussion), each print in Wheatley's series

> pictures a pleasantly rumpled man or a remarkably well-dressed and rosy-checked girl with the appropriate cry ("Turnips & Carrots ho," "Round and Sound Five pence a Pound Duke Cherries," etc.) inscribed beneath. Needless to say, there are no lame old men or harlots in Wheatley's series; and while the architectural backgrounds in his prints feature some of London's more palatial edifices and church spires, none are blackened or bloodied.[35]

That is, Wheatley's prints imply that the power and value produced by language-as-labor in the mouths of attractive street vendors is sufficient to their needs and desires. The vendors are, after all, in good health and well turned out. Like enlistees in the armed forces, these vendors are seeing the world while being all that they can be, and having fun in both pursuits in the bargain.

As Thompson goes on to observe, "Antinomianism, and in particular Muggletonianism, can be seen as an extreme recourse open to the excluded. It challenged the entire superstructure of learning and of moral and doctrinal teaching as ideology." At least as interesting as the fact that Antinomianism and Muggletonianism in particular posed such as challenge is the matter of *how* they posed the challenge: in the form of language-as-labor represented by the book. The Muggletonian commitment to keeping the sect's works in print and safe from destruction verged on the obsessive. And no wonder: "Muggletonians eschewed evangelism unless by the printed word. It was in print that the faith must be preserved, and through which conversions might be made."[36]

To return to Los's project: at one point in *Jerusalem*, "Albion"—England embodied and figured in the form of its imaginative collectivity—"is sick to death" (*J*, pl. 36 [40], l. 12). As a consequence, humanity faces the threat of being consigned to a situation of everlasting inarticulateness by reason of having its linguistic labor (and the resulting hope for transcendence) preempted, and of being "wrap'd in an endless curse, / Consuming and consum'd for-ever in flames of Moral Justice" (pl. 36 [40], ll. 29–30). Albion—and by extension, the humanity that resides everlastingly in his bosom—is saved by the exemplary, self-sacrificial intervention of the Divine Family, figured by twenty-four humanized cathedrals of Britain,[37] and most prominently in this instance as "Selsey, true friend! who afterwards submitted to be devourd / By the waves of Despair" (pl. 36 [40], ll. 48–49).

As Harold Bloom's commentary on these lines and the two following suggests, they "form an interesting and charming miniature myth of salvation, based on the transfer of the see of Selsey to Chichester in 1075, caused by coast erosion."[38] Blake, in other words, equates the Divine Family's self-sacrificing redemptive descent and redemption of Albion to Selsey's self-sacrificing descent into the sea of space and time, so that the church that is the repository of everlasting life might live, and in it all who are, in the several senses of the term, its members. But both "Winchester,"[39] the next prayerful offering, which stands "devoting itself for Albion," and "Submitting to be call'd the son of Los the terrible vision" (*J*, pl. 36 [40], ll. 52–53), and, indeed, "Selsey," are properly "the son[s] of Los," just as religion is the offspring of poetry.[40] But unlike the "men [who] forgot that All deities reside in the human breast" (*MHH*, pl. 11), Selsey and Winchester are fully cognizant of the imperishable divine immanence of the word made flesh that works in them.[41] Put in another Blakean way, in an action that stresses the sacrificiality, sacramentality, and mutuality of artistic labor: Los becomes as his sons are, that they may be as he is.[42]

Accordingly, not only does Winchester acquiesce in spirit to a redemptive descent into the realm of human law and commerce,[43] but he makes a bodily commitment to the enterprise as well,

> his Emanations
> Submitting to be call'd Enitharmons daughters, and be born
> In vegetable mould: created by the Hammer and Loom
> In Bowlahoola & Allamanda where the Dead wail night & day.
> (*J*, pl. 36 [40], ll. 54–57)

It is the poet/artist who lays what is both literally and figuratively the groundwork of an articulate, intelligible culture, making the labor that signals the exertions of the desiring imagination the basis of language, art, and the work of articulation more generally. Remarking on the nomenclature of the passage quoted above, Blake confides in a parenthetical aside,

> (I call them by their English names: English, the rough basement.
> Los built the stubborn structure of the Language, acting against
> Albions melancholy, who must else have been a Dumb despair.[44]

The structure of poetic language—its architectonics, the plan for building Jerusalem in England's green and pleasant land[45]— begins with its (re)design, from the bottom ("rough basement") up. The process in question is recurrent rather than singular. As Blake says earlier in *Jerusalem*,

> All things acted on Earth are seen in the bright Sculptures of
> Los's Halls & every Age renews its powers from these Works
> With every pathetic story possible to happen from Hate or
> Wayward Love & every sorrow & distress is carved here
> Every Affinity of Parents Marriages & Friendships are here
> In all their various combinations wrought with wondrous Art.
> (*J*, pl. 16, ll. 61–66)

That (re)design is hard work, for the medium is difficult, but that (re)design is ineluctably stub-born (or stub-borne): it is begotten of the pencil stub or burin stub acting on the paper or plate to reappropriate the product of language-as-labor and to do away with any prescriptive interdictions of this process. The doubling of this reappropriation is Los acting on Enitharmon to do away with the sort of spectrous interdictions that Satan or Urizen bring to bear, to the end of insuring that Albion's depression ("melancholy") has as one of its features aphasia.

So much—everything for Blake, in fact—depends on what is stub-born (or stub-borne).[46]

Thoughout *Milton* and *Jerusalem*, Los labors to give the English language articulate and architectonic form. For his prophetic undertaking to succeed, however, Los must move his audience—"The Twenty-eight" (*J*, pl. 37 [41], l. 23),[47] and the middle-class and radical artisan reading publics more generally— to do what the namesake of Blake's *Milton* was moved to do: to speak out the language of the inspired individual instead of being spoken for by the prescriptive language of preexistent codes, to break silence and make a start toward reclaiming their illicitly prescribed and co-opted language by speaking out.[48]

Within two plates of his "rough basement" speech, Los confronts "The Twenty-eight" with their failures. The first of these is the failure to realize that the divine donation of "the breath of life" (Genesis 2:7) marks God's immanent power and presence ensouled in humanity.

> Then Los grew furious raging: Why stand we here trembling around
> Calling on God for help; and not ourselves, in whom God dwells
> Stretching a hand to save the falling Man [i.e., Albion]?
> (*J*, pl. 38 [43], ll. 12–14)

After detailing the horrors that follow from this failure of nerve, among other things, Los implores "The Twenty-eight" once more.

> Have you caught the infection of Sin & stern Repentance?
> I see Disease arise upon you! Yet speak to me and give
> Me some comfort: why do you all stand silent? I alone
> Remain in permanent strength. (*J*, pl. 38 [43], ll. 75–78)

Moved by Los, "They [i.e., 'The Twenty-eight'] Albion surround with kindest violence and bear him back / Against his will thro Los's Gate to Eden, Four-fold; loud!" (*J*, pl. 39 [44], ll. 2–3). Eden is the originary site of "the breath of life" and the site of Adam's ensoulment by Jehovah, not to mention being the site where Adam, in naming the animals (Genesis 2:19–20), utters the first human speech.[49] Although Los's minions have made a good start, the time has not yet come for the millennial resurrection of Albion, who retreats into the rational and conventional realm of mechanics and mathematics. "Albion dark, / Repugnant; rolld his Wheels backward into Non-Entity" (pl. 39 [44], ll. 5–6). The right time for that resurrection is the end of time, or at least the beginning of an era beyond a scenario of historical contingency interpreted and acted upon by those in control of prescriptive codes.

That moment marks the return of "the breath of life" in its unmediated, edenic form. Los announces, "Time was Finished! The Breath Divine Breathed over Albion" (*J*, pl. 94, l. 18). With this reensoulment comes the return of the unfallen speech that is Jehovah's donation to Adam, inflected with the prophetic wrath that Albion deems necessary to put the fallen world in order. Albion is portrayed in terms that confirm Los's earlier contention that it is "ourselves in whom God dwells," terms that liken his actions to those of Jehovah in Exodus as he works to help end the bondage of the Israelites.

> The Breath Divine went forth over the morning hills Albion rose
> In anger: the wrath of God breaking bright flaming on all sides around
> His awful limbs: into the Heavens he walked clothed in flames
> Loud thundring, with broad flashes of flaming lightning & pillars
> Of fire, speaking the Words of Eternity in Human Forms, in direful
> Revolutions of Action & Passion, thro the Four Elements on all sides
> Surrounding his awful Members.[50]

Albion's speech does put the world in order,

> Compelling Urizen to his Furrow; & Tharmas to his Sheepfold;
> And Luvah to his Loom: Urthona he beheld mighty labouring at
> His Anvil, in the Great Spectre Los unwearied labouring & weeping.
> (*J*, pl. 95, ll. 16–18)

But Albion's speech is of the order of dictation, not conversation. If left uninflected by the language of the other, Albion's language threatens to become a fixed text—reified, an ideology, a Bakhtinian common language—rather than giving way to the textual free play of heterology and dialogism.[51]

Slightly earlier in chapter 4 of *Jerusalem*, Los specifies the conditions of conversation beyond the contingencies of space and time.

> When in Eternity Man converses with Man they enter
> Into each others Bosom (which are Universes of delight)
> In mutual interchange. (*J*, pl. 88, ll. 3–5)

188

The bosom is the seat of God-in-humanity, the place where "the breath of life" (or "The Breath Divine") dwells, the site of ensoulment. The sort of conversation that Los describes takes dialogism to its utmost limit of possibility: each speaker literally puts himself or herself in the place of the other.

The model for this sort of exchange is Blake's Jesus, who, as the figure of "Poetic Genius," "becomes as we are, that we may be as he is" (*NNR[b]*, *CPP*, p. 3). Having put the world in order in his Jehovah aspect, Albion fears the textualized, reified outcome. He fears that his order is the only order; his commandments, the only commandments; his vision, the single vision. In the throes of his despair, Albion unwittingly imitates Jesus by confiding in him. And in imitating Jesus by confiding, Albion is both (re)created and redeemed by Jesus.

> O Lord what can I do! my Selfhood cruel
> Marches against thee deceitful from Sinai & from Edom
> Into the Wilderness of Judah to meet thee in his pride
> I behold the Visions of my deadly Sleep of Six Thousand Years
> Dazzling around thy skirts like a Serpent of precious stones & gold
> I know it is my Self: O my Divine Creator & Redeemer.
> (*J*, pl. 96, ll. 8–13)

Jesus's response continues in the vein of mutuality, as he declares that he will offer himself for Albion, even as Albion, in imitating Jesus, offers himself.

> Fear not Albion unless I die thou canst not live
> But if I die I shall arise again & thou with me
> This is Friendship & Brotherhood without it Man Is Not.
> (*J*, pl. 96, ll. 14–16)

Although the allusive echoes are faint—if, indeed, they exist at all—Albion's association, by means of heavy and ongoing allusion, with the Mosaic Pentateuch, and Jesus's comments on the nature of authentic speech as the source of the authentic and enduring text point the way to Paul's comments, in 2 Corinthians, on the letter versus the spirit. According to Paul, Jesus, "the Word . . . made flesh" (John 1:14), who himself never wrote down anything that he is reported to have said, is the "epistle written in our hearts, known and read of all men." He is an epistle "written not with ink, but with the Spirit of the living

God; not in tables of stone, but in fleshy tables of the heart." This same Jesus, according to Paul, "also hath made us able ministers of the new testament; not of the letter, but of the spirit: for the letter killeth, but the spirit giveth life" (2 Corinthians 3:2–6).

A universal ministry based on a readily accessible text of which Paul speaks stands in marked contrast the the restrictive priesthood of the Old Testament, which reifies and fetishizes its God materially by means of veiling. Paul, alluding to the rending of the veil covering the Ark that took place at the moment of Jesus's death (see also Matthew 27:51; Mark 15:38; Luke 23:45), argues, "But even unto this day, when Moses is read, the vail is upon their [i.e., the Children of Israel's] heart. Nevertheless when it shall turn to the Lord, the vail shall be taken away. Now the Lord is that Spirit: and where the Spirit of the Lord is, there is liberty" (3:15–17).[52]

The way to transcending the "vail," to attaining what Paul terms the "liberty" of speech that marks the presence of "the Spirit of the Lord," lies in speaking freely about preexistent texts, much as Jesus spoke freely about the Old Testament; in celebrating such manifestations of "spirit" as appear in them; and in noting the reifying, fetishizing—and, above all, the ideologizing— tendencies in them that are attributable to "the letter."[53] Whatever Paul has to say about obedience to the text as an operative concept elsewhere, it does not figure prominently here.[54]

For Blake as well, texts exist not to obey but to converse with, not as Old Testament versions of the Merkabah[55] but as the transferential vehicles by which one enters into the bosom of the other in the manner exemplified by Jesus. If nothing else, his lifelong habit of annotation attests to this postulation.[56] When "The innumerable Chariots of the Almighty appear[d] in Heaven / And Bacon & Newton & Locke & Milton & Shakespeare & Chaucer" (*J*, pl. 98, ll. 8–9), it is as such transferential vehicles, not as spectrous precursor-texts to be obeyed. These apocalyptic manifestations signal their transferential status by owning the play of life forces in them—by standing "Fourfold" (pl. 98, l. 12). In so doing, they adumbrate the oft-cited conversation "in Visionary forms dramatic" (pl. 98, ll. 28–40) that follows. This is language- as-labor made language-as-free-play—language free and enfranchised to create the universe anew repeatedly, "Creating Space, Creating Time according to the wonders Divine / Of Human

Imagination" (pl. 98, ll. 31–32). From such a perspective, the long list of ideological formations that runs from "the Covenant of Priam" to "the Spectrous Oath" (pl. 98, ll. 46–53) is seen for the collection of self-serving preemptions of authentic human speech that it is. The collectivity of these linguistic creations— from one exemplar of humanity to another—constitutes the "Emanations" identified in the closing line of *Jerusalem* as no more, and no less, than the city of God itself. "And I heard the Name of their Emanations they are named Jerusalem" (pl. 99, l. 5).

Notes

INTRODUCTION

1. See Paul R. Gross and Norman Levitt, *Higher Superstition: The Academic Left and Its Quarrels with Science* (Baltimore: Johns Hopkins University Press, 1994).

2. Joseph Carroll, "T. H. Huxley and Stephen Weinberg: Science and Culture at a Century's Distance," *SLS Abstracts* (Atlanta: Society for Literature and Science, 1996), 90.

3. See John Sallis, *Being and Logos: The Way of Platonic Dialogue* (Pittsburgh: Duquesne University Press, 1975), 401–12. In founding "the fourth city, the city of the philosopher" in the *Republic*, Socrates "will found this city, not just in *logos* [language, experience, but in *ergon* [work], by educating Glaucon" through the work of dialectic. What Socrates educates Glaucon to, according to Sallis, is *he tou agathon*, the idea of the good.

4. Gerry O'Sullivan, "Strategies of Power in Aristotle's Poetics," in *Culture/Criticism/Ideology: Proceedings of the Northeastern University Center for Literary Studies*, vol. 4 (Boston: Northeastern University Press for the Northeastern University Department of English, 1986), 1–16.

5. Michel Serres, *Hermes: Literature, Science, Philosophy*, ed. Josue V. Harrari and David F. Bell (Baltimore: Johns Hopkins University Press, 1982), 67.

6. Stephen Toulmin, *The Return to Cosmology: Postmodern Science and the Theology of Nature* (Berkeley and Los Angeles: University of California Press, 1982), 239.

7. Toulmin, *Return to Cosmology*, 238. Paul K. Feyerabend lays out a similar argument in much greater detail in *Against Method: An Anarchistic Theory of Knowledge* (Atlantic Highlands, N.J.: Humanities Press, 1975).

8. Toulmin, *Return to Cosmology*, 238. See also Alexandre Koyré, *Newtonian Studies* (Cambridge, Mass.: Harvard University Press, 1965), 261–72.

9. See Frank E. Manuel, *A Portrait of Isaac Newton* (Cambridge, Mass.: Harvard University Press, 1968), 23–35, 51–67. Manuel makes much of the following notebook anagram in which Newton identifies himself with a one-personed God: "Isaacus Neutonus—Ieova Sanctus et Unus."

10. *Sir Isaac Newton's Mathematical Principles of Natural Philosophy*, trans. Andrew Motte, rev. Florian Cajori (1934; rpt., Berkeley and Los Angeles: Univ of California Press, 1966), 544.

11. William Blake, *The [First] Book of Urizen*, pl. 3, ll. 6–7, in *The Complete Poetry and Prose of William Blake*, ed. David V. Erdman, commentary by Harold Bloom, rev. ed (Garden City, N.Y.: Anchor Books, 1982). All references to Blake's works follow this edition, hereafter cited as *CPP*, and cite either page or plate and line numbers.

12. In the Gospel According to John, Jesus is figured as *Logos*. "In the beginning was the Word (*Logos*), and the Word was with God, and the Word was God" (1:1). This fact, taken in conjunction with the endings of *Milton* and *Jerusalem*, suggests the following etymology for Los's name: it is a contraction of *Logos*. *Contraction* is a word that figures prominently in the story of the Fall set forth in *Milton*, where it denotes the bodily condition of a fallen humanity that has reached the limiting nadir of its fall: "Contraction was named Adam" (13 [14].21). As long as a fallen humanity exists in this condition, Logos is Los, the Word, but with no "go."

Los may be seen as what he really (and eternally) is—*Logos*—at the end of these poems, because it is at the end that the "go" reappears manifested in Los, who participates in effecting the change back from contraction to plenitude. For example, at the end of *Milton*, on the verge of imaginative apocalypse, "All Animals upon the Earth, are prepard in all their strength / *To go forth* to the Great Harvest & Vintage of the Nations" (pl. 42 [49], l. 39–pl. 43 [50], l. 1; my emphasis). And at the end of *Jerusalem*, Los proclaims,

> All Human Forms identified even Tree Metal Earth & Stone. all
> Human Forms identified, living *going forth* & returning wearied
> Into the Planetary lives of Years Months Days & Hours reposing
> And then Awaking into his Bosom in the Life of Immortality.
>   (pl. 99, ll. 1–4; my emphasis)

13. Throughout *Milton* the seven-planet solar system, only recently increased to that number with the discovery of Uranus by William Herschel in 1787, is referred to as "the Starry Eight," because Blake wishes to play on the centrality, radiance, and influence of the sun-son on the seven planets. As with poetic genius, the sun-son becomes those planets, that they may be as he is. Thus it should come as no surprise that near the conclusion of *Milton*, "with one accord the Starry Eight became / One Man Jesus the Saviour" (pl. 42 [49], ll. 10–11).

14. See John Milton, *Complete Poetry and Selected Prose*, ed. Merritt Y. Hughes (New York: Odyssey Press, 1957), 720. "Iron tablets," in addition to symbolizing the least inspired of the four ages of poetry (gold, silver, bronze, iron), a connection Blake picks up in "To Winter" in *Poetical Sketches* (1783), suggests the galley and chase of the printing press. Blake is taking aim not only at ostensible doctrine of *Paradise Lost*, which he claims Milton wrote as "a true

poet and of the Devils party without knowing it" (*MHH*, pl. 5), but also at Milton's pamphleteering generally, and perhaps *Areopagitica* (1644) in particular. One of the things that occurs in *Milton* is Milton's return from the status of a silent, metonymic book to a vocal, metaphoric speaking presence. Hence Blake may be making a sidelong comment on Milton's remark that "he that destroys a good book, kills reason itself, kills the image of God, as it were, in the eye."

15. Harold Bloom sees Rahab as being "to Milton here as Leutha was to Satan, chief of his emanations. The other wives and daughters are the daughters of the sonless Zelophehad (Numbers 26:33). Milton, in his old age, was sonless, and left his legacy to the Female Will or the sensuous tyranny of the fallen natural world. The daughters of Zelophehad prevailed upon Moses to legalize female inheritance, which Blake interpreted as yielding to the Female Will. Rahab presides then over Milton's five fallen senses, and the legend of Milton dictating to his womenfolk is transformed into an extraordinary stony vision of a Mosaic Milton, the Rock Sinai, dictating law to six lesser masses of stone" (*CPP*, p. 916).

16. In the passage in *Milton*, "The Divine hand found the Two Limits: first of Opacity, then of Contraction / Opacity was named Satan, Contraction was named Adam" (pl. 13 [14], ll. 20–21).

17. "Mad Song," in *Poetical Sketches* (1783), offers a marvelous vignette of the Mosaic mind-set, as Blake later elaborates it.

> I turn my back to the east,
> From whence comforts have increas'd;
> For light doth seize my brain
> With frantic pain. (ll. 21–24)

18. The recurrence of the nonstandard period after the word "Eternity" is Blake's adumbration, by means of a sight pun, of what he later formulates this way:

> Every Time less than the pulsation of the artery
> Is equal in its period and value to Six Thousand Years.
> For in this Period the Poets Work is Done: and all the Great
> Events of Time start forth & are concievd in such a Period
> Within a Moment: a Pulsation of the Artery. (*M*, pl. 28 [30],
> l. 62–pl. 29 [31], l. 3).

19. Balaam's parable is echoed in the last stanza of Blake's "Mock on Mock on Voltaire Rousseau," one of the poems in Blake's Notebook (1800–1808?):

> The Atoms of Democritus
> And Newtons Particles of light
> Are sands upon the Red sea shore
> Where Israels tents do shine so bright. (ll. 9–12)

20. See Hayden V. White, "The Irrational and the Problem of Historical Knowledge in the Enlightenment," in *Tropics of Discourse: Essays in Cultural Criticism* (Baltimore: Johns Hopkins University Press, 1978), 142–43. Discussing "the distinction" that Enlightenment historians "drew between

mythical thought and scientific thought," White notes that "that distinction was not unique to Enlightenment thought; it was as old as Greek philosophy and was a mainstay even of Christian theology during the Patristic period." One might observe the distinctly Mosaic cast of that theology, with its strictures, hypothetical cases, and codifications.

21. Michel Foucault, *The Order of Things: An Archaeology of the Human Sciences* (New York: Random House, 1973), 303–43.

22. David Simpson, *The Academic Postmodern and the Rule of Literature: A Report on Half-Knowledge* (Chicago: University of Chicago Press, 1995), 79, 149. Of Blake, Simpson observes, "Writers with firm religious commitments, like Blake . . . could find eternity anywhere and at any time."

23. See Simpson, *Academic Postmodern*, 121–34. See also Clifford Geertz, *The Interpretation of Culture* (New York: Basic Books, 1973), 17–18, and *Local Knowledge: Further Essays in Interpretive Anthropology* (New York: Basic Books, 1983), 19.

24. See Simpson, *Academic Postmodern*, 136. See also Philippe Lacoue-Labarthe and Jean-Luc Nancy, *The Literary Absolute: The Theory of Literature in German Romanticism*, trans. Philip Barnard and Cheryl Lester (Albany: SUNY Press, 1988), 6.

25. Hayden V. White, "The Irrational," 136, 141–42.

26. See Simpson, *Academic Postmodern*, 79. In discussing the intellectual events that lead to Foucault's "analytic of finitude," Simpson implicates no less a pillar of the Enlightenment than Descartes as one who is similarly poised on the brink of the abyss of subjectivity: "Failure and success, virtue and vice, innocence and guilt, being and nonbeing, all become critically subjective. And as soon as there is subjectivity, there is the problem of subjectivity. It is there in the dalliance with solipsism and performativism in Descartes's *Discourse on Method*, and it explains why models of universal psychology are always most vigorously proposed when they are already and visibly collapsing (witness the short cycle from Kant through Hegel to Marx, Nietzsche, and Freud)."

27. White, "The Irrational," 145.

28. See Joseph Viscomi, *Blake and the Idea of the Book* (Princeton, N.J.: Princeton University Press, 1993), 4–8, 20–32, for a discussion of Blake's idea of artistic, as opposed to poetic, invention.

29. Blake's discussion of line in *A Descriptive Catalogue* (1809) makes it clear that he understands invention (or in-vention) in precisely this sense. His thesis "is this: That the more distinct, sharp, and wirey the bounding line, the more perfect the work of art. . . . Great inventors, in all ages, knew this. Protogenes and Apelles knew each other by this line. Rafael and Michael Angelo, and Albert Durer are known by this and this alone." In Blake's understanding, line serves to divide and differentiate hitherto undivided and undifferentiated mass or matter, and this sort of division recapitulates the divisions by which God accomplishes the Creation. "Leave out this l[i]ne," Blake argues, "and you leave out life itself; all is chaos again, and the line of the almighty must be drawn out upon it before man or beast can exist" (p. 550). Blake's second remark reprises the beginning of Genesis: "And the earth was without form, and void; and darkness was upon the deep. And the Spirit of God moved upon the face of the waters" (1:2). God, manifested

as "Spirit" (L. *spirare*, "to breathe"), invents the world in in-venting, in other words.

30. In *A Descriptive Catalogue* Blake makes two comments worth recalling in this context. First, in a discussion of the "lineaments of universal human life," Blake argues for unchanging human types. "Names alter, things never alter. . . . As Newton numbered the stars, and as Linneus numbered the plants, so Chaucer numbered the classes of men" (p. 533). That the reader is to consider these three as poets of a kindred type, and not as philosophers, natural or otherwise, is made clear subsequently, in Blake's comments on his depiction of the Clerk of Oxenford. "This character varies from that of Chaucer, as the contemplative philosopher varies from the poetical genius. There are always these two classes of learned sages, the poetical and the philosophical" (p. 537).

CHAPTER 1. BLAKE AND NEWTON

Reprinted from *Studies in Eighteenth-Century Culture*, vol. 10, ed. Harry Payne (Madison: University of Wisconsin Press, 1981).

1. The present essay grows out of a discussion and dialogue begun with George S. Rousseau in the meeting of the Literature and Science section of the 1978 MLA convention, where I delivered a paper entitled "Visionary Semantics: Blake, Newton, and the Language of Scientific Authority." Rousseau himself delivered "Literature and Science: Decoding the State of the Field" in a special session convened to discuss the implications of his paper and the papers of those presenting in the section for new and future directions in literature and science. Rousseau's paper, slightly reworked, appears as "Literature and Science: The State of the Field," *Isis* 9 (1978): 583–91. In it, he claims that the vogue of structuralist and poststructuralist approaches to the history of ideas have rendered traditional approaches to literature and science moribund, if not obsolete. For example, the rise to prominence of Michel Foucault, "all of whose books inherently deal with literature and science," had the result of repelling "most serious students then [i.e., in the 1960s] . . . and had the further effect of transforming old categories, in a sense rendering them obsolete. The question for someone writing about science and literature changed from 'what type of critic are you?' to 'how much self-consciousness do you have about your methodology?' " (589). This essay constitutes a response to Rousseau's gloomy portrayal of the field and, it is hoped, one conceptual approach to the field that can arrogate to itself the close analysis of rhetoric that is at the heart of the structuralist and poststructuralist methodologies, while at the same time dealing with recognizable scientific and literary texts in a manner that is plausible, if not wholly conventional. In its original form, the essay was presented at the seminar "Conceptual Approaches to Literature and Science in the Eighteenth Century," chaired by John Neubauer and convened at the 1979 meeting of the American Society for Eighteenth-Century Studies, held in Atlanta.

2. See Marjorie Hope Nicolson, *Science and Imagination* (Ithaca, N.Y.: Cornell University Press, 1956), chapter 5, "The Scientific Background of Swift's *Voyage to Laputa*," 110–54.

3. Newton's conception of absolute space is made clear in book 1, section 11, of the *Principia*. The passage quoted in the text of the essay may be found

in Sir Isaac Newton, *Principia*, trans. Andrew Motte, rev. Florian Cajori, 2 vols. (Berkeley and Los Angeles: University of California Press, 1934), 549. Subsequent references to the *Principia* will be to this edition and will be made by page number only in the text of the essay. The rationale for omitting the volume number is that the Cajori edition uses running pagination, even though it is printed in two volumes. Newton's conception of absolute time, i.e., a framed, six-thousand-year Biblical chronology, is made clear elsewhere, in *Observations on the Propitecies of Daniel and the Apocalypse of St. John in Two Parts*, 2 vols. (London: J. Roberts, 1733).

4. See note 3 for Newton on absolute space and time.

5. See Marjorie Hope Nicolson, *Newton Demands the Muse: Newton's "Opticks" and the Eighteenth Century Poets* (Princeton, N.J.: Princeton University Press, 1946); Richard B. Schwartz, *Samuel Johnson and the New Science* (Madison: University of Wisconsin Press, 1971); and Margaret C. Jacob, *The Newtonians and the English Revolution, 1689–1720* (Ithaca, N.Y.: Cornell University Press, 1976).

6. On Pope and Addison, see Nicolson, *Newton Demands the Muse*, 123–64. On Johnson, see Schwartz, *Samuel Johnson*, 59–93.

7. A fuller elaboration than can be made here has been made in my "Blake on Space, Time and the Artist," *Science/Technology and the Humanities* 2 (1979): 246–63. Briefly, it might be noted that the Four Zoas, as they approach the condition of instantaneous change at the end of *Jerusalem*, also approach the condition of light, under circumstances in which the newly merged categories of space and time become one and the same, existing in a continuum. The energy exhibited by the Four Zoas, which appears as consuming fire to the fallen and as delight to the redeemed, is derived from the ability of the "matter" of the Zoas to change instantaneously—with the speed of light, in fact. The space-time continuum Blake is describing in his visionary way, a continuum in which energy is liberated by matter moving at the speed of light, is, in its essentials, close to the continuum described by Einstein in his world-shaking equation $E = mc^2$.

8. For a pithy restatement of this position for a modern critical audience, see Stanley E. Fish, "Normal Circumstances, Literal Language, Direct Speech Acts, the Ordinary, the Everyday, the Obvious, What Goes without Saying, and Other Special Cases," *Critical Inquiry* 4 (1978): 625–44.

9. For Gleckner's discussion, see "Most Holy Forms of Thought: Some Observations on Blake and Language," *ELH: English Language History* 41 (1974): 555–77. My "Visionary Semantics" is discussed in note 1.

10. *OED* 7:309. The sense is that of a *corpus*, the term used by linguists to describe a body of utterances made and recorded diachronically, as opposed to the total number of possible utterances in the language deployed synchronically. See Claude Lévi-Strauss, *Le cru et le cuit* (Paris: Plon, 1964), especially the conclusion. See also Jonathan Culler, *Structuralist Poetics* (Ithaca, N.Y.: Cornell University Press, 1975), 43ff.

11. *The Marriage of Heaven and Hell*, pls. 22–23, makes as much clear. According to Blake, "The Worship of God is. Honouring his gifts in other men, each according to his genius." And "if Jesus is the Greatest man, you ought to love him in the greatest degree." The Gospels were written by those who loved

such a "man of genius," and thus the Gospels exhibited the genius of those who wrote them.

12. See Donald D. Ault, *Visionary Physics: Blake's Response to Newton* (Chicago: University of Chicago Press, 1974); his "Incommensurability and Interconnection in Blake's Anti-Newtonian Text," *Studies in Romanticism* 16 (1977): 277–303; and F. B. Curtis, "Blake and the 'Moment of Time': An Eighteenth-Century Controversy in Mathematics," *Philological Quarterly* 51 (1972): 460–70.

13. See Ault, *Visionary Physics*, and Nicolson, *Newton Demands the Muse*.

14. William Powell Jones, *The Rhetoric of Science: A Study of Scientific Imagery and Ideas in Eighteenth-Century English Poetry* (Berkeley and Los Angeles: University of Caiifornia Press, 1966), 97.

15. For a full discussion of this "father-son" relationship, see Frank E. Manuel, *A Portrait of Isaac Newton* (Cambridge, Mass.: Harvard University Press, 1968), 23–35, 51–67.

16. See Ault, "Incommensurability and Interconnection." See also J. E. McGuire and P. M. Rattansi, "Newton and the 'Pipes of Pan,'" *Notes and Records of the Royal Society of London* 21 (1966): 108–43, also cited by Ault, 277n.

17. Newton begins by talking of the *"five primary planets, Mercury, Venus, Mars, Jupiter, and Saturn"* (*Principia*, 403), then proves that the Earth exhibits similar properties of motion, talking finally of the six in the "General Scholium" (543).

18. See note 8.

19. Ault, *Visionary Physics*, 96–140.

20. In a letter to his brother James, dated 30 January 1803, Blake writes that he goes "on Merrily with my Greek & Latin . . . as I find it very Easy" (in *CPP*, p. 696). For a fuller discussion of Newton's meaning and his dilemma, see Colin Murray Turbayne, *The Myth of Metaphor* (1962; rpt., Columbia: University of South Carolina Press, 1970), 44–45.

21. *Harper's Latin Dictionary*, ed. Charlton T. Lewis and Charles Short, rev. ed. (1879; rpt., New York: Harper, 1907), 750.

22. The connotation is consistent and of long standing, going all the way back to Blake's earliest preserved writings. See, for example, the Ossianic fragment "then She bore Pale desire," contemporaneous with *Poetical Sketches* (1783), in *Blake*, ed. Erdman, 437–39.

23. For Ault's comments, see *Visionary Physics*, 155–56.

24. Newton, *Principia*, 398–400. These rules attempt to standardize the causes of apparently similar phenomena, the covert motivation being to move toward a view of the universe in which formal cause and efficient cause proceed from one and the same source—God.

25. "The mind is its own place, and in it self / Can make a Heav'n of Hell, a Hell of Heav'n" (2.254–55).

26. The speaker of that poem puts his selfhood into the seemingly selfless task of tending a tree, rather than confronting the friend who angers him. As the result of his choice of strategies, the tree produces an apple that, like the apple in the Garden, is a deceptive form of selfhood.

And I waterd it in fears,
Night & morning with my tears:
And I sunned it with my smiles,
And with soft deceitful wiles (ll. 5–8)

When the speaker's friend steals, and presumably eats, the apple, he is seen to be "outstretchd beneath the tree" (l. 16)—"dead" in the sense of having been deprived of his free and autonomous selfhood. For the speaker, now "inside" his erstwhile friend, has taken over that selfhood. Without the full Gothic trappings, the concept seems very much like that of the vampire, interest in which grew and evolved during the late eighteenth and nineteenth centuries. On the other hand, Blake may be viewed as being caught up in the same currents of thought that led Sade to write of the utter possession of one individual by another. See Michel Foucault, "Language to Infinity," in *Language, Counter-Memory, Practice: Selected Essays and Interviews*, trans. Donald F. Bouchard and Sherry Simon (Ithaca, N.Y.: Cornell University Press, 1977), 53–67, esp. 60–63, 65–66.

CHAPTER 2. BLAKE AND ANTI-NEWTONIAN THOUGHT

Reprinted from *Beyond the Two Cultures: Essays on Science, Technology, and Literature*, ed. Joseph W. Slade and Judith Yaross Lee (Ames: Iowa State University Press, 1990).

1. For a synopsis of force-body models and the changes rung upon them by Thomas Young in the early nineteenth century, see Loyd S. Swenson Jr., *The Genesis of Relativity: Einstein in Context* (New York: Franklin, 1979), 13–18, 71. For Newton's clearest exposition of the relationship, see his "Rules of Reasoning in Philosophy" and "General Scholium," at the beginning and end, respectively, of book 3 of the *Principia*; rpt. in *Sir Isaac Newton's Mathematical Principles of Natural Philosophy and His System of the World*, trans. Andrew Motte, rev. Florian Cajori 1 vol. in 2 (1934; rpt., Berkeley and Los Angeles: University Of California Press, 1966), 398–99, 543–47.

2. Giambattista Vico, *The New Science of Giambattista Vico*, trans. Thomas Goddard Bergin and Max Harold Fisch, rev. ed. (Ithaca, N.Y.: Cornell University Press, 1968), 129, 118 (secs. 405, 377).

3. For thorough discussion of these ideas, see my "Science's Fictions: The Problem of Language and Creativity," in *Creativity and the Imagination: Case Studies from the Classical Age to the Twentieth Century*, ed. Mark Amsler, Studies in Science and Culture, vol. 3 (Newark: University of Delaware Press, 1987), 134–67.

4. Hans Eichner, "The Rise of Modern Science and the Genesis of Romanticism," *PMLA* 97 (1982): 24.

5. Newton, *Mathematical Principles*, 547.

6. The application of an essentially Newtonian explanation to history is epitomized by Edward Gibbon's famous chapter 15 of *The History of the Decline and Fall of the Roman Empire* (1776), which explains the early fortunes of Christianity in terms of forces, bodies, and the principle of oppositional force. Henry Brooke presents a mechanistic, Newtonian explanation of neurophysiology

in *Universal Beauty: A Poem* (1735), 4.243–48; this excerpt is cited in George S. Rousseau, "Science and the Discovery of the Imagination in Enlightened England," *Eighteenth-Century Studies* 4 (1970): 115. David Hartley's *Observations on Man, His Frame, His Duties, His Expectations* (1749), rpt., ed. Theodore L. Huguelet (Delmar, N.Y.: Scholars' Facsimiles and Reprints, 1976), 5ff., offers the theory of the association of ideas on the basis of an essentially Newtonian and behaviorist explanation of human psychology.

7. Epistle 2, ll. 31–34, in Alexander Pope, *An Essay on Man*, ed. Maynard Mack, vol. 3 of *The Twickenham Edition of the Poems of Alexander Pope*, ed. John Butt, 6 vols. (New Haven, Conn.: Yale University Press, 1950–53), 59–60.

8. Newton, *Mathematical Principles*, 399.

9. See Isaac Newton, *Opticks, or A Treatise on the Reflections, Refractions, Inflections, and Colours of Light, Based on the Fourth Edition, 1730* (New York: Dover, 1952), 400. Arguing against "occult Qualities" in the thirty-first query, Newton allows that "it seems probable . . . that God in the Beginning form'd Matter in solid, massy, hard, impenetrable, moveable particles, of such Sizes and Figures, and with such other Properties, and in such Proportion to Space, as most conduced to the end for which he form'd them." Newton refers to the particles subsequently as "what God himself made . . . in the first Creation," suggesting that any change to such particles will signal the end of theodical time as we know it. "While the Particles continue entire, they may compose Bodies of one and the same Nature and Texture in all Ages: But should they wear away, or break in pieces, the Nature of Things depending on them, would be changed" (400).

10. See Vico, *New Science*, 117–19 (secs. 377–79), and Johann Gottfried Herder, *Essay on the Origin of Language* (1772), trans. Alexander Gode, rpt. in *On the Origin of Language*, ed. John H. Moran and Alexander Gode (New York: Ungar, 1966), 149.

11. Francis Bacon, *The Advancement of Learning*, ed. William Aldis Wright, 5th ed. (Oxford: Clarendon Press, 1926), 1.6.6.

12. *The Correspondence of Isaac Newton*, ed. H. W. Turnbull, 7 vols. (Cambridge: Cambridge University Press for the Royal Society, 1959–77), 2:333.

13. Vico, *New Science*, 129, 118 (secs. 405, 377).

14. Herder, *Origin of Language*, 133.

15. I. A. Richards, *The Philosophy of Rhetoric* (Oxford: Oxford University Press, 1936), 92–107.

16. Vico, *New Science*, 60 (sec. 122).

17. Paul Ricoeur "The Metaphorical Process as Cognition, Imagination, and Feeling," in *On Metaphor*, ed. Sheldon Sacks (Chicago: University of Chicago Press, 1979), 151.

18. There are interesting affinities between Blake's portrait of Urizen and the depiction of the scientific personality in Gerald Holton, *The Scientific Imagination: Case Studies* (New York: Cambridge University Press, 1978), esp. 237.

19. Blake suggests that "priesthood" imposes arbitrary material and spiritual standards alike. The document authorizing standard weights and measures in England is not *Philosophical Transactions*, however, but the Magna

Carta. Chapter 35 proclaims, "Let there be one measure of wine throughout the whole realm; and one measure of ale, and one measure of corn, to wit, 'the London quarter'; and one width of cloth (whether dyed, or russet, or 'halberget'), to wit, two ells between the selvedges; with weights also let it be as with measures." See William Sharp McKechnie, *Magna Carta: A Commentary on the Great Charter of King John*, 2d. ed. (New York: Franklin, 1958), 356.

20. According to Donald Ault, "Incommensurability and Interconnection in Blake's Anti-Newtonian Text," *Studies in Romanticism* 16 (Summer 1977): 277, "Blake . . . saw that such a 'coherent' world (which Newton nevertheless believed needed to be explained) required, at the level of explanation, the rejection, suppression, and ruling out of massive aspects of human experience."

21. The allusion is suggested by Ault in *Visionary Physics: Blake's Response to Newton* (Chicago: University of Chicago Press, 1974), 106.

22. In an extremely fortuitous example of this usage, *The Interpreter's Dictionary of the Bible*, ed. George Arthur Buttrick et al., 4 vols. (New York and Nashville: Abingdon Press, 1962), 2:521, cites Isaiah 35:3. It is certain Blake read and approved of this verse, since he proclaims, near the conclusion of "The Argument" in *The Marriage*, "Now is the dominion of Edom, & the return of Adam into Paradise; see Isaiah xxxiv & xxxv Chap." (*MHH*, pl. 3).

23. M. H. Abrams, *Natural Supernaturalism: Tradition and Revolution in Romantic Literature* (New York: Norton, 1971), 54–55, discusses Blake's affinities with "inner light" Protestantism. *Paradise Lost*, in *John Milton: Complete Poems and Major Prose*, ed. Merritt Y. Hughes (New York: Odyssey, 1957), 12.587.

24. Newton mounts his argument in the "Generai Scholium," in *Mathematical Principles*, 543ff. I discuss the dispute and its effect on Blake in "Blake on Space, Time, and the Artist," *Science/Technology and the Humanities* 2 (1979): 246–63. Dennis M. Welch, "Center, Circumference, and Vegetation Symbolism in the Writings of William Blake," *Studies in Philology* 75 (1978): 223–42, discusses Blake's vortex as a heuristic for overcoming the delusion of material priority.

CHAPTER 3. BLAKE, FREEMASONRY, AND THE BUILDER'S TASK

Reprinted from *Mosaic: Journal for the Interdisciplinary Study of Literature* 17, no. 3 (University of Manitoba, summer 1984).

1. Margaret C. Jacob, *The Radical Enlightenment: Pantheists, Freemasons, and Republicans* (London: Allen and Unwin, 1981), 67.

2. For a not quite accurate account of Freemasonry in its modern dispensation, see Joseph Fort Newton, *The Builders: A Story and Study of Freemasonry* (1914; rpt., Richmond, Va.: Macoy, 1951). A better account is A. S. Frere, *The Grand Lodge* (Oxford: Oxford University Press, 1967).

3. The Old Charges are discussed at some length in Alex Home, *King Solomon's Temple in the Mosaic Tradition* (Wollingborough, Northamptonshire: Aquarian, 1972), 89–113.

4. Desaguliers and Pope are cited in Newton, *The Builders*, 181, 255, respectively. Swift, Pope, and Sterne are mentioned by Paul Nettl, *Mozart and Masonry* (New York: Philosophical Library, 1957), 5.

5. Nettl, *Mozart and Masonry*, 118, 95ff., 40, 114ff., 9ff.

6. See Newton, *The Builders*, 232–47.

7. *M*, pl. 1. For a discussion of Blake's lifelong struggle against an esthetics of consensus and for the expressive privilege and power of the artist, see Morris Eaves, William Blake's Theory of Art (Princeton, N.J.: Princeton University Press, 1982).

8. Newton, *The Builders*, 177; Home, *Solomon's Temple*, 53. Jacob, *Radical Enlightenment*, 35, 41, notes Bacon's influence on the development of Freemasonry. She discusses the consequences of that influence after the English Revolution on pages 67, 71, and 74.

9. Newton, *The Builders*, 222. Jacob, *Radical Enlightenment*, 118, has her doubts. "Throughout the eighteenth century, English Masons claimed Locke as one of their own, and the eighteenth-century Portrait Gallery of the Grand Lodge includes him. . . . but the evidence for Locke's Masonic membership—one letter of 1696 of very dubious origin—hardly qualifies him."

10. Newton, *The Builders*, 255, argues for the quoting and linking of the "Universal Prayer" to Freemasonry. For a discussion of Blake's understanding of the Newtonian Pantokrator, see chapter 1.

11. The self-denial of selfhood is most pointedly present at the outset of Milton. Jacob, *Radical Enlightenment*, 93, notes that "For Blake, with his unique vision, Newtonians were the true 'Materialists' in that they subjected people to the rule of an impersonal and mechanized nature divorced from the human order."

12. All cited in Home, *Solomon's Temple*, 31, 36, 35.

13. As cited in Newton, *The Builders*, 214n. Jacob, *Radical Enlightenment*, 154, notes that "Thomas Paine, quite possibly a Freemason himself, argued that Masonry was derived from 'the religion of the ancient Druids, who like the Magi of Persia or the Priests of Heliopolis in Egypt, were priests of the Sun,' while radical republicans in the new American republic were known to set up druidical lodges."

14. Horne, *Solomon's Temple*, 251, refers to this indirectly.

15. Anne K. Mellor, *Blake's Human Form Divine* (Berkeley and Los Angeles: University of California Press, 1974), 320.

16. As reprinted in Home, *Solomon's Temple*, 229.

17. Newton, *The Builders*, 254.

18. As cited in Jacques Chailley, *The Magic Flute: Masonic Opera*, trans. Herbert Weinstock (New York: Knopf, 1971), 132. The continuity of the tradition is demonstrated by Home, *Solomon's Temple*, 276.

19. See Mellor, *Form Divine*, 146, for a discussion of Blake's difficulties with the Vitruvian conception of bodily proportions and the style of architecture that that conception gives rise to.

20. The pyramid is associated with the rite of Mizraim. Home, *Solomon's Temple*, 84, cites an argument by G. Ernest Wright that the Temple of Solomon is a "typical Phoenician temple."

21. For a fuller discussion of Blake's quarrel with Newtonian calculus, see F. B. Curtis, "Blake and the 'Moment of Time': An Eighteenth-Century Controversy in Mathematics," *Philological Quarterly* 51 (1972): 460–70.

22. See chapter 1.

23. The language is obviously deconstructive; the source, obviously Derrida. See *Of Grammatology*, trans. Gayatri Chakravoorty Spivak (Baltimore: Johns Hopkins University Press, 1974), 6–26.

24. Chailley, *The Magic Flute*, 127.

25. In *The Early Masonic Catechisms*, as cited in Home, *Solomon's Temple*, 121.

26. See B. H. Fairchild, *Such Holy Song: Music as Idea, Form, and Image in the Poetry of William Blake* (Kent, Ohio: Kent State University Press, 1980), 9–10, for a discussion of the analogy between music and the visual arts, and the subversion of line by "technique" in each. See Morris Eaves, "Blake and the Artistic Machine: An Essay on Decorum and Technology," *PMLA* 92 (1977): 903–27, for a discussion of the depredations wrought by "technique" in the visual arts specifically.

27. Prichard's *Masonry Dissected*, as cited in Home, *Solomon's Temple*, 249.

28. Horne, *Solomon's Temple*, 60.

29. For a fuller discussion of the topos of "the edifice of art," see my "A Program Toward Prophecy: Eighteenth-Century Influences on the Poetry of William Blake," Ph.D. diss. (University of Washington, 1974), ch. 2 (pp. 88–109).

30. Samuel Johnson, "Preface" to the 1750 edition of William Lauder's *Essay on Milton's Use and Imitation of the Moderns*, as cited in *Selections from Samuel Johnson*, ed. R. W. Chapman (London: Oxford University Press, 1962), 143–44.

31. Harold Bloom, *The Anxiety of Influence* (New York: Oxford University Press, 1973).

32. Donald Pease, "Blake, Crane, Whitman, and Modernism: A Poetics of Pure Possibility," *PMLA* 96 (1981): 64–85.

CHAPTER 4. BLAKE, PRIESTLEY, AND THE "GNOSTIC MOMENT"

Reprinted from *Literature and Science: Theory and Practice*, ed. Stuart Peterfreund (Boston: Northeastern University Press, 1990).

1. Hans Eichner, "The Poise of Modern Science and the Genesis of Romanticism," *PMLA* 97, no. 1 (1982): 8–30, esp. 25.

2. See Boris Hessen, *The Economic Roots of Newton's "Principia"* (1931; rpt., New York: Fertig, 1971). For a more balanced social analysis of approximately the same vintage, see Robert Merton, *Science, Technology, and Society in Seventeenth-Century England* (New York: Columbia University Press, 1938), J. D. Bernal, *The Social Foundations of Science* (New York: Macmillan, 1939); or Edgar Zitsel, "The Sociological Roots of Science," *American Journal of Sociology* 47 (1942): 544–62. A good and more recent collection dealing with the social construction of scientific discourse is *The Social Production of Scientific Knowledge*, ed. Everett Mendelsohn, Peter Weingart, and Richard Whitley (Dordrecht: Reidel, 1977).

3. Richard Rorty, *Philosophy and the Mirror of Nature* (Princeton, N.J.: Princeton University Press, 1979), 42, 346. Citing book 2 of Bacon's *Advancement of Learning* as well as Shakespeare, Rorty observes, "Our Glassy Essence—the 'intellectual soul' of the scholastics—is also Bacon's 'mind of man'

which 'far from the nature of a clear and equal glass, wherein the beams of things should reflect according to their true incidence . . . is rather like an enchanted glass, full of superstition and imposture if it be not delivered and reduced.'" Rorty problematizes "the distinction between the *Geistes- and Naturwissenschaften*," stating in the process that "this . . . distinction is supposedly coextensive with the distinction between hermeneutical and other methods."

4. Ibid., 4, 315, 346. Rorty does not see hermeneutics as a successor to epistemology. On the contrary: he characterizes hermeneutics as "an expression of hope that the cultural space left by the demise of epistemology will not be filled." But "the demise of epistemology" does not automatically entail the onset of a warm and fuzzy aquarian age. Rorty undertakes to debunk "the claim that hermeneutics is particularly suited to the 'spirit' or to 'the sciences of man,' whereas some other method (that of 'objectivizing' and positive sciences) is appropriate to 'nature.'"

5. See *Cratylus* 438c, in *Plato, with an English Translation*, rev. ed., trans. H. N. Fowler, vol. 6 (1939; rpt., Cambridge, Mass.: Harvard University Press, 1953), 182, 183; speaking to Socrates, Cratylus states his opinion that "the truest theory of the matter . . . is that the power which gave the first names to things is more than human, and therefore the names must necessarily be correct." See *Valerius Terminus*, in *The Works of Francis Bacon*, ed. James Spedding, Robert Leslie Ellis, and Douglas Denon Heath, 2d ed., 7 vols. (London: Longmans, 1870), 3:222: "the true end . . . of knowledge is a restitution and reinvesting (in great part) of man to the sovereignty and power (for whensoever he shall be able to call the creatures by their true names he shall again command them) which he had in his first state of creation."

6. Fredric Jameson, *The Political Unconscious: Narrative as a Symbolic Act* (1981; rpt., Ithaca, N.Y.: Cornell University Press, 1986), 63.

7. Ibid., 84. See Tzvetan Todorov, *Mikhail Bakhtin: The Dialogical Principle*, trans. Wlad Godzich, Theory and History of Literature, vol. 13 (Minneapolis: University of Minnesota Press, 1984), 57.

8. For a discussion of the politics of this creed, see Elaine Pagels, *The Gnostic Gospels* (New York: Random House, 1979), 28.

9. So common, in fact, that it is the example for metonymy given in Sylvan Barnet, Morton Berman, and William Burto, *Introduction to Literature: Fiction, Poetry, Drama*, 7th ed. (Boston: Little, Brown, 1981), 428.

10. Consider Newton's characterization of the "Lord God Pantokrator" in the "General Scholium" of the *Principia*: "In him are all *things* contained and mooved." See Isaac Newton, *Mathematical Principles of Natural Philosophy*, trans. Andrew Motte, rev. Florian Cajori (1934; rpt., Berkeley and Los Angeles: University of California Press, 1966), 545.

11. Early Christian Rome is discussed in Pagels, *Gnostic Gospels*. Sixteenth- and early seventeenth-century Italy is discussed in Frances Yates, *Giordano Bruno and the Hermetic Tradition* (1964; rpt., New York: Vintage Books, 1969). Early seventeenth-century England is discussed in Christopher Hill, *The Intellectual Origins of the Puritan Revolution* (Oxford: Oxford University Press, 1965), and *The World Turned Upside Down* (New York: Viking, 1972). According to Eric Voegelin, in *Science, Politics, and Gnosticism*

(Chicago: Regnery, 1968), 83, the late nineteenth and early twentieth centuries have also been a "gnostic moment" of sorts, during which the practice of self-validating interpretation originated by Spinoza has given rise to a plethora of oppressive and reductive -isms, including Marxism, Freudianism, and Nazism.

12. Kurt Rudolph, *Gnosis: The Nature and History of Gnosticism*, trans. Robert McLachlan Wilson (San Francisco: Harper & Row, 1983), 56–57. I take my understanding of these terms from Rudolph, and he takes his in turn from the Congress on the Origins of Gnosticism, held in Messina in 1966. "According to this view we should understand by 'Gnosis' a 'knowledge of divine secrets which is reserved for an elite' (and thus has an esoteric character), but 'Gnosticism' should be used in the above-mentioned sense for the gnostic systems of the second and third centuries." Obviously, my use of the term "gnostic moment" is an attempt to remain true to the letter of these definitions while quarreling with the spirit of the latter one. The quarrel is in some measure sanctioned by another of the pronouncements of the Congress of Messina, concerning gnosticism's centering myth:

> the idea of the presence in man of a divine "spark" . . . which has proceeded from the divine world and has fallen into this world of destiny, birth and death and which must be reawakened through its own divine counterpart in order to be finally restored. This idea . . . is ontologically based on the conception of a downward development of the divine whose periphery (often called *Sophia* or *Ennoia*) has fatally fallen victim to a crisis and must—even if only indirectly—produce this world, in which it cannot be disinterested, in that it must once again recover the divine spark (often designated as *pneuma*, "spirit").

It seems clear that this same myth pervades and informs, with some variation, the "gnostic moments" discussed in this essay.

13. James M. Robinson, "Introduction," *The Nag Hammadi Library in English* (hereafter cited as *NHLE*), trans. members of the Coptic Gnostic Library Research Project of the Institute for Antiquity and Christianity, ed. Marvin W. Meyer (San Francisco: Harper & Row, 1977), 2, 19.

14. *NHLE*, 450. All further citings of the Nag Hammadi codices themselves are parenthetical, by codex number, binding order, chapter, and verse.

15. See Amos Funkenstein, *Theology and the Scientific Imagination from the Middle Ages to the Seventeenth Century* (Princeton, N.J.: Princeton University Press, 1986), 273.

16. See Alan P. Cottrell, *Goethe's View of Evil and the Search for a New Image of Man in Our Time* (Edinburgh: Floris, 1982), 26. Cottrell documents convincingly the argument that Goethe's response to the problem of evil has a good deal to do with his early reading in esoterica, including "Gnostic, Hermetic, cabalistic, Neoplatonic and other esoterical literature of the pansophical stream."

17. Yates, *Giordano Bruno*, 358–59, speculates that the dialogical form of Galileo's *Dialogo* (1632) owes something to the similarly dialogical form of Bruno's *Cena de la ceneri* (1584), but the case rests on the fact that both Bruno and Galileo were in Padua at nearly the same time in 1592 and that Galileo used

the library of Vincenzo Pinelli, an associate of Bruno's and a collector of Hermetica. However, Galileo was no gnostic. if anything, his advocacy of a corpuscular model of matter, which implicitly denied the principle of consubstantiality and thereby caused his problems with the Jesuits and the Inquisition, was opposed to the immanentist concept of *pneuma* central to gnosticism. See Pietro Redondi, *Galileo Heretic*, trans. Raymond Rosenthal (Princeton, N.J.: Princeton University Press, 1987).

Newton's fascination with hermetic lore, chiefly in the context of his fascination with alchemy, is well documented in Betty Jo Teeter Dobbs, *The Foundations of Newton's Alchemy, or "The Huntyng of the Greene Lyon"* (1975; rpt., New York: Cambridge University Press, 1984). Once again, however, Newton's heresies, such as they are, are inimical to gnosticism. Richard S. Westfall, *Never at Rest: A Biography of Isaac Newton* (New York: Cambridge University Press, 1980), 292, 524–25, corroborates Dobbs's identification of the significance of Hermetica for Newton's alchemical studies in the mid-1670s. But Westfall (313–14) notes that, during virtually the same period, Newton was hard at work refuting the doctrine of *homoousia* (consubstantiality) because of its implications both for his corpuscular model of light and for his attempt to reconcile his optics with the cosmogony depicted in the *P* account in Genesis (1:1–2:4a). That account implicitly denies the concept of *pneuma*, which is central to the *J* account (2:4b–2:25).

18. See note 14 above.
19. Pagels, *The Gnostic Gospels*, 142, 150.
20. Funkenstein, *Scientific Imagination*, 273; Rudolph, *Gnosis*, 30.
21. Funkenstein, *Scientific Imagination*, 273. Cottrell, *Goethe's View of Evil*, 26, notes the influence of counterhistory in general and of Arnold's account in particular on the young Goethe's understanding of the problem of evil.

Through the ministrations of an intimate of Goethe's mother, the Pietist Fräulein Susanne Katharina von Kietterberg (1723–1774), the young man was introduced to an array of mystical, alchemical, theosophical books from the Gnostic, Hermetic, cabalistic, Neoplatonic and other esoterical literature of the pansophical stream. In his father's library he found the second edition (1729) of the *Kirchen- und Ketzergeschichte* (History of the Church and of Heretics) by Gottfried Arnold (1666–1714), whose discussion of church history from the time of the Apostles to Pietism convinced Goethe that those figures condemned as heretical might be viewed in a more positive fight.

22. Rudolph, *Gnosis*, 30.
23. Pagels, *Gnostic Gospels*, 150, observes that "radical visionaries like George Fox, themselves unfamiliar, in all probability, with gnostic tradition, nevertheless articulated analogous interpretations of religious experience." Although Pagels's speculation that such visionaries were not familiar with gnostic tradition is questionable, she is correct in understanding the ready compatibility of gnosticism with a radical political and religious position. In this last regard, see Stephen Shapin, "History of Science and Its Sociological Reconstructions," *History of Science* 20 (1982): 157–211, esp. 82. Speaking of the Digger Gerrard Wistanley, whose "inner light" metaphysics and politics

were very close to those of the overtly gnostic John Everard, Shapin correctly notes the importance of immanentism for that metaphysics and politics.

His argument was founded upon a vision of God's relationship to the universe in which divinity was immanent in material nature just as it was immanent within each believer. Divine power was thus accessible to all; revelation was democratized and the hierarchical order which made nature dependent upon an external spiritual Deity, the believer dependent upon an external spiritual intermediary, and civil society dependent upon supervision by a divine-right monarch was collapsed and rejected.

24. Keith Thomas, *Religion and the Decline of Magic* (New York: Scribners, 1971), 225. The imprint date on the supposedly reprinted first edition of Everard that I cite in note 33 below is 1650, not 1649 as Thomas has it. Yates, *Giordano Bruno*, 398–99, concurs with Thomas's assessment of the effect Casaubon's dating had on the decline of Renaissance magic. Rudolph, *Gnosis*, 26, notes that the tractate "which bears the name 'Poimandres' ('shepherd of men') . . . which for the first time gave its name to the whole work [i.e., the *Corpus Hermeticum*]" was first translated into Latin by Ficino in 1463, then published under the patronage and protection of Cosimo de Medici in 1471, after which date "it exercised a great influence on Renaissance philosophy in Italy. Several editions appeared in the course of the sixteenth and seventeenth centuries, of which that of 1554 offered the Greek text for the first time." Patrizi's *New Philosophy* (1591) "even attempted to supplant the Catholic school philosophy of Aristotle, since he saw in the teachings of Hermes something that was in conformity with Christian thought." Rudolph does not even begin to take into account the writings of Pico della Mirandola, Cornelius Agrippa, Giordano Bruno, and Tommaso Campanella, all of whom are discussed by Yates, *Giordano Bruno*, passim. Clearly, then, Everard's *Pymander*, although its heretical implications are no less than those of Patrizi's *New Philosophy*, has its place in a long line of Renaissance philosophical humanism that is profoundly at odds with the line of Christian orthodoxy.

25. See, for example, *A Reformation of Schools* (1642), 47–48, as cited in Dobbs, *The Foundation of Newton's Alchemy*, 61: "Also the practise of the Chymists came into my mind, who have found out a way so to cleare, and unburden the essences, and spirits of things from the surcharge of matter, that one drop extracted out of Mineralls, or Vegetables containes more strength, and vertue in it, and is used with better successe, and efficacy than can be hoped for from the whole, and entire lumpe."

26. Ibid., 60–61. Yates, *Giordano Bruno*, 432–55, esp. 443, comments on Fludd's controversies with the likes of Mersenne and Kepler, calling into question Fludd's grasp of the mathematical rudiments necessary to pursue his scientific program. "Fludd's mathematics are really 'mathesis' and 'vana geometria' which he utterly confuses with 'Chymia' and with 'Hermes.' Kepler is concerned not with 'Pythagorean intentions' but with reality (*res ipsa*). He uses mathematics as a mathematician, while Fludd uses them 'more Hermetico.' "

27. On the Codex Brucianus, see Pagels, *Gnostic Gospels*, xxiv: "in 1769 . . . a Scottish tourist named James Bruce bought a Coptic manuscript

near Thebes (modern Luxor) in upper Egypt" and brought it back to England, where he deposited it in the Bodleian Library at Oxford as the Codex Brucianus no later than 1778. On the Codex Brucianus and the Codex Askewianus, see Rudolph, *Gnosis*, 27. A certain Dr. Askew deposited in the British Museum Library another manuscript, known as the Codex Askewianus, also no later than 1778. Both codices "were first brought to the attention of scholars by C. G. Woide in 1778."

Morton D. Paley, *Energy and the Imagination: The Development of Blake's Thought* (Oxford: Clarendon Press, 1970), 66, suggests that in his use of the concept of creation-as-fall, "Blake need not have gone to esoteric sources of this and other Gnostic doctrines, for they are summarized in J. L. Mosheim's *Ecclesiastical History*, first published in English translation in 1764. He could also have found a succinct exposition of Gnostic theology reprinted from Mosheim in Priestley's *Matter and Spirit.*"

28. Michael Ferber, *The Social Vision of William Blake* (Princeton, N.J.: Princeton University Press, 1985), 93.

29. "The Eleventh Book of Hermes Trismegistus: Of the Common Mind to Tat," in [John Everard], *The Divine Pymander of Hermes Mercurius Trismegistus in XVII Books*, vol. 2 of *Collectanea Hermetica*, ed. W. Wynn Westcott (1650; rpt., London: Theosophical Publishing Society, 1894), 86. That "the operation of life" is an immanent, vital energy is clear from the authoritative version of the text. See *Corpus Hermeticum*, ed. A. D. Nock, trans. A. J. Festugière, 4 vols. (1945–54; rpt., Naris: Société d'Edition "Les Belles Lettres," 1960), 1:180–81. In this translation of what is, in this edition, the twelfth rather than the eleventh book, Festugière renders "the operation of life" as "l'énergie de la vie," taking his lead from Nock's Greek original, where the term is *energeia*.

30. Everard, *Pymander*, 88–89. See also *Corpus Hermeticum* 1:183. Festugière renders the passage last quoted as follows: "Et si elle est mise en oeuvre, par qui l'est elle? Car ses énergies qui opèrent, nous l'avons dit, sont parties de Dieu." Nock's original reads *tinos energeitai* for "mise en oeuvre," and *energeias* for "énergies."

31. See note 2 above.

32. *Blake Records*, ed. G. E. Bentley Jr. (London: Oxford University Press, 1969), 545. A number of others have commented on Blake's gnostic proclivities, including Paley (see note 27 above); Ferber (see note 28 above); Stuart Curran, "Blake and the Gnostic Hyle: A Double Negative," *Blake Studies* 4 (spring 1972): 117–33; and Leslie Tannenbaum, "Blake's Art of Crypsis: *The Book of Urizen* and Genesis," *Blake Studies* 5 (fall 1972): 141–64. Tannenbaum further elaborates Blake's relation to gnosticism in *Biblical Tradition in Blake's Early Prophecies* (Princeton, N.J.: Princeton University Press, 1982), 4, 6, 15, 202, 257–58.

33. Joseph Priestley, *Disquisition Relating to Matter and Spirit* (London: Joseph Johnson, 1777), 50, xxxix; hereafter cited as *DMS*.

34. William Blake, *Europe*, in *CPP*, pl. iii, ll. 1–7. See also Everard, *Pymander*, 37. The predicament that Blake describes shows some striking affinities with the account of "the wickedness of the Soul" given by Trismegistus [i.e., Hermes] in "The Fourth Book Called 'The Key'": "And the

wickedness of the Soul is ignorance; for the Soul that knows nothing of the things that are, neither the nature of them, nor that which is good, but is blinded, rusheth and dasheth against the bodily Passions, and unhappy as it is, not knowing itself, it serveth strange Bodies, and evil ones, carrying the Body as a burden, and not ruling, but ruled. And this is the mischief of the Soul."

35. *The History and Present State of Electricity* (1767), xiii, as cited in Joseph Priestley, *Autobiography*, ed. Jack Lindsay (Teaneck, N.J.: Fairleigh Dickinson University Press, 1971), 19.

36. *A Scientific Autobiography of Joseph Priestley*, ed. Robert E. Schofield (Cambridge, Mass.: MIT Press, 1966), 117, 122. Two recent articles attempt to revise, or at least to readjust, the positions of Priestley and Lavoisier and the lineage leading up to them. J. B. Gough, "Lavoisier and the Fulfillment of the Stahlian Revolution," *Osiris* n.s. 4 (1988): 15–33, esp. 23, 32, seeks to identify Lavoisier as the last and greatest in the line of French Stahlians who participated in "the Chemical Revolution of the eighteenth century . . . a revolution concerning the composition of the chemical molecule." To make this argument, Gough must deal with the obvious fact that Stahl, along with Becher, is one of the authors of the phlogiston theory. This he does by insisting that "phlogiston was but a small part of Stahlian theory." Alistair M. Duncan, "Particles and Eighteenth Century Concepts of Chemical Combination," *British Journal for the History of Science* 21 (1988): 447–53, esp. 448, 453, deemphasizes "the tradition derived from Becher and Stahl, and continuing through the modifications of the phlogiston theory," as well as "the extremes of Newtonianism [?] such as the theory of Boscovich," in order to argue that "the model of chemical change as consisting of interactions between particles, adapted by chemists to suit their own needs rather than as dictated to them by mechanical philosophers, acquired considerable explanatory power in the late eighteenth century." Although neither article is unreconstructedly internalist in its orientation, trying to separate Stahl from phlogiston in order to make him the intellectual progenitor of Lavoisier rather than Priestley, not to mention making Stahl, the source of Priestley's anti-Newtonian conception of electricity as an immanentist phenomenon, into a Newtonian extremist, raises more questions than are answered.

37. Arguably, Blake's discussion of "Poetic Genius" (*CPP*, p. 2) in *All Religions Are One* (1788) is the earliest such discussion.

38. See Eichner, "The Rise of Modern Science," 24.

39. In *Milton* (1804), Blake names "Satan [who] is Urizen / Drawn down by Ore & the Shadowy Female into Generation" (*M*, pl. 10 [11], ll. 1–2), "Prince of the Starry Wheels" (pl. 3, l. 43). This title, coupled with Los's recognition that Satan is "Newton's Pantocrator weaving the woof of Locke" (pl. 4, l. 1)— that is, the "*Lord God Pantrokrator, or Universal Ruler,*" of the "General Scholium" to the *Principia* (see Newton's *Mathematical Principles*, trans. Motte, rev. Cajori, 544), who is closely modeled on the creator-God of Genesis 1—invites the comparison of Urizen to Yaldabaoth. "The word is of Semitic (Aramaic) origin and probably means Begetter of Sabaoth (= Abaoth)' i.e. 'the heavenly powers'; evidently an esoteric description of the God of the Jews who corresponding to the biblical tradition occupies in the gnostic systems the role of the creator" (Rudolph, *Gnosis*, 73).

As described in the gnostic codex *On the Origin* (*NHLE*, 161–79), Yaldabaoth is, in several senses, the spiritless "afterbirth" or miscarriage" of Pistis Sophia (Faith Wisdom). But lacking spirit (*pneuma*) and therefore "ignorant of the power of Pistis," Yaldabaoth knows nothing of his parent. He rules "lion-like in appearance, androgynous, and having a great authority within himself but not knowing whence he came into being (II, 5: *99*, 25–*100*, 20). Blake seems to have this scenario or one very much like it in mind in Urizen's description of his struggle to create the material world in a place that is the womb of Pistis whence he sprang: "A void immense, wild dark & deep, / Where nothing was: Natures wide womb" (*U*, pl. 4, ll. 16–17) is how he describes the place, ignorant that his description shows him to be "ignorant of the power of Pistis."

Perhaps even more than Urizen's description, Blake's illustrations Of him suggest his identity with Yaldabaoth: "the perfect ones called him 'Ariael' because he was a lion-likeness" (II, 5: *100*, 25–26). Blake, for his part, usually depicts Urizen with a leonine mane of hair and as often as not hunched or squatting in a manner suggestive of a big cat preparing to pounce. Yet another name for Yaldabaoth is "'Samuel,' that is, 'the blind god'" (II, 5: *103*, 18). Blake nearly always depicts and describes Urizen with obstructed vision—gaze averted, eyes filled with tears, pleading the dimness of the light, and so on.

40. *Trimorphic Protennoia* (*NHLE*, 461–70) explains the entity thusly: "[I] am [Protennoia, the] thought that [dwells] in the Light. I am the movement that dwells in the [All, she in whom the] All takes its stand, [the first]-born among those who [came to be, she who exists] before the All. . . . I am intangible, dwelling in the intangible. I move in every creature" (XIII, 1: 35, 1–13).

41. Joseph Priestley, *An History of the Corruptions of Christianity*, 2 vols. (London: Joseph Johnson, 1782), 1:6; hereafter cited as *History*.

42. Pagels cites the *Tripartite Tractate* (1, 5: 99ff.; *NHLE*, 54–97) in elaborating the contrast between the orthodox, who embrace the doctrine of particular immanence and the consequence of hierarchy, and the gnostics, who share the bond of equality effected by the working of a pervasive immanence in them.

> The *Tripartite Tractate* . . . contrasts those who are gnostics, "children of the Father," with those who are uninitiates, offspring of the demiurge. The Father's children . . . join together as equals, enjoying mutual love, spontaneously helping one another. But the demiurge's offspring—the ordinary Christians—"wanted to command one another, outrivalling one another in their empty ambition"; they are inflated with "lust for power," "each one imagining that he is superior to the others." (40–41)

43. Pagels, *Gnostic Gospels*, 41.

44. Ibid., 28.

45. *Shelley's Prose, or The Trumpet of a Prophecy*, ed. David Lee Clark, corrected ed. (Albuquerque: University of New Mexico Press, 1966), 188, 279. Shelley's own gnostic sympathies are readily apparent in his prose fragment "The Assassins."

46. Pagels, *Gnostic Gospels*, 28.

47. See note 7 above.
48. Robert Alter, *The Art of Biblical Narrative* (New York: Basic Books, 1981), 145, contrasts the *P* account of the creation (Genesis 1:1–2:4a) with the *J* account (2:4b–2:25) in the following terms: "*P* is interested in the large plan of creation; *J* is more interested in the complicated and difficult facts of human life in civilization, for which he provides an initial explanation through the story of what happened in Eden. Man culminates the scheme of creation in *P*, but man is the narrative center of *J*'s story, which is quite another matter."
49. Pagels, *Gnostic Gospels*, 32–33.

CHAPTER 5. BLAKE ON CHARTERS, WEIGHTS, AND MEASURES

Reprinted from *Studies in the Literary Imagination* 22, no. 1 (Georgia State University, spring 1989).

1. Stewart Crehan, *Blake in Context* (Atlantic Highlands, N.J.: Humanities Press, 1984), 74, 84. Crehan contrasts the "charter'd streets" of "London" with the "opening streets" of *Jerusalem*, noting in the latter "that at least there is the possibility of *imaginatively* breaking out of the system."
2. Michael Ferber, "'London' and Its Politics," *ELH: English Literary History* 48 (1981): 310–38, esp. 311.

> Repetitiveness, almost a theme of the poem, is enacted in the drearily repeated every and in the repeated pairings of words and clauses, themselves subsumed in hierarchies of pairs which take us begond repetition or seriality . . . to a sense of inclusiveness or totalization. . . . The infinite series of encounters sums to an integral formula. Even the pairs by themselves are summary or totalizing: street and river, man and infant, church and state, harlot and bride, man and woman, birth and death.

3. See Donald D. Ault, "Incommensurability and Interconnection in Blake's Anti-Newtonian Text," *Studies in Romanticism* 16 (1977): 277–303.
4. David V. Erdman, *Blake: Prophet against Empire*, rev. ed. (Garden City, N.Y.: Anchor Books, 1969), 276. The fair copy is found on p. 109 of the Notebook; the "charter'd/cheating" variant, on p. 113. See also *SE*, 46.1–2.
5. Erdman, *Prophet*, 276–77.
6. See Northrop Frye, *Fearful Symmetry: A Study of William Blake* (1947; rpt., Princeton, N.J.: Princeton University Press, 1969), 180–81; E. D. Hirsch Jr., *Innocence and Experience: An Introduction to Blake* (New Haven, Conn.: Yale University Press, 1964), 262–63; D. G. Gillham, *Blake's Contrary States* (Cambridge: Cambridge University Press, 1966), 9–10; Jack Lindsay, *William Blake: His Life and Work* (New York: Braziller, 1979), 68; and Crehan, *Blake in Context*, 65–66. Frye, missing the irony of the fragment, characterizes it as being "simply 'Rule Britania' in blank verse." Gillham sees the irony in "London" but does not identify the dramatic fragment as a precedent. Lindsay sees the irony in "London" as being directed not against civil charters but against "the chartered companies, the big money-powers, which he sees as owning the city and its people." Crehan concurs with Lindsay.

7. Second Part of *The Rights of Man*, in *The Writings of Thomas Paine*, ed. Moncure Daniel Conway, 26 vols. (1894–96; rpt., New York: AMS, 1967), 2:436–37.

8. Erdman, *Prophet*, 313.

9. William Sharp McKechnie, *Magna Carta: A Commentary on the Great Charter of King John, with an Historical Introduction*, 2d ed. (New York: Franklin, 1958), p. 241.

10. Ibid., 242–47.

11. Erdman, *Prophet*, 159. According to Erdman, "Blake could not have failed to have some acquaintance with the famous Society for Constitutional Information." According to Scrivener, *Radical Shelley: The Philosophical Anarchism and Utopian Thought of Percy Bysshe Shelley* (Princeton, N.J.: Princeton University Press, 1982), 4, "The SCI had three basic demands: (1) political rights for Dissenters by repealing the Test and Corporation Acts: (2) annual parliaments; (3) better representation of the middle class."

12. Scrivener, *Radical Shelley*, 4–5. Erdman, *Prophet*, 161–62, notes Blake's "familiarity with the Ideas of the Paine set," adding that an early poem such as *Visions of the Daughters of Albion* (1793) "suggest[s] a stronger affinity for the artisan radicalism of the Constitutional and Corresponding Societies than for the more Whiggish radicalism of younger men such as Wordsworth and Coleridge."

13. See Ronald Edward Zupko, *British Weights and Measures: A History from Antiquity to the Seventeenth Century* (Madison: University of Wisconsin Press, 1977), 18–19. "In the case of wine and ale it never named the capacity measures, but it stated that the London quarter (the Saxon seam or pack-load) was the model for corn. . . . During the reign of Henry III [1216–72], however, the viceroy and the council ordered observance of the London standards."

14. McKechnie, *Magna Carta*, 356.

15. Zupko, *British Weights*, 19.

16. Ibid., 37–38, 59–62.

17. Morton D. Paley, *Energy and the Imagination: The Development of Blake's Thought* (Oxford: Clarendon Press, 1970), 67. Given the Mosaic overtones of Urizen's proclamation, it is all the more interesting to find in Mosaic law anticipations of the mind-set evident in chapter 35. Leviticus 19:35–36 proclaims, "Ye shall do no unrighteousness in judgment, in meteyard, in weight, or in measure. Just balances, just weights, a just ephah, and a just hin, ye shall have." And Deuteronomy 25:13–15 proclaims, "Thou shalt not have in thy bag divers weights, a great and a small. Thou shalt not have in thy house divers measures, a great and a small. *But* thou shalt have a perfect and just weight, a perfect and just measure shalt thou have."

18. Crehan, *Blake in Context*, 75, observes, "By his 'marking' the speaker relates to others at a less than human level, in a city where all are strangers." E. P. Thompson, "London," in *Interpreting Blake*, ed. Michael Phillips (New York: Cambridge University Press, 1978), 10–14, notes that "the word 'mark' would have had a number of associations for Blake's reader. Revelations 13:17 speak of 'the mark of the beast' on those who buy and sell." Ferber, " 'London' and Its Politics," 316–18, argues for Thompson's source (and against the "precise

source" proposed by Harold Bloom and Heather Glen after him: Ezekiel 9:3–4). In Ferber's words, "The main abomination here is buying and selling, the commercialism of the imperial capitals of London and Babylon."

19. As cited in Frank Donovan, *Prepare Now for a Metric Future* (New York: Weybright and Talley, 1970), 20. Zupko, *British Weights*, 20, comments, "Its exact date is not known and its authorship is still in doubt. It must, however, have been drawn up after the Assize of Bread and Ale of 1266 and before the Treatise on Weights and Measures (*Tractatus de ponderibus et mensuris*) of Edward I in 1303."

20. See Richard S. Westfall, *Never at Rest: A Biography of Isaac Newton* (New York: Cambridge University Press, 1980), 567–75.

21. Zupko, *British Weights*, 21–22.

22. Ibid., 22–24.

23. Ibid., 89. Zupko notes that, during the reign of Elizabeth I, copies of avoirdupois and troy weights were distributed to the "principal cities and boroughs of England and Wales," but that standards were deposited in the Tower. Alexander Wood and Frank Oldham, *Thomas Young: Natural Philosopher, 1773–1829* (Cambridge: Cambridge University Press, 1953), 294, note that the English standard yard was so severely damaged as to necessitate its replacement when the House of Commons burnt down in 1835. Donovan, *Prepare Now*, 8, notes that "The Hebrews, in common with other ancient peoples, made the priests the custodians of weights and measures and kept their basic standards of weight and capacity in the temples."

24. Erdman, *Prophet*, 80–81.

25. Zupko, *British Weights*, 60–67.

26. Ferber, "London," 321–22.

27. As discussed in Erdman, *Prophet*, 277.

28. James Engell, *The Creative Imagination: Enlightenment to Romanticism* (Cambridge, Mass.: Harvard University Press, 1982), 220–22, compares Blake's sense of this form-giving power to Schelling and Herder's sense of it, subsumed under the rubric of *Bildungstrieb*, "the creative force in God and in man."

29. See Crehan, *Blake in Context*, 75. Speaking of "London," Crehan observes, "The freedom to buy and sell shackles 'everyman'—including the speaker—in a depersonalising system based, not on genuine human contact, but on the exchange of goods and money. There is no possibility within the speaker's mode of perception, trapped as he is in this impersonal system, of hearing a street-cry, say, as a poetic utterance, an assertion of something human behind the figure of the seller."

30. Donovan, *Prepare Now*, 5.

31. Zupko, *British Weights*, 18–19, states that "The ulna was the Latin equivalent of the Saxon elne, or 'elbow,' hence 'forearm length.'"

32. Zupko, Ibid., 10. "The North German foot—the standard for linear measurement—was defined as the length of 12 thumbs, or of 36 barleycorns laid end to end."

33. Blake's conception of good immanence in general and *pneuma*, which in *Jerusalem* (1804–20) becomes "The Breath Divine" (*J*, pl. 95, l. 5), is tied to his self-proclaimed Gnosticism noted in *Blake Records*, ed. G. E. Bentley Jr.

(London: Oxford University Press, 1969), 545. See also chapter 4 in the present volume.

34. Donovan, *Prepare Now*, 38.

35. Ibid., 43.

36. Act of the Assembly passed in 1795, as cited in ibid., 40.

37. See Wood and Oldham, *Thomas Young*, 290–94.

38. Ibid., 83. Opposition on irrational grounds of various sorts has continued into the twentieth century. For one wretched instance, see Frederick A. Halsey, *The Metric Fallacy: An Investigation of the Claims Made for the Metric System and Especially of the Claim That Its Adoption Is Necessary in the Interest of the Export Trade*, 2d ed. (New York: The American Institute of Weights and Measures, 1920).

39. As cited in Donovan, *Prepare Now*, 86–87. Donovan characterizes these positions as some of "the antimetric arguments that were most prevalent in the eighteenth century . . . summed up by one writer thusly," but does not identity their compiler.

40. Gerald W. Chapman, *Edmund Burke: The Practical Imagination* (Cambridge, Mass.: Harvard University Press, 1967), 223. Chapman cites Burke's "To a Member of the National Assembly" and "Policy of the Allies."

41. Ibid., 181. Chapman dates the work November 1790. Other datings range from October to December.

42. Peter J. Stanlis, *Edmund Burke and the Natural Law* (1958; rpt., Ann Arbor: University of Michigan Press, 1965), 125–27, notes that Burke, from the time of *A Vindication of Natural Society* (1756), "perceived the revolutionary tendency of the state of nature theory, which in his last years was to destroy the established order." Stanlis notes further that "the pamphleteers who responded to Burke's *Reflections* put forth in perfect seriousness many things Burke had argued ironically thirty-five years earlier. In his early satire Burke pretended to believe that 'truth' in religion, government, and law, as revealed by mathematical logic systematically extended, was always simple, plain, direct, uniform, and universal."

Maurice Crosland, "The Image of Science as a Threat: Burke versus Priestley and the 'Philosophic Revolution,'" *British Journal for the History of Science* 20:3:66 (July 1987): 287–307, has argued that Burke, from the time of *Reflections* on, argued with increasing stridency against the fanaticism, reductionism, and universalizing tendencies that he perceived as characterizing not only the intellectual basis of the revolution but also the thought of its supporters closer to home—Joseph Priestley in particular.

43. Edmund Burke, *Reflections on the Revolution in France* (Garden City, N.Y.: Doubleday, 1961), 43–44; subsequent citations by page number appear in the text. As Crosland observes ("Image of Science," 279n.), "It is to be regretted that . . . there is not yet a standard scholarly edition of his works." Not coincidentally, Zupko, *British Weights*, 17, notes the instrumentality of Henry I in "perfecting the scope and function of assizes . . . to promulgate the issuance of physical standards and to regulate inspection, verification, and enforcement procedures."

44. Donovan, *Prepare Now*, 39–40, discusses the survey. Rousseau himself worked as a surveyor in 1732, as part of a tax survey commissioned by King

Victor Amadeus and completed by his son, Charles Emmanuel III. See Jean-Jacques Rousseau, *The Confessions*, trans. J. M. Cohen (1953; rpt., New York: Penguin Books, 1985), 168–69 (i.e., book 4).

45. See Karel Berka, *Measurement: Its Concepts, Theories and Problems*, trans. Augustin Riszka, Boston Studies in the Philosophy of Science, vol. 72 (Boston: Reidel, 1983), 9. "The transition from a qualitative view of reality to a quantitative one is therefore regarded as the beginning of modern science. . . . Many historians of science claim that modern science arises from measurement and that it is inconceivable without it."

46. Also discussed in Chapman, *Edmund Burke*, 187–88.

47. Gillham, *Blake's Contrary States*, 13.

48. The reference to Bacon and Newton as the intellectual lineage that gave rise to such notions as those of gravity and "action at a distance" seems clear enough; the reference to Pitt, who resigned in 1795, less so, although it is worth noting, as Erdman, *Prophet*, 221, 277, does in his discussion of "London," that Pitt's prescriptive initiatives, which resulted among other things in the proclamation against seditious writings, are, for Erdman, "the bans, linked with an order to dragoons 'to assemble on Hounslow Heath' and 'be within one hour's march of the metropolis.'" Stanlis, *Edmund Burke*, 183–84, notes that Burke "praised . . . the virtues of Lord Chatham, Charles Townshend, Lord North, Erskine, Dundas, and the younger Pitt, men with whom he often strongly disagreed. . . . Burke's private letters are filled with glowing tributes to the moral and intellectual integrity and the liberal and humanized company of his peers."

49. Thomas S. Kuhn, "The Function of Measurement in Modern Physical Science," in *The Essential Tension: Selected Studies in Scientific Tradition and Change* (Chicago: University of Chicago Press, 1977), 178–224, esp. 216–18.

50. Ault, "Incommensurability," 280. In Ault's words, "features are smuggled back in and distorted in the sense that they are explained by properties of light other than those originally postulated."

51. Isaac Newton, *Opticks, or A Treatise on the Reflections, Refraction, Inflections, and Colours of Light*, based on the 4th ed., 1730, ed. Duane H. D. Roller (New York: Dover, 1952), 375–406.

52. See Thomas Young, "The Bakerian Lecture on the Theory of Light and Colours," *Philosophical Transactions of the Royal Society of London* 92, no. 1 (1801): 12–48.

53. Berka, *Measurement*, 9.

54. Newton, *Opticks*, 400.

CHAPTER 6. POWER TROPES

Reprinted from *New Orleans Review* 18, no. 1 (spring 1991): 27–35.

1. Stewart Crehan, *Blake in Context* (Atlantic Highlands, N.J.: Humanities Press, 1984), 125.

2. E. D. Hirsch, *Innocence and Experience: An Introduction to Blake* (New Haven, Conn.: Yale University Press, 1964), 244, and Roderick Huang, "William Blake's 'Tyger': A Re-Interpretation," *Humanities Association Bulletin* 18 (1969): 31–33.

3. Morton D. Paley, "The Tyger of Wrath," *PMLA* 81 (1966): 540–51; rpt. as "Tyger of Wrath," chapter 2 of *Energy and the Imagination: The Development of Blake's Thought* (Oxford: Clarendon Press, 1970), 30–60.

4. Paul Miner, " 'The Tyger,' " *Criticism* 4 (1962): 59–73; Kathleen Raine, "Who Made the Tyger?" *Encounter* 2 (1954): 44n; and Larry Swingle, "Answer to Blake's Tyger: A Matter of Reason or Choice?" *Concerning Poetry* 2 (1968): 61–71.

5. Harold Pagliaro, *Selfhood and Redemption in Blake's Songs* (University Park, Pa.: Pennsylvania State University Press, 1987), 84.

6. Jonathan Culler, *The Pursuit of Signs: Semiotics, Literature, Deconstruction* (Ithaca, N.Y.: Cornell University Press, 1981), 189.

7. *SE*, 42.3–4. Joel Fineman, "The Structure of Allegorical Desire," in *Allegory and Representation*, ed. Stephen Greenblatt (Baltimore: Johns Hopkins University Press, 1981), 26–40, esp. 44, argues that "Every metaphor is always a little metonymic because in order to have metaphor there must be a structure, and where there is structure there is already nostalgia for the lost origin through which structure is thought. Every metaphor is a metonymy of its own origin, its structure thrust into time by its very structurality." In the case under consideration, the metaphor of creator as inspired artisan depends on the tacit acceptance of the metonymic relationship that sees the created universe as material effect of a divine first cause.

8. Umberto Eco, *A Theory of Semiotics* (Bloomington: Indiana University Press, 1976), 281, insists, quite rightly, that one take metonymy on its own logical terms, as distinguished from those terms applicable to synecdoche. "Distinctions such as *pars pro toto, totum pro parse, genus pro specie, species pro genere*, etc. (concerning synecdoche) and *causa pro effecto, effectus pro causa, a possessore quod possidetur, inventas ab inventore, ab eo quod continet quod continetur*, etc. (concerning metonymy) seem to be rather important from a semantic point of view." Eco is virtually alone in insisting that metonymy be distinguished from synecdoche and that neither of these terms be treated merely as "weak" or "loose" variants of metaphor. For example, John R. Searle, *Expression and Meaning* (Cambridge: Cambridge University Press, 1979), 108, offers an "account of metaphor" in which "it becomes a matter of terminology whether we want to construe metonymy and synecdoche as special cases of metaphor or as independent tropes." And Liselotte Gumpel, *Metaphor Reexamined: A Non-Aristotelian Perspective* (Bloomington: University of Indiana Press, 1984), 230, follows Quintilian's translator and commentator, John Selby Watson, in claiming "that synecdoche and metonym 'are not very different.' "

9. M. H. Abrams, *A Glossary of Literary Terms*, 5th ed. (New York: Holt, Rinehart and Winston, 1988), 66.

10. *Sir Isaac Newton's Mathematical Principles of Natural Philosophy and His System of the World*, trans. Andrew Motte, rev. Florian Cajori (1934; rpt., Berkeley and Los Angeles: University of California Press, 1966), 398.

11. For a useful comparison of the *P*-account and the alternative *J*-account (Genesis 2:4b–25), see Robert Alter, *The Art of Biblical Narrative* (New York: Basic Books, 1981), 140–47.

12. In part because he rejects the Aristotelian notion of occult qualities as causes, in part because it has the potential to be subverted to trinitarian uses

(such as arguments for consubstantiality), and in part because his antipathy to Cartesianism will not allow Newton to accept the distinction between ensouled humans possessing the cogito and animal automata lacking it, Newton marginalizes the whole question of ensoulment as a criterion of difference between animals and humans. There is no soul in his universe—no ghost in the machine. Rather, the machine is in the ghost, at least insofar as that ghost is synonymous with the "Lord God *Pantokrator*" Newton unveils in the "General Scholium" of the *Principia*. "In him are all things contained and moved," Newton says. Only at the very end of the "General Scholium" does Newton allude to "a certain most subtle spirit which pervades and lies hid in all gross bodies." But Newton begs off, stating that "these are things that cannot be explained in a few words, nor are we furnished with that sufficiency of experiments which is required to an accurate determination and demonstration of the laws by which this electric and elastic spirit operates" (*Mathematical Principles*, 544–47).

13. See *The Correspondence of Isaac Newton*, ed. H. W. Turnbull (Cambridge: Cambridge University Press for the Royal Society, 1959–77), 1:362–66, esp. 364. In the context of his "Hypothesis explaining the Properties of Light," first transmitted to Oldenburg for presentation to the Royal Society in the letter of 7 December 1675, Newton proposes the existence of "an aethereall Medium much of the same constitution with air, but far rarer, subtiler & more strongly Elastic." This medium is conceived, like atmosphere air, as being compounded of "the maine flegmatic body of ether [and] partly of other various aethereall Spirits. . . . For the Electric & Magnetic effluvia and gravitating principle seem to argue such variety." The final cause of both this ethereal medium and the matter which it informs is God. "Perhaps the whole frame of nature [may be nothing but aether condensed by a fermental principle] . . . after condensation wrought into various formes, at first by the immediate hand of the Creator, & ever since by the power of Nature, wch by vertue of the command Increase & Multiply, became a complete Imitator of the copies sett her by the Protoplast."

14. In the letter of January 1680/1 to Bishop Burnet, Newton discusses these verses. The latter concedes that, with specific reference to the relative size of the sun, moon, and earth versus their apparent size as viewed from the earth, and with specific reference to the notion of the "day" as cosmological unit, Moses "adapt[ed] a description of ye creation as handsomly as he could to ye sense & capacity of ye vulgar" rather than describing events as a natural philosopher might. Yet Newton insists that "the things signified by such figurative expressions are not Ideall or moral but true" (*Correspondence* 2:331, 333).

15. Sir Isaac Newton, *Opticks, or A Treatise of the Reflections, Refractions, Inflections, and Colours of Light*, ed. H. D. Roller, based on the 4th ed., 1730 (New York: Dover, 1952), 400.

16. Amos Funkenstein, *Theology and the Scientific Imagination from the Middle Ages to the Seventeenth Century* (Princeton, N.J.: Princeton University Press, 1986), 3–9, discusses science in the sixteenth and seventeenth centuries as constituting, in several senses, a "secular theology."

17. *The Works of Robert Boyle*, 3d ed., ed. Thomas Birch (London: T. and J. Rivington, 1772), 6:724–25.

18. *Paley's Natural Theology, with Illustrative Notes*, ed. Henry Brougham and Charles Bell (London: Knight, 1836), 3–4.

19. Nor is the reification of the clockwork universe the only such instance of metonymic logic of Newtonian science leading to reification. See Zenon W. Pylyshyn, "Metaphorical Imprecision and the 'Top-Down' Research Strategy," in *Metaphor and Thought*, ed. Andrew Ortony (Cambridge: Cambridge University Press, 1979), 420–36, esp 435. Pylyshyn identifies Newton as the scientist responsible for "the reification of geometry . . . accepting the axioms of Euclid as a literal description of physical space," an action that "profoundly affected the course of science" by proposing "a literal account of reality . . . that . . . enables scientists to see that certain further observations are possible and others are not." Speaking of "the physical universe" as understood by Newton and Leibniz, Funkenstein states that "it was an ideal clock—whether, as Newton thought, a clock that needed periodical rewinding or, as Leibniz insisted, a clock that runs perpetually with equal precision." As a specific result of the reification of the clockwork universe by Newton and Leibniz as well, "the mechanical philosophers of the seventeenth century came close to believing that, even if we can never hope to know all the facts about the universe, we know nonetheless enough of its dynamic principles to reconstruct its making in the way that God does" (*Theology*, 317, 323).

20. Blake's most powerful evocation of what happens when reified institutions invoke the "chartered" authority to speak for others is "London," where church and state use the authority vested in them by the Magna Carta (Great Charter) to speak for the chimney sweep and soldier, respectively; see chapter 5.

21. See Joseph Priestley, *The History and Present State of Electricity, with Original Experiments* (London: J. Dodsley, 1767), xiii; quoted in *Autobiography of Joseph Priestley*, ed. Jack Lindsay (Teaneck, N.J.: Fairleigh Dickinson University Press, 1971), 19. Hans Eichner, "The Rise of Modern Science and the Genesis of Romanticism," *PMLA* 97 (1982): 8–30, esp. 24, notes that a significant shortcoming of "the mechanical philosophy" was "the impossibility of accounting for the interaction of mind and matter." Benedict Spinoza, *Ethic*, trans. W. Hale White, rev. Amelia Hutchison Stirling (London: Oxford University Press, 1923), 22–23, argues in proposition 18 of that work that "*God is the immanent, and not the transitive* [i.e., transcendent] *cause of all things.*"

22. In Blake's three terms, especially "Spirit," there is a strong suggestion that he favors the *J*-account of the creation over the *P*-account, and more particularly, that he favors a gnostic reading of both accounts. For a fuller discussion of these proclivities, see chapter 4.

23. Richard S. Westfall discusses Newton's Biblical criticism of the 1670s, which was premised on the understanding "that a massive fraud, which began in the fourth and fifth centuries, had perverted the legacy of the early church," turning it away from the truth of a unitarian creed to trinitarian apostasy. See *Never At Rest: A Biography of Isaac Newton* (New York: Cambridge University Press, 1980), 312–24, esp. 313.

24. See Donald Ault, *Narrative Unbound: Re-Visioning William Blake's "The Four Zoas"* (Barrytown, N.Y.: Station Hill Press, 1990), 196, 214. Something like this perversity underlies the fact that in Night IV "Los consistently

has been performing Tharmas' directions *precisely in reverse order.*" So, too, "Night VI involves a counter-clockwise quest (backwards in time, thus repetitive)."

25. A number of commentators have identified "The Tyger" as an important and allusive locus of "natural or organic thoughts." For example, Rodney M. Baine, "Blake's 'Tyger': The Nature of the Beast," *Philological Quarterly* 46 (1967): 488–98, identifies Buffon's *Histoire Naturelle*, Goldsmith's *Animated Nature*, and Lavater's *Essays in Physiognomy* as influences on the poem's symbolism. To Baine's attributions of influence, less Lavater, Coleman O. Parsons, "Tygers before Blake," *Studies in English Literature, 1500–1900* 8 (1968): 573–92, adds Linnaeus's *Animal Kingdom* and Smellie's *Philosophy of Natural History.* William S. Doxey, "William Blake and William Herschel: The Poet, the Astronomer, and 'The Tyger,'" *Blake Studies* 2 (1969–70): 5–13, reads the poem against William Herschel's astronomical publications.

26. The linkage between the passage in "The Tyger" and the passage in *The Four Zoas* was first remarked by David V. Erdman, *Blake: Prophet against Empire*, 2d ed. (Princeton, N.J.: Princeton University Press, 1969), 194–95.

27. See Anne Kostelanetz Mellor, *Blake's Human Form Divine* (Berkeley and Los Angeles: University of California Press, 1974), 65. "By 1793, Blake had often associated stars with the oppressions of monarchy and with a Newtonian, mechanistic conception of the universe." Elaine Pagels, *The Gnostic Gospels* (New York: Random House, 1979), 48–69, discusses the battle waged between the early Church Fathers and their gnostic opponents over God's gender and the gender-based worldly authority deriving therefrom.

28. Abrams, in defining *metonymy*, observes, "typical attire can signify the male and female sexes: 'doublet and hose ought to show itself courageous to petticoat'" (Shakespeare, *As You Like It* 2.4.6 [66])." Urizen does not take part in this stand-down. He continues to exercise hegemonic male authority. Eighteen lines after the stars fled, "Urizen arose & leaning on his Spear explord his dens" (*4Z*, p. 67, l. 1). *Spear* itself may be viewed as a metonym, in the same sense that "a thousand guns" is a metonym for an armada of ships mounting that number of guns.

29. Ault, in commenting on *The Four Zoas* (p. 70, ll. 39–45), observes, "Urizen's Children perceive his words as landscape" (*Narrative Unbound*, 218). That is, by dint of metonymic logic they reason from material effect to verbal cause.

30. There are interesting affinities between the image of Urizen leaning on his spear and Blake's color print of Newton. Discussing the print, W. J. T. Mitchell, *Blake's Composite Art: A Study of the Illuminated Poetry* (Princeton, N.J.: Princeton University Press, 1978), 49, asks, "Is this a night scene, a subterranean realm, or an undersea world?" One possible answer is that it is a print of Newton exploring his dens, much as Urizen explores his. That Newton leans on a pair of dividers rather than a spear poses no extreme difficulty. The dividers, a geometrical tool, is Newton's weapon of choice. Then too, if one follows the logic of *Milton*, it is plausible to argue that Newton, like Blake's Satan, who is "Newton Pantocrator, weaving the Woof of Locke" (*M*, pl. 4, l. 11), and who has not "the Science of Wrath, but only of Pity," creates the material universe of his dens in his own divided image, one that sees "Wrath"

and "Pity," i.e., soul and body, corpuscle and immanent, immaterial principle, "Rent . . . asunder" (*M*, pl. 9, ll. 46–47). Without wrath, that is, Satan/Newton/Urizen's spear is a divided spear, or dividers.

31. John E. Grant, "The Art and Argument of 'The Tyger,'" *Texas Studies in Language and Literature* 2 (1960): 1–17.

32. William Blake, *Songs of Innocence and of Experience*, ed. Geoffrey Keynes (1794; rpt., New York: Oxford University Press, 1977), pl. 42.

33. *The Illuminated Blake*, ed. David V. Erdman (Garden City, N.Y.: Doubleday, 1974), 121.

34. Blake may also intend an oblique jab at Newton, whose *Observations on the Prophecies of Daniel, and the Apocalypse of St. John* (1727) sets forth an exegetical method that takes the prophecies to be enciphered history and reads them as historical narrative for the literal truth of the matter.

35. Daniel recounts a dream of "four great beasts," beginning with "This first [which] was like a lion" (Daniel 7:3–4).

CHAPTER 7. BLAKE AND THE IDEOLOGY OF THE NATURAL

This study, reprinted from *Eighteenth-Century Life*, n.s., 18, no. 1 (February 1994): 91–119, was completed under the auspices of an NEH Summer Seminar for College Teachers held at Harvard University during the summer of 1991. I am especially grateful to Leopold Damrosch Jr., the Seminar Director, for his conversation and comments, and to my colleagues in that seminar as well.

1. *CPP*, p. 670.

2. *De dignitate et augmentis scientiarum* (1623), in *The Works of Francis Bacon*, new ed., ed. James Spedding, Robert Leslie Ellis, and Douglas Denon Heath, 14 vols. (London: Longmans, 1870), 4:296. Subsequent references to Bacon are to this edition, unless otherwise noted, by volume and page. In *De augmentis* Bacon argues that there should be nothing sacred or secret in nature. Addressing James I, his dedicatee, Bacon argues that, concerning "the further disclosing of the secrets of nature. Neither ought a man make a scruple of entering and penetrating into these holes and corners."

See also John Locke, *An Essay Concerning Human Understanding*, ed. Peter H. Nidditch (Oxford: Clarendon Press, 1975), 48–103. Subsequent references to Locke are to this edition, by book, chapter, section, and page. In the *Essay* (1690; 1706), Locke argues throughout chapters 2–4 of book 1 that the mind is uninformed by any "innate principles."

See finally *Sir Isaac Newton's Mathematical Principles of Natural Philosophy and His System of the World*, trans. Andrew Motte, rev. Florian Cajori (1934, rpt. Berkeley and Los Angeles: University Of California Press, 1966), 399, 547. Newton's "Rules of Reasoning in Philosophy," which preface book 3 of the *Principia* (1687; 1729), propose a model of corpuscular matter with no interiority, no potential for immanent causation. "The extension, hardness, impenetrability, mobility, and inertia of the whole, result from the extension, hardness, impenetrability, mobility, and inertia of the parts," Newton argues. However, the "General Scholium," on which book 3 ends, suggests the arbitrariness of Newton's corpuscular model. There he allows that "we might add something concerning a most subtle spirit which pervades and lies hid in all gross bodies," but concludes, "we [are not] furnished with that sufficiency of experiments which is required to an accurate determination and demonstration of the laws by which this electric and elastic spirit operates."

3. As discussed by Robert Alter, *The Art of Biblical Narrative* (New York: Basic Books,1981), 143–45.

4. Leopold Damrosch Jr., *Symbol and Truth in Blake's Myth* (Princeton, N.J.: Princeton University Press, 1980), 40–41.

5. See Leslie Brisman, "'The Mysterious Tongue': Shelley and the Language of Christianity," *Texas Studies in Literature and Language* 23 (1981): 389–417, esp. 389. Brisman points out that the word *metaphor* itself is derived from the Greek *metapherein*, "to transfer." See also Jerrold E. Hogle, *Shelley's Process: Radical Transference and the Development of His Major Works* (New York: Oxford University Press, 1988), 230. Hogle characterizes "the distribution of transference" as "a continuous going-out to others beyond the present circle." To give Blake the last word on the importance of transference: "If it were not for the Poetic or Prophetic character. the Philosophic & Experimental would soon be at the ratio of all things & stand still. unable to do other than repeat the same dull round over again" (*CPP*, p. 3).

See also Monroe K. Beardsley, "The Metaphoric Twist" (1962), rpt. in *Philosophical Perspectives on Metaphor*, ed. Mark Johnson (Minneapolis: University of Minnesota Press, 1979), 105–21, esp. 116.

6. On Blake's language as ontologically constitutive, see Robert N. Essick, *William Blake and the Language of Adam* (Oxford: Clarendon Press, 1989), 224–36.

7. Hogle, *Shelley's Process*, 302.

8. See ibid. Hogle makes the same point about Shelley's treatment of death in *Adonais* (1821). There death's "core is apprehendable only in the 'dwelling place' that is its refiguration, and the dwelling is always in the process of reappearing in some other container or form of itself."

9. In *Jerusalem* Blake says of his onomathesis:

> (I call them by their English names: English, the rough basement.
> Los built the stubborn structure of the Language, acting against
> Albion's melancholy, who must else have been a Dumb despair).
> (*J*, pl. 36 [40], ll. 58–60)

See also Essick, *Blake*, 71–72.

10. Blake's Beulah draws on *The Pilgrim's Progress* (1678–84). See John Bunyan, *The Pilgrim's Progress*, ed. Louis L. Martz (1949; rpt., New York: Holt, Rinehart, 1966), 321. "More pilgrims are come to town," exclaims one of Beulah's residents. "And another would answer, saying, And so many went over the water, and were let in the gates to day."

11. See Plotinus, *The Enneads*, trans. Stephen McKenna, 4th ed., rev. B. S. Page (New York: Pantheon Books, 1969), 1.7 (p. 64), which adumbrates Blake's ideas.

12. See Proclus, *The Elements of Theology*, ed. and trans. E. R. Dodds (Oxford: Clarendon Press, 1933), 513. Blake's elaboration of "Poetic Genius" owes a good deal to propositions 5–11 in Proclus. An extreme statement of Blake's position is found in the letter of 2 October 1800 to Thomas Butts, where

the effect of "Genius" as both a creative and a humanizing principle is taken to its tropaically logical conclusion. Blake recounts a vision in which even "Cloud Meteor & Star / Are Men Seen Afar" (ll. 31–32).

13. Newton, *Mathematical Principles*, 544–45. See also Amos Funkenstein, *Theology and the Scientific Imagination from the Middle Ages to the Seventeenth Century* (Princeton, N.J.: Princeton University Press, 1986), 97. "Like his medieval predecessors, he [i.e., Newton] was concerned not to forget God's transcendence over his immanence."

14. As Bacon writes in *De augmentis*, "For like as a man's disposition is never well known or proved till he be crossed, nor Proteus ever changed shapes till he was *straitened and held fast*, so nature exhibits herself more clearly under the trials and vexations of art [mechanical devices, i.e., torture] than when left to herself" (4:298).

15. See chapter 6.

16. Umberto Eco, *A Theory of Semiotics* (Bloomington: Indiana University Press, 1976), 281; and see Liselotte Gumpel, *Metaphor Re-examined: A Non-Aristotelian Perspective* (Bloomington: Indiana University Press, 1984), 134; Roman Jakobson, "Concluding Statement," in *Style in Language*, ed. Thomas A. Sebeok (Cambridge, Mass.: MIT Press, 1960), 375, and "Two Aspects of Language and Two Aspects of Aphasic Disturbances," in *Selected Writings* (The Hague: Mouton, 1971), 255–56; *John Milton: Complete Poems and Major Prose*, ed. Merritt Y. Hughes (New York: Odyssey, 1957); M. H. Abrams, *A Glossary of Literary Terms*, 5th ed. (New York: Holt, Rinehart, and Winston, 1988), 66–67; and Paul de Man, *Allegories of Reading: Figural Language in Rousseau, Nietzsche, Rilke, and Proust* (New Haven, Conn.: Yale University Press, 1979), 71.

Resistance to recognizing the difference between metonymy and synecdoche is the result of failing to recognize the operation of anything like an ideology of the natural. Roman Jakobson, an apostle of the distinction between "the metaphoric style of romantic poetry" and "the metonymic style of realistic prose," distinguishes between metaphor and metonymy by contrasting the former, which renders "whole for whole," with the latter, which renders "part for whole." Jakobson sees metonymy where he should see synecdoche; however, the distinction is hardly academic. The apparently "natural" power relations often (re)marked by synecdoche—for example, the power relations of the apostolic succession, rejected by Milton in *Lycidas* (1637) with a fleeting reference to "blind mouths" (l. 119)—are ordained by metonymy. Just as metonyms such as " 'the crown' or 'the scepter' can stand for a king," according to Abrams, and can be seen as effects within a causal chain that begins with God's decision to have the king function as his vice gerent, the "blind mouths" can be seen, by one who does not regard them as blind, as the final effect of a causal chain that begins with God's decision to send his Son to redeem humankind and continues through the Son's decision to gather about himself apostles dedicated to spreading the Son's word.

One of the most interesting attempts to deflect critical focus from metonymy's self-concealing ideological entailments is Paul de Man's. He attempts to elide metaphor and metonymy, and to blame "the complementary and totalizing power of metaphor"—"the seduction of metaphor" as he calls it—on the failed synthesis of "intra- and extra-textual movements." The failure, according to de Man, arises out of "the relationship between the literal and the figural senses of a metaphor [which] is always, in this sense, metonymic."

17. Essick, *Blake*, 224.

18. Theories of tropaic decline were fairly common by the middle of the eighteenth century. See, e.g., William Warburton, *Divine Legation of Moses Demonstrated* (1738–41), Giambattista Vico, *The New Science*, 3d ed. (1744); and Jean-Jacques Rousseau, *Essay on the Origin of Languages* (ca. 1755). See also Percy Bysshe Shelley, *A Defence of Poetry* (1821), in *Shelley's Poetry and Prose: Authoritative Texts, Criticism*, ed. Donald H. Reiman and Sharon B. Powers (New York: Norton, 1977), 482. Shelley, Blake's poetic near-contemporary, articulates a theory of tropaic decline from the "vitally metaphorical" language of transferentiality to metonymic "signs for portions and classes of thoughts instead of integral thoughts."

19. See Essick, *Blake*, 15, for a parallel synopsis of the "contraction of the word into words."

20. See Ronald Schleifer, *Rhetoric and Death: The Language of Modernism and Postmodern Discourse Theory* (Urbana: University of Illinois Press, 1990), 4, 65. Schleifer takes "metonymy (and the 'surface' of discourse) to stand more generally, synecdochically, for the materiality of language. All discourse and meaning must take up material signifiers to articulate and communicate itself, and such materiality, like death, is both a 'part' of language and the 'other' of language."

21. See Glen E. Brewster, "Blake and the Metaphor of Marriage," *Nineteenth-Century Contexts* 16 (1992): 65–89, esp. 81–83. Speaking of the changes Blake rings on Matthew 22:30 ("for in the resurrection they neither marry, nor are given in marriage, but are as the angels of God in heaven") in *Jerusalem*, pl. 30, l. 15 ("In Eternity they neither marry nor are given in marriage"), Brewster argues that Blake "moves toward a new formulation" in which "true unification comes about not through a marriage of the sexes, nor . . . as the marriage of the Lamb and His Bride. Instead, we are given a vision of a Family of Friends." Brewster does admit that friendship cannot exist without the occurrence of certain prior consummations. For example, "Britannia (the unified form of Jerusalem and Vata)" must enter "Albions bosom rejoicing" (*J*, pl. 95, l. 22). In this act, the relationship between Albion and his erstwhile garment is transformed, much as Christ's relationship to his grave clothes is transformed after his resurrection. What formerly had been all around Christ is now within he who has become all in all.

22. Michael Ferber, *The Social Vision of William Blake* (Princeton, N.J.: Princeton University Press, 1985), 8, 10–11; also Abrams, *Glossary*, 66. The reference to "a part into the whole" suggests that Ferber views the operation of ideology as figural, and that he draws no sharp distinction between the figures of synecdoche and metonymy. Elsewhere, in his discussion of how ideological argument operates, Ferber observes, "The name 'Milton' might mean a safe religious writer or a republican and a regicide, according to what associations a context triggers." As Abrams observes, " 'Milton' can signify the writings of Milton," and in that signifying capacity it operates as a metonym.

23. Michael Ryan, "The Marxism-Deconstruction Debate in Literary Theory," *New Orleans Review* 11 (1984): 29–35, esp. 33.

24. See Mary Wollstonecraft, *A Vindication of the Rights of Woman*, 2d ed., ed. Carol H. Poston (New York: Norton, 1988), 28.

25. See Abrams, *Glossary*, 66; Diane Long Hoeveler, *Romantic Androgyny: The Women Within* (University Park: Pennsylvania State University Press, 1990), 207. Of the Romantic topos of the veiled (female) muse, Hoeveler observes, "The veil conceals at the same time it reveals, however; her sexual power is subsumed by the male and in its place he leaves drapery, the vestiges of her fearfulness. The veiled woman stands, then, as then ultimate embodiment of the woman as fetishistic commodity."

26. See Newton, *Mathematical Principles*, p. 398. Newton's two rules are "*We are to admit no more causes of natural things than such as are both true and sufficient to explain their appearances,*" and "*Therefore to the same natural effects we must, as far as possible, assign the same causes.*" I make the Mosaic connection at great length in my "Saving the Phenomenon or Saving the Hexameron? Mosaic Self-Presentation in Newtonian Optics," *The Eighteenth Century: Theory and Interpretation* (1991): 139–65.

27. See Paul de Man, "The Rhetoric of Temporality," in *Interpretation: Theory and Practice*, ed. Charles S. Singleton (Baltimore: Johns Hopkins University Press, 1969), 191. De Man has shown that "around the same time that the tension between symbol and allegory finds expression in the works and theoretical speculations of the early romantics, the problem of irony receives more and more self-conscious attention." See also Angus Fletcher, *Allegory: The Theory of a Symbolic Mode* (1964; rpt., Ithaca, N.Y.: Cornell University Press, 1982), 73–84. Although Fletcher condemns the uncritical assumption "that allegory is metaphorical in a 'normal' way," he does go to some length to show both the way that allegory was metaphorical for classical rhetoricians and the way in which allegory is metaphorical by current criteria, although he insists that there are insuperable difficulties in "the equation of allegory and metaphor."

28. Manlius Severinus Boethius, *The Consolation of Philosophy*, trans. W. V. Cooper, rev. J. J. Buchanan (New York: Ungar, 1957), 1–3.

29. Charles Taylor, *Sources of the Self: The Making of the Modern Identity* (Cambridge, Mass.: Harvard University Press 1989), 222.

30. See Stephen Toulmin, *The Return to Cosmology: Postmodern Science and the Theology of Nature* (Berkeley and Los Angeles: University of California Press, 1982), 232. "Many of those writers who were most active in the new scientific movements of the seventeenth and eighteenth centuries were also devout Protestants, and they saw their work for science as contributing equally to 'true religion.' . . . In their view, God's Hand had written the book of Nature as surely as it had the Book of Scripture; and you could 'read God's mind' in the one as surely as in the other."

31. See Taylor, *Sources of the Self*, 244; *The Works of Robert Boyle*, ed. Thomas Birch, 6 vols. (London, 1772), 6:724–25. Boyle refers to "the world being, as it were, a great piece of clockwork"; thus "the naturalist, as such, is but a mechanician."

32. See Carolyn Merchant, *The Death of Nature: Women, Ecology, and the Scientific Revolution* (San Francisco: Harper and Row, 1983), 164–90, for a discussion of Bacon's misogyny as the motivation for his scientific enterprise.

33. Francis Bacon quoted in Moody C. Prior, "Bacon's Man of Science," in *The Rise of Science in Relation to Society*, ed. Leonard C. Marsak (New York: Macmillan, 1964), 45.

34. See Sir Isaac Newton, *Optick, or A Treatise on the Reflections, Refractions, Inflections, and Colours of Light*, ed. Duane H. D. Roller (New York: Dover, 1952), 400. Newton has the following to say in the 31st query about corpuscles—little bodies that comprise the feminized "frame of Nature": "While the particles continue entire, they may compose bodies in one and the same nature and texture in all ages; but should they wear away, or break in pieces, the nature of all things depending on them would be changed. Water and earth, composed of old worn particles and fragments of particles, would not be of the same nature and texture now, with water and earth composed of entire particles in the beginning."

35. David Hume, *Dialogues Concerning Natural Religion and the Posthumous Essays on the Immortality of the Soul and Suicide*, ed. Richard H. Popkin (Indianapolis: Liberty Classics, 1980), 79, 88; Leopold Damrosch Jr., *Fictions of Reality in the Age of Hume and Johnson* (Madison: University of Wisconsin Press, 1989), 130–43.

36. Ibid., 5, 178.

37. That Blake does not use the classical nomenclature "to name" these strategies should not be surprising, given his strictures, in *Milton* and elsewhere, against "the Stolen and Perverted Writings of Homer & Ovid: of Plato & Cicero. which all Men ought to contemn: [and which] are set up by artifice against the Sublime of the Bible" (*M*, pl. 1). This reference to the Bible suggests Blake's acquaintance with Robert Lowth's *Lectures on the Sacred Poetry of the Hebrews* (1787). For a fuller discussion of this connection, see Morton Paley, *Energy and the Imagination: The Development of Blake's Thought* (Oxford: Clarendon Press, 1970), 20–21, 46–47.

38. Morris Eaves, *William Blake's Theory of Art* (Princeton, N.J.: Princeton University Press, 1982), 20–22.

39. "Of or pertaining to the shore; existing, taking place upon, or adjacent to the shore," (*OED*, 2d ed., 8:1145). According to the *OED*, *Littoral* was in the English word hoard by 1656. A 1657 entry actually uses the spelling that Blake uses.

40. Blake would appear not to distinguish between the immediate and the theodical. As he states in "A Vision of the Last Judgment" (1810), "whenever any Individual Rejects Error & Embraces Truth a Last Judgment passes upon that Individual" (p. 84).

41. See n. 33 above.

42. John Wilmot, Earl of Rochester, in "Upon Nothing" (1680), his satiric rejoinder to Abraham Cowley's "Hymn to Light" (1656), characterizes Nothing in terms similar to those used by Blake. To take but one example, the womb imagery:

> But turn coat time assists the foe in vain,
> And, bribed by Time, assists thy short-lived reign.
> And lo thy hungry womb drives back thy slaves again. (19–21)

Add to this similarity the fact that Cowley was a Baconiast and an apologist for the Royal Society, the history of which is prefaced by his ode (1662), which makes Bacon out to be a type of Moses, the similarities become more intriguing still. It is not impossible that Rochester's poem, in print since 1680 and in the reliable Tonson edition since 1713, may have informed the imaging of the cosmogony that is recounted in *The Book of Urizen*.

43. F. B. Curtis, "Blake and the 'Moment of Time': An Eighteenth-Century Controversy in Mathematics," *Philological Quarterly* 51 (1972): 460–70.

44. See Thomas R. Frosch, *The Awakening of Albion: The Renovation of the Body in the Poetry of William Blake* (Ithaca, N.Y.: Cornell University Press, 1974), 87–135. Frosch's is the best extended discussion of how renovation operates in Blake's prophetic works. His thesis, worth restating here, is "that the redemptive potentiality exists within nature, specifically in the fallen artist and in the fallen senses" (87).

45. Locke, *Essay*, 4.2.11 [535]. See also Taylor, *Sources of the Self*, 167.

46. Feet with strongly phallic overtones, it should be noted: to this day the slang term in Irish English for *penis* is *footie*, a fact not lost on later poets such as Theodore Roethke. The refrain to the second section of "Praise to the End!," the title poem of his 1951 collection, is "What footie does is final."

47. Frances Yates, *Giordano Bruno and the Hermetic Tradition* (1964; rpt., New York: Vintage Books, 1969), 455.

48. See Schleifer, *Rhetoric and Death*, 196. Quoting Eve Tavor Bannet, Schleifer argues that "what such speech is 'full' of . . . is not meaning, but the activity of signification; it is 'full' of 'the fact that it is a word which has been uttered by the subject. . . .' 'But . . . in Lacan this experience of full speech has few implications for interpersonal relations outside the analytic situation, for Lacan believes that such disalienating encounters are possible only between an analyst and analysand.'"

Blake seems to agree in the matter of meaning versus signification. In the concluding visionary conversation of *Jerusalem*, signification is the only game in town and is, in fact, the very basis of creating the dialectic of self and other that is a precondition of transferentiality:

> every Word & Every Character
> Was Human according to the Expansion or Contraction, the
> Translucence or
> Opakeness of Nervous fibres. (*J*, pl. 98, ll. 35–37)

But transferentiality is more universalizable than transference. The Four Zoas, who contain within themselves the immanent potential for any and all encounters,

> walked
> To & fro in Eternity as One Man reflecting each in each &
> clearly seen
> And seeing: according to fitness & order. (*J*, pl. 98, ll. 38–40)

49. Damrosch, *Symbol and Truth*, 182.

50. Abrams, *Glossary*, 66.

51. Eco, *Theory of Semiotics*, 281.

52. See Proclus, *Elements*, 214. Glossing propositions 26–27 of *Elements of Theology*, Proclus's editor, E. R. Dodds, observes, "The law of emanation is . . . qualified in Neoplatonism by a further law, viz. that in giving rise to the effect the cause remains undiminished and unaltered. This doctrine is older than Plotinus."

53. John Everard, *The Pymander of Hermes*, ed. W. Wynn Westcott (London: Theosophical Publishing Society, 1894), 2:14 (p. 23). For discussions of the place of gnosticism in Blake's thought see Damrosch, *Symbol and Truth*, passim; Paley, *Energy and Imagination*, 66–67; and chapter 4 of the present volume.

54. See n. 24 above.

55. See n. 25 above.

56. Tilottama Rajan, *The Supplement of Reading: Figures of Understanding in Romantic Theory and Practice* (Ithaca, N.Y.: Cornell University Press, 1990), 301.

CHAPTER 8. THE DIN OF THE CITY

Reprinted from *ELH: English Literary History* 64 (1997): 99–130.

1. *J*, pl. 12, ll. 38–41, pl. 16, ll. 3–13. A similar passage from the first book of *Milton* is the one portraying "Golgonooza the spiritual Four-fold London eternal / In immense labours & sorrows, ever building, ever falling" (*M*, pl. 6, ll. 1–35, esp. 1–2).

As regards the first of the two excerpts from *Jerusalem* quoted in the text, see E. P. Thompson, *Witness against the Beast: William Blake and the Moral Law* (New York: New Press, 1993), 148. Citing J. Bellamy's *Jesus Christ the Only God* (1792), a Swedenborgian tract, Thompson observes, "Swedenborg affirmed that 'human nature cannot be transmuted into the Divine Essence, neither commixed therewith.'' Therefore a distinction must be maintained in Christ's genesis between the 'human nature of the mother' and the Divine Essence from the divine influx, or from the Father (i.e., the male principle which infused his soul). What Mary supplied was 'a covering, called the maternal human, or a body like our own, so that the divine human (which was eternal and infinite) dwells in the maternal human, which was finite.'"

2. See Dorothy Marshall, *Dr. Johnson's London* (New York: Wiley, 1968), 23–24; George Rude, *Hanoverian London, 1714–1808* (Berkeley and Los Angeles: University of California Press, 1971), 4–5.

3. See David V. Erdman, *Blake: Prophet against Empire*, rev. ed. (Garden City, N.Y.: Anchor Books, 1969), 474. Of Paddington, Erdman observes that "as a village of poverty-stricken Irish laborers, Paddington was sufficiently mournful in any case." He cites Mary Dorothy George's *London Life in the 18th Century* (1935) to the effect that "in 1812 Paddington 'had an evil reputation.' Its 'extensive waste . . . was occupied by the most wretched huts, filled with squatters of the lowest of the community.'"

4. *The Letters of William and Dorothy Wordsworth: The Early Years, 1787-1805*, 2d ed., ed. Ernest de Selincourt, rev. Chester L. Shaver (Oxford: Clarendon Press, 1967), 312.

5. Rude, *Hanoverian London*, 5-19.

6. See "A Description of a City Shower," in *The Poems of Jonathan Swift*, 3 vols., ed. Harold Williams (Oxford: Clarendon Press, 1937), vol. 1, ll. 53-63:

> Now from all Parts the swelling Kennels flow,
> And bear their Trophies with them as they go:
> Filth of all Hues and Odours seems to tell
> What Street they sail'd from, by their Sight and Smell.
> They, as each Torrent drives, with rapid Force
> From *Smithfield*, or *St. Pulchre's* shape their course,
> And in one huge confluent join at *Snow-Hill* Ridge,
> Fall from the Conduit prone to *Holborne-Bridge*.
> Sweepings from Butchers Stalls, Dung, Guts, and Blood,
> Drown'd Puppies, stinking Sprats, all drench'd in Mud,
> Dead Cats, and Turnip-Tops come tumbling down the Flood.

7. Erdman, *Prophet against Empire*, 7-8, 396-97. Blake supposedly witnessed the Gordon Riots first hand. Erdman also notes that in 1803 Blake and his wife took lodgings in South Molton Street: "The Blakes' new residence was at 'Calvarys foot Where the Victims were preparing to sacrifice their Cherubim,' because just outside their door, 'between South Molton Street & Stratford Place,' ran Tyburn Road or Oxford Street leading to 'Tyburns fatal tree,' the ancient gallows, and leading to the reviewing ground where 'Satans Druid sons' were taught to offer 'Human Victims' on Albion's rocky tomb."

8. See Nelson Hilton, *Literal Imagination: Blake's Vision of Words* (Berkeley and Los Angeles: University of California Press, 1984); David Fuller, *Blake's Heroic Argument* (New York: Croom Helm, 1988), 287; Erdman, *Prophet against Empire*, 403-12, 476-77; Morton D. Paley, *The Continuing City: William Blake's Jerusalem* (Oxford: Clarendon Press, 1983), 272; and S. Foster Damon, *A Blake Dictionary* (Providence, R.I.: Brown University Press, 1965), 107, 260. Fuller wrongly castigates Hilton for his attempt "to show that puns and other forms of verbal play are common in Blake's poetry." Having excepted instances of broad farce, such as *An Island in the Moon*, and "the naming of some of the figures of his myth," Fuller states that "Blake's impulse is to resist this potential rather than to exploit it. It is in his fallen state that Los utters 'ambiguous words blasphemous' (*FZ*, 53.26): the inspired Los demands 'explicit words' (*J*, 17.60)."

Fuller's first mistake is to equate the ambiguous with the polysemous. In fact, if one reconstructs the context out of which Fuller wrenches his first quote, it becomes apparent that ambiguity is a good deal closer to indefiniteness than to polysemousness. Los speaks during the course of "the binding of Urizen," an operation in which Los, in effect, becomes Urizen and appropriates his language.

> The Prophet of Eternity beat on his iron links & links of brass
> And as he beat round the hurtling Demon. terrified at the Shapes

> Enslavd humanity put on he became what he beheld
> Raging against Tharmas his God & uttering
> Ambiguous words blasphemous filld with envy firm resolvd
> On hate Eternal. (*FZ*, p. 53, ll. 22–27)

Fuller's second mistake is to miss the etymological pun in *explicit*. *Explicitus*, the Latin root, is a variant on *explicatus*, unfolded. The passage from which Fuller wrenches his second quote begins with Los instructing his specter in ways that that specter, like Fuller, understands imperfectly, to "Go . . . to Skofield: ask him if he is Bath or if he is Canterbury" (*J*, pl. 17, l. 59). That is, Los wishes to know if Skofield, who in life was John Schofield, one of the dragoons who deposed against Blake for making treasonous antiwar statements, has come to his senses and become one of the party of Richard Warner, both a poet and the minister of Bath's Saint James's parish, who in 1804 published a sermon entitled *War Inconsistent with Christianity*, and who in 1808 published *A Letter to the People of England: On Petitioning the Throne for the Restoration of Peace*. If Skofield is not of Bath's party, he must still be of Canterbury's, Canterbury of course being the seat of the archbishop of England and thus the seat of the established religion that sanctions the war.

Los will have his answer not so much by means of *what* Skofield says as by means of *how* he says it. If Skofield is "dubious"—that is, if, like Los struggling with his specter, Skofield utters "Ambiguous words blasphemous"—then it will be clear that Skofield is Canterbury. If, on the other hand, Skofield speaks "explicit words" (*J*, pl. 17, l. 60)—that is, if he truly exfoliates what is in his heart and soul—then it will be clear that Skofield is Bath. But Los's question presupposes the answer "Canterbury," because the malady at this point in *Jerusalem* is that individuals feel as though they lack the heart or soul to exfoliate. Blake's scholium on Los's instructions to his specter confirms this lack.

> From every-one of the Four Regions of Human Majesty,
> There is an Outside spread Without, & an Outside spread Within
> Beyond the Outline of Identity both ways, which meet in One:
> An orbed Void of doubt, despair, hunger, & thirst & sorrow.
> (*J*, pl. 18, ll. 1–4)

The situation is markedly different at the end of *Jerusalem*, where the Four Zoas, engaged in conversation in "Visionary forms dramatic, which bright / Redounded from their Tongues in thunderous majesty," walk "To & fro in Eternity as One Man reflecting each in each & clearly seen / And seeing: according to fitness & order" (pl. 98, ll. 28–29, 39–40).

The extent of the deep-seated and irrepressible punning in *Jerusalem* may be inferred from Paley's identification of Gwendolen's anatomy "from Mam-Tor to Dovedale" (pl. 82, l. 45) as that part extending "from breasts to vagina." Leaving aside for a moment the puns latent in actual geographic characteristics of Mam-Tor, "part of a double peak in Derbyshire," and "nearby Dovedale . . . a narrow limestone valley," as Damon identifies these, there are linguistic puns—albeit found linguistic puns—to conjure with as well. *Mam-* is the root syllable of the Latin word for breast, and *tor* is a British word for a hill. From Blake's perspective, Gwendolen's unquestioning etymological mingling of Latin and native British speech to speak this name is an index of her fallenness. Dovedale is a name that looks back to the story of the Flood, where the dove is gendered exclusively female (Genesis 8:9-11), as well as back to the Song of Solomon, where the female beloved is described as having "doves' eyes within thy locks" (4:1). A "dove-dale," then, is the valley of the female both geographically and with reference to prior biblical genderings.

9. Shelley did, too. See *Prometheus Unbound*, 4.129-34, 415-17, in *Shelley's Poetry and Prose: Authoritative Texts, Criticism*, ed. Donald H. Reiman and Sharon B. Powers (New York: Norton, 1977). For example, in the gigantic choral ode on which Shelley's visionary drama concludes, a "Chorus of Spirits and Hours" enjoin all to

> weave the web of the mystic measure;
> From the depths of the sky and the ends of the Earth
> Come swift Spirits of might and of pleasure,
> Fill the dance and the music of mirth
> As the waves of a thousand streams rush by
> To an Ocean of splendour and harmony.

As the Earth herself, observes,

> Language is a perpetual Orphic song
> Which rules with Daedal harmony a throng
> Of thoughts and forms, which else senseless and shapeless were.

10. Erdman, *Prophet against Empire*, 479-80, 482, discusses these associations in relation to other passages in Jerusalem.

11. See John Mee, *Dangerous Enthusiasm: William Blake and the Culture of Radicalism in the 1790s* (Oxford: Clarendon Press, 1992), 11; and Thompson, *Witness against the Beast*, 222. As Mee observes, "At the root of Blake's attitude to the Bible lies a hostility to the very notion of the pure text, the text which gains authority from its claim to be sacred, invariable, and original."

The *caudex-codex* association has its parallel in the Muggletonian tradition: "the Tree was taken to stand for Knowledge of Good and Evil: that is, the Moral Law of tablets and commandments as opposed to the gospel of forgiveness of sins, moralism as opposed to love, or, as Muggleton had it in his onslaught against George Fox, the Reason of Pilate which 'delivered up the Just One to be crucified by reasonable men.'"

12. I make a similar argument about "London" in chapter 5.

13. Ball bearings are cast in just this manner.

14. The globule of "living fluids" reappears in *Milton* as a palimpsest or cipher connecting the visionary productions of time to eternity:

> For every Space larger than a red Globule of Mans blood.
> Is visionary; and is created by the Hammer of Los
> And every space smaller than a globule of Mans blood. opens
> Into Eternity of which this vegetable Earth is but a shadow.
>   (*M*, pl. 29 [31], ll. 19-22)

15. See Leopold Damrosch Jr., *Symbol and Truth in Blake's Myth* (Princeton, N.J.: Princeton University Press, 1980), 321. Speaking of a slightly

different sort of fabrication—that of Golgonooza, which takes place immediately prior to the Lambeth passage cited above—Damrosch notes that there are limits attaching to any sort of fabrication in the fallen world of time, space, and matter. "Golgonooza represents the best that can be done with physical materials—with material materials—but in using them at all it confesses its distance from Eden."

16. See Erdman, *Prophet against Empire*, 218, 424–26; David G. Riede, *Oracles and Hierophants: Constructions of Romantic Authority* (Ithaca, N.Y.: Cornell University Press, 1991), 38, 80; Stewart Crehan, *Blake in Context* (Atlantic Highlands, N.J.: Humanities Press, 1984), 172, 181; and Paul Mann, "Apocalypse and Recuperation: Blake and the Maw of Commerce," *ELH: English Literary History* 52, no. 1 (1985): 1–32, esp. 9. The identities of Rintrah and Palamabron amd their historical roles, according to Erdman, remain constant from the time of *Europe* (1794) to that of *Milton*. Although Erdman has no comment on their role in *Jerusalem*, the identities and roles of Rintrah and Palamabron seem unchanged there as well.

Riede observes of Blake that "up to the mid-1790s, his work was very clearly written within the context of fervid political debate. His sources of 'inspiration' were not so much from eternity as from the daily press." Riede, however, takes Crehan's point that, "by the time of the late prophecies Blake was no longer speaking so much from the revolutionary perspective of the artisan class as from the loftier perspective of the exalted artist." Mann suggests implicitly that Blake's movement away from that "revolutionary perspective" has to do with his "main error"—assuming "that his ability to produce his work in entirely distinctive material forms would grant him unmediated access to his desired audience; as it turned out, to liberate oneself from the social machinery of production was to liberate oneself from the audience which was also its production (and its producer)".

17. See Erdman, *Prophet against Empire*, 344–46. Discussing Night Nine of *The Four Zoas* (1796–1807? [pp. 817–18]), Erdman connects it, among other things, to a "food crisis" that occurred in 1800, in an England subject to harsh political repression, and at the same time that the Second Coalition's war against Napoleon was faring badly. "All England was astir, coupling demands for bread with a cry for peace. In June there had been a 'serious riot' when army officers were stoned out of a Nottingham theatre for trying to make the audience sing 'God Save the King.'" Erdman notes further that "In several communities gunfire between people and dragoons brought casualties."

Then there is the matter of the Corn Laws, import tariffs imposed by the government to make sure that relatively plentiful supplies of foreign grain did not ruin English grain farmers by driving down the price of such grain as a spate of poor harvests did yield. Within the historical frame of *Jerusalem*, England amended the Corn Law, thereby raising the tariff in 1815, the very year of its greatest land victory to date at Waterloo. It is no wonder that Blake connects "the Cornfield" to "The Soldiers fife."

18. My argument here is that Blake's visionary project turns the restoration of the alienated labor of the individual to that individual, irrespective of whether that labor takes articulate form as visual sign or verbal language. Both share with some differences, Blake's focus of "form" and "line." See Minna Doskow, "The Humanized Universe of Blake and Marx," in *William Blake and the*

Moderns, ed. Robert J. Bertholf and Annette S. Levitt (Albany: State University of New York Press, 1982), 225–40, esp. 225; Morris Eaves, *The Counter-Arts Conspiracy: Art and Industry in the Age of Blake* (Ithaca, N.Y.: Cornell University Press, 1992), 153–272, esp. 165, 170; Olivia Smith, *The Politics of Language, 1791–1819* (Oxford: Clarendon Press, 1984), 1–34, esp. 2, 30; and Michael Ferber, *The Social Vision of William Blake* (Princeton, N.J.: Princeton University Press, 1985), 202–11, esp. 208–9.

The dilemma of the human subject for Blake, and the relation between his understanding of this dilemma and Marx's understanding, has been admirably treated by Doskow. As she notes, "Both William Blake and Karl Marx address themselves to the central philosophical problem of their times, the relation of human subjectivity to the external world." That relationship is problematic if one conceives the external world as nothing more or less than the sum of its materiality. Eschewing "the mechanistic world view," Blake and Marx propose "a humanistic alternative. . . . They propose a human definition of man and his world, for both believe that the world has no meaning isolated from man, and it is only man's work upon the world which gives it shape, substance, and meaning."

Making a start out of Blake's *Public Address* (1809–10), Eaves identifies Blake's critique of the arts "industry" as arising out of a critique of the division and alienation of labor under conditions of intermeasurability. Blake's is a "contemptuous treatment of mindless physical labor. Though fundamental, the opposition is not absolute. Physical labor can be better or worse—as in the contrast between the journeyman's bungling and the master's touch—as it is more or less informed by thought. . . . The mental may dignify the physical; the reverse seems inconceivable." Blake's vision of a remedy in the form of a nascent Christian middle class, "As it criticizes the exploitive class hierarchy built around the 'Arts of Trading Combination' (*PA*, E 577) . . . implicitly promises a classless society upon the model of integrated labor."

Smith documents how, from the 1750s onward, the study of language "derived from the presupposition that language revealed the mind. To speak the vulgar language demonstrated that one belonged to the vulgar class; that is, that one was morally and intellectually unfit to participate in the culture." Acting on this presupposition, those in power intentionally restricted and mystified the study of language as they marginalized the lower classes by depriving them of access to a grammar school education. Ultimately, as Smith notes, "Between 1793 and 1818 (and later as well), Parliament dismissively refused to admit petitions because of the language in which they were written. . . . political arguments were contained and then dismissed in the context of ideas about language."

As Ferber notes, "Blake's vision of restored 'natural' speech" is most fully articulated in *Jerusalem*. "We may see at work in *Jerusalem*, finally, a dramatization of linguistic *apocatastasis*, a rescuing of words from Satan's labyrinth, even a conversion of Satanic words into verbal weapons against him."

19. Threatened to, but did not: the lower classes, although admittedly imperfectly self-taught, read and imbibed values from such diverse texts as Volney's *Ruins of Empire* (1791; 1822) and *The Law of Nature* (1793; 1822), on the one hand, and Shelley's *Queen Mab* (1813) and *The Revolt of Islam* (1818), on the other. See Mee, *Dangerous Enthusiasm*, 121; Thompson, *Witness against*

the Beast, 199–203, 207–8, 211–15; Adrian Desmond, "Artisan Resistance and Evolution in Britain, 1819–1848," *Osiris*, n.s., 3 (1987): 77–110; Michael Scrivener, "Shelley and Radical Artisan Poetry," *Keats-Shelley Journal* 42 (1993): 22–36; and Mann, "Apocalypse and Recuperation," 5–6, 9.

Despite the attempts at the linguistic and political marginalization of the lower classes from which the artisans came, then, those artisans cultivated the very life of the mind that gave them an intellectual basis for resistance. Mee observes that "Blake's mythography shares . . . the radical impulses of those speculators like Erasmus Darwin and C. F. Volney (and, indeed, the earlier work of John Toland) whose syncretism was part of an attempt to break up the Christian hegemony in the 1790s." And Thompson explicitly connects Blake's *The Marriage of Heaven and Hell* (1790–93) to "Volney's *Ruins*[, which] belonged decisively, not to an academic, but to a revolutionary tradition: he pressed always his arguments to conclusions both republican and hostile to state religion."

Although recourse to texts in common such as Darwin and Volney helped the artisans in their struggle against marginalization, there was no such recourse to Blake's texts, and that absence of recourse is problematic. "The question of audience is," according to Mann, "the most egregiously underasked question in Blake studies. There are, to be sure, continual references to a reader whose faculties are roused to visionary activity by Blake's subversive narrative strategies, to a reader who responds to Blake's self-presentation with love and friendship, and so on." As Mann insightfully observes, however, Blake ironically and unintentionally alienated the very audience he strove to reach:

20. See my "The Problem of Originality and Blake's *Poetical Sketches*," *ELH: English Literary History* 52 (1985): 673–705.

21. Compare the conclusion of *There Is No Natural Religion [b]* (1788): "Therefore God becomes as we are, that we may be as he is" (*CPP*, p. 3).

22. Riede, *Oracles and Hierophants*, 50, captures finely the tendency of even inspired prophecy to become dogma: "Though Paul is seen as an ally for all who would subvert the established order, for Blake the Church Paul represents the hardening of Paul's discourse into dogmatic authority by passive, obedient readers who take the letter as law."

23. To "be as gods" would require "tak[ing] also of the tree of life, and eat[ing], and liv[ing] for ever" (3:22).

24. Robert F. Gleckner, *The Piper and the Bard* (Detroit: Wayne State University Press, 1959), 232–33, notes the connections between the introduction to *Experience* and Genesis 3:8–9.

25. See chapter 5.

26. Thompson, *Witness against the Beast*, 130–31 notes that his "annotations show a distinct modification in Blake's response to Swedenborg. His annotations to *Heaven and Hell* (1784) are desultory and languid. His annotations to *Divine Love* (1788) suggest a thorough-going and sympathetic scrutiny, with Swedenborg's doctrines set against Blake's own already developed and strongly formed system. His annotations to *Divine Providence* (1790) suggest ridicule or indignant rejection."

27. See Paley, *Continuing City*, 237, 306; Jerome J. McGann, *A Critique of Modern Textual Criticism* (Chicago: University of Chicago Press, 1983), 48;

and Thompson, *Witness against the Beast*, 5–6. Paley notes that "of all the major figures of the long poems of the Romantic period, Los is the only one who can call himself a 'labourer.' His incessant work . . . is symbolic, but it is also real metalwork, meticulously described." As with the figure, so with the theme: "The active labour of Los with his tools at his furnaces is one of the great themes of *Jerusalem*." McGann argues that Blake's conception of language-as-labor implies a critique of the "literary institution," most especially its means of production, consumption, and valorization.

Thompson deploys a series of dichotomies—Faith versus Works, Morality versus the Cross, Legality versus the Gospel of Forgiveness of Sins, and Bondage versus Freedom. To illustrate the first of these, Thompson cites a 1780s sermon by one William Huntington, S.S. (Sinner Saved), a former coal heaver who was at first a Baptist, then later "his own evangelist and prophet." "In contrast to mere 'workmongers,'" argues Huntington (and Thompson after him), "the Saved must know that 'the Saviour's laws are written within us.'" For Blake, such knowledge does not take the form of amazing grace descending, but rather the form of artistic exfoliation. At the conclusion of *Milton*, the poem's namesake announces this project.

> To bathe in the Waters of Life; to wash off the Not Human
> I come in Self-annihilation & the grandeur of Inspiration
> To cast off Rational Demonstration by Faith in the Saviour
> To cast off the rotten rags of Memory by Inspiration
> To cast off Bacon, Locke & Newton from Albions covering
> To take off his filthy garments, & clothe him with Imagination.
>   (*M*, pl. 41 [48], ll. 1–6)

28. John Sallis, *Being and Logos: The Way of Platonic Dialogue* (Pittsburgh: Duquesne University Press, 1975), 401–12. Compare Blake's position that "Without Contraries is no progression. Attraction and Repulsion, Reason and Energy, Love and Hate, are necessary to Human existence" (*MHH*, pl. 3).

29. T. Bedingfield, "Pains and Gains," ll. 1–4, 21–24; in *Elizabethan Lyrics from the Original Texts*, ed. Norman Ault (1949; rpt., New York: Capricorn Books, 1960), 74–75.

30. See Raymond Williams, *Culture and Society, 1780–1950* (1958; rpt., New York: Harper and Row, 1966), 315, 320. In surveying English culture from approximately 1600 to the mid-twentieth century, Raymond Williams, although holding that "the area of culture . . . is usually proportional to the area of a language rather than to the area of a class," allows that "it is true that a dominant class can to a large extent control the transmission and distribution of the whole common inheritance; such control, where it exists, needs to be noted as a fact about that class."

Williams also suggests just how deeply and durably rooted the problem is. "It is clear," he observes, "that even in contemporary [circa 1950] democratic communities the dominative attitude to communication is still paramount. Almost every kind of leader seems to be genuinely afraid of trusting the processes of majority discussion and decision. As a matter or practice this is usually whittled away to the merest formula. For this, the rooted distrust of the majority, who are seen as masses or more politely as the public, is evidently responsible."

31. *John Milton: Complete Poetry and Selected Prose*, ed. Merritt Y. Hughes (New York: Odyssey Press, 1957), 631, 720, 730. Milton subsequently makes it clear that licensing depends on the doctrine of infallibility and ignores what is, for him, the historical fact of the Fall. He asks, "if learned men be the first receivers out of books and dispreaders both of vice and error, how shall the licensers themselves be confided in, unless we confer upon them, or they assume to themselves above all others in the land, the grace of infallibility and uncorruptedness?"

In "Of Education" (1644; 1673) Milton characterizes language-as-labor as "the instrument conveying to us things useful to be known" and distinguishes between such linguistic labor as befits an educated person and linguistic common labor. "And though a linguist should pride himself to have all the tongues that Babel cleft the world into, yet, if he have not studied the solid things in them as well as the words and lexicons, he were nothing so much to be esteemed a learned man as any yeoman or tradesman competently wise in his mother dialect only."

Riede, *Oracles and Hierophants*, 40, 51, notes that Blake appropriates as the epigraph to *Milton* the same verse from Numbers (11:29) that Milton uses in his *Areopagitica*, "A favorite text of the radical Protestant tradition." Riede also notes a tendency that Milton shares with such predecessors as Paul to become one of "the fallen sons of prophecy," to become "the Church Milton" instead of "Milton." "Paul's transformative typological readings of the Old Testament and Milton's combative utterances in *Areopagitica* become models for the Blakean mode of mental warfare that replaces the divinely authoritative voice of *Paradise Lost* with a contentious heteroglossia in which Blake, Milton, and Paul contend with and against one another, with and against the myriad voices of the living Judeo-Christian tradition."

32. Thompson, *Witness against the Beast*, 109–10. See also Mee, *Dangerous Enthusiasm*, 112. Mee notes that such distinctions extend into the realm of language and down to the level of the dictionaries themselves. "[Francis] Grose produced his *Classical Dictionary of the Vulgar Tongue* (1785) in direct competition with Johnson's *Dictionary*. Where the latter attempted to limit 'the language properly so-called' to literary sources and polite usage, Grose's dictionary was orientated toward the language as spoken by the people and included scurrilous and often indecent entries." Early on, Blake burlesqued these notions of propriety and a proprietary culture in *An Island in the Moon* (1784).

33. Smith, *The Politics of Language*, 30. See also Susan Allen Ford, " 'A Name More Dear': Fathers, Daughters, and Desire in *A Simple Story, The False Friend,* and *Mathilda*," in *Re-Envisioning Romanticism: British Women Writers, 1776–1837*, ed. Carol Shiner Wilson and Joel Haefner (Philadelphia: University of Pennsylvania Press, 1994), 51–71, esp. 65. Ford notes that "in all these novels, language functions as a tool of power," adding to Smith's point the necessary if obvious corollary that linguistic power relations in the period under discussion are deployed along gender and generational as well as class lines.

34. See Robert N. Essick, *William Blake and the Language of Adam* (Oxford: Clarendon Press, 1989), 137; Eaves, *Counter-Arts Conspiracy*, 36–37, 234–35. Although Eaves has nothing to say about Colnaghi, he does note that

Wheatley (1747–1801) was one of the major figures in the creation of Boydell's Shakespeare Gallery and Bowyer's Historic Gallery, projects noteworthy to Blake chiefly because "his 'Talents,' plural, as painter and engraver had been passed over," as he states the case in a letter of 11 December 1805 to William Hayley (*CPP*, p. 767). According to Eaves, in the hands of one of Blake's archvillains such as Francesco Bartolozzi, the stipple technique could be "threatening to its technical competitors. The gray scale is more refined, the residual evidence of reproduction above the threshold—the optical noise is less, and the manufacturing process, requiring less labor and less skill, is cheaper."

35. See Essick, *Language of Adam*, 137; Thompson, *Witness against the Beast*, 187. Thompson notes a thematic organization in "London" similar to the one remarked by Essick. According to the former, "First and simply, it [i.e., "London"] is organised about the street-cries of London."

36. Thompson, *Witness against the Beast*, 110, 117.

37. Erdman, *Prophet against Empire*, 474. It is worth noting that one of the quests of *Jerusalem* is to declare "All Human Forms identified even Tree Metal Earth & Stone" (*J*, pl. 99, l. 57).

38. *CPP*, p. 936. See also Erdman, *Prophet against Empire*, 475–76. Erdman reads the Selsey passage as part of the project of "reconversion from State Religion to true Christianity," noting that "Signs of any actual work on this great project of restoration are meager," but adding that "London, speaking as a City and a 'father of multitudes,' is still willing to give himself for Albion, as London and Bristol gave themselves for the nations in 1780; and his very 'Houses are Thoughts.' Edinburgh, too, keeps alive in prophetic memory . . . the first victims of Antijacobin 'Justice,' the leaders of the British Convention of Reformers who were tried in Scottish courts in 1793 and 1794."

39. See Thompson, *Witness against the Beast*, 226–27. Neither Erdman nor Bloom comments on "Winchester," which is, of course, a cathedral town. But there may be another strand of association at work in the passage under discussion. Thompson discusses one Elhanan Winchester, the "prophet" of "The Universalists, who emerged in the Swedenborgian nexus." Winchester "republished in 1792 a translation of Siegvolk's *The Everlasting Gospel*, and by 1794 the Universalists had their own hymn-book in which the New Jerusalem was announced. . . . And Winchester himself had published in the previous year a poem in twelve books, of which Book IX described the Millennium."

40. Blake makes this line of descent clear in *The Marriage of Heaven and Hell* (1790–93). "The ancient Poets" began by "animat[ing] all sensible objects with Gods or Geniuses, calling them by the names and adorning them with the properties of woods, rivers, mountains, lakes, cities, nations, and whatever their enlarged & numerous senses could percieve." Subsequently, "a system was formed, which took advantage of & enslav'd the vulgar by attempting to realize or abstract mental dieties from their objects: thus began Priesthood" (*MHH*, pl. 11).

41. See DeLuca, *Words of Eternity*, 34–35. "For Blake, language is not only the glory of our humanity but its essence, and in the apocalypse described at the end of *Jerusalem*, the form of the sign and the human form become one. Albion speaks 'Words of Eternity in Human Forms,' and 'every Word & Every Character / Was Human' (*J*, 95.9; 98.35–36)."

42. Compare the following passage from *There Is No Natural Religion [b]*:

> If it were not for the Poetic or Prophetic character. the Philosophic &
> Experimental would soon be at the ratio of all things & stand still, unable to
> do other than repeat the same dull round over again
>   Therefore God becomes as we are. that we may be as he is. (*CPP*, p. 3)

In *Milton* Blake is, if anything, even more explicit.

> For God himself enters Death's Door always with those that enter
> And lays down in the Grave with them, in Visions of Eternity
> Till they awake & see Jesus & the Linen Clothes lying
> That the Females had Woven for them, & the Gates of their Fathers House.
>   (*M*, pl. 32 [35], ll. 40–43)

43. Of Bowlahoola, Blake observes,

> Bowlahoola is namd Law. by mortals, Tharmas founded it:
> Because of Satan, before Luban in the City of Golgonooza.
> But Golgonooza is namd Art & Manufacture by mortal men.
>   (*M*, pl. 24 [26], ll. 48–50)

Once produced, Golgonooza's "Art & Manufacture" enters

>   Allamanda calld on Earth Commerce, [which] is the Cultivated land
> Around the City of Golgonooza in the Forests of Entuthon:
> Here the Sons of Los labour against Death Eternal.
>   (*M*, pl. 27 [29], ll. 42–44)

Taken together, Bowlahoola and Allamanda compose "Science[, which] is
divided into Bowlahoola & Allamanda" (*M*, pl. 27 [29], l. 63). Science, in its
turn, is the temporal form of what in "Eternity" is known as "Architecture" (*M*,
pl. 27 [29], ll. 55–56). The architectural metaphor returns prominently
throughout *Jerusalem*—for example, in the passage having to do with "Los's
Halls" (*J*, pl. 16, ll. 61–69), and in the description of how Los builds his
"stubborn structure of the Language" (pl. 36, ll. 58–60).

44. *J*, pl. 36 [40], ll. 58–60. See Damrosch, *Symbol and Truth*, 327; Paley,
Continuing City, 262. Discussing these three lines, Damrosch notes that
"Blake's fascination with mythological traditions shows his recognition of this
truth: every word, every thought, is built up by human usage, and any serious
attempt at reconstruction calls for a thoroughgoing rethinking of tradition. In
doing so, the artist frees language from unexamined rigidities and makes it live
again."

Paley cites this passage as demonstrating that "Los, in his capacity as the
poetic imagination, is the embodiment of the Logos or primordial word. It is
he who creates the English language so that an intellectual structure may exist
to contain the results of the Fall."

45. See Essick, *Language of Adam*, 11–12. Commenting on *Milton*, pl. 28
[30], ll. 1–7, which describes how "Some Sons of Los" create "the beautiful
house for the piteous sufferer," Essick observes that "the architectural
metaphor in this passage builds, for the modern reader, an associative link with

Martin Heidegger's contention that 'language is the house of Being,' since 'the word alone gives being to the thing.' "

46. See Ferber, *Social Vision*, 203. "If English is a rough basement, we may note, it is not only the ruin of a once glorious linguistic mansion but the foundation of its reconstruction."

47. Erdman, *Prophet against Empire*, 475; Paley, *Continuing City*, 204. Erdman identifies this aggregation as the "twenty-four . . . 'Friends of Albion,' and another four, 'Verulam, London, York, Edinburgh, mourning one towards another' [*J* 41(46).24], as including all the rest."

Paley notes that Edinburgh was not a cathedral city, but that Blake chose to include it as a way of registering "sympathy for the Scottish radicals convicted during the years that Jerusalem was being written."

48. See chapter 7. See also Jon Klancher, *The Making of English Reading Audiences, 1790–1832* (Madison: University of Wisconsin Press, 1987), 173. "The newly self-conscious middle class and radical artisan publics that emerged after 1790 began to represent at least two possible relations between reader and audience. Either the reader's social belonging must be declared in an increasingly class conscious radical discourse that helped give rhetoric its bad name by the very explicitness of its rhetorical assumptions, or the individual reader must be defined as a textual presence in a discourse where he constitutes himself as 'reader' by becoming aware of his distinction from all social, collective formations that he learns to 'read' as a social text." It would seem that Blake works both sides of this street, at once identifying the rhetorical turn and sending it up by his excesses in this regard, and exhorting Los's audience— and his own, by extension—to become the sort of "textual presence" of which Klancher speaks.

The whole of *Milton* is about Milton's redemptive descent from a position "Unhappy tho in heav'n," where "he obey'd, he murmur'd not. he was silent" (*M*, pl. 2, l. 18). That descent involves reassuming speech, and in so doing becoming Milton the living transferential presence (Milton-as-metaphor) that works in Los rather than Milton the dead cause (Milton-as-metonym) that prescribes Los.

49. See Essick, *Language of Adam*, 10, 15. Essick begins his discussion with a detailed analysis of Blake's pen-and-tempera *Adam Naming the Beasts* (1810), which he correctly observes "is a painting about language. By so emphatically foregrounding Adam, Blake stresses the man-centered event rather than the diversity of nature overwhelming Adam in other illustrations of the scene. . . . Adam's closed lips diminish the importance of physical utterance and emphasize the mental processes essential for the act of naming." But the lesson of this painting is easily enough forgotten after the act of naming, which becomes the record of a past presence that threatens to overwhelm the present itself through language's ability to represent—and in so doing, to reify—the past. Speaking of the fall from a Blakean perspective, Essick correctly observes that "the serpent's ability to lie to Eve has its structural foundation in the power of language to call to mind that which is not present."

50. *J*, pl. 95, ll. 5–11; "broad flashes of flaming lightning" recalls one of the plagues: "And Moses stretched forth his rod toward heaven: and the LORD sent thunder and hail, and the fire that ran along upon the ground" (Exodus 9:23).

239

"Pillars / Of fire" recalls the exodus itself: "And the LORD went before them by day in a pillar of a cloud, to lead them the way; and by night in a pillar of fire, to give them light" (13:21).

51. See *The Dialogic Imagination: Four Essays by M. M. Bakhtin*, ed. Michael Holquist, trans. Caryl Emerson and Michael Holquist (Austin: University of Texas Press, 1981), 84–85.

52. In his Annotations to Lavater's *Aphorisms on Man* (1788), Blake apparently takes Paul at his word, commenting that "man is the ark of God the mercy seat is upon the ark cherubims guard it on either side & in the midst is the holy law. man is either the ark of God or a phantom of the earth & the water" (*CPP*, p. 596).

53. See Mee, *Dangerous Enthusiasm*, 3; Riede, *Oracles and Hierophants*, 50–51; and Thompson, *Witness against the Beast*, xvi. Mee usefully notes, after Lévi-Strauss, that Blake mobilizes the tactic of bricolage, "an approach which unapologetically recombines elements from across discourse boundaries such that the antecedent discourses are fundamentally altered in the resultant structures."

Riede notes the tendency of Paul to lapse into dogma, to become "the Church Paul." It is a tendency shared by Milton—indeed, by Blake himself. The antidote is the ceaseless intellectual contention that shows the dogmas in question as the reified ideological formations that they are.

According to Thompson, Blake spoke freely in just this manner. He "would look into a book with a directness which we might find to be naïve or unbearable, challenging each one of its arguments against his own experience and his own 'system.' . . . He took each author (even Old Testament prophets) as his equal, or as something less. And he acknowledged as between them, no received judgements as to their worth, no hierarchy of accepted 'reputability.' "

54. In 1 Corinthians 7, Paul goes on at some length about the proper conduct of relations between men and women, foreshadowing the apostolic succession rather than interpretive "liberty." The following is perhaps the most extreme example of how arrogates interpretive authority to himself: "And unto the married I command, yet not I, but the Lord, Let not the wife depart from the husband" (7:10).

55. See Damrosch, *Symbol and Truth*, 306. "Christian typology interpreted the Merkabah as a Christophany: the living creatures are the cherubim who bear Christ aloft, and are associated with the four evangelists. But Blake is always on the watch for the perverted doctrine of cherubs who guard the inaccessible deity, identifying them with the 'Covering Cherub' of Ezekiel 28:14 and with the cherubim who guard the holy of holies in the Temple."

56. See note 53 above.

Index

Titles of works by authors other than Blake are identified with the authors' names in parentheses. Page numbers for illustrations are in italics.

Index

Index

Boscovich, Ruggiero Giuseppe, 98
Bowlahoola, 81, 82, 83, 238n.43
Boyle, Robert, 129, 131, 134, 152
Breath Divine, The, 18, 51, 123, 188, 189
Breathing fields, 51, 164
Breath of life, 164, 187, 188, 189
Bretland, Joseph, 98
Browning, Robert, 152
Bruno, Giordano, 90
Builder's task, 60, 78–81, 84
Bunyan, John, 152
Burke, Edmund, 119–23, 215n.42
Butts, Thomas, Blake's letters to, 38, 45, 69, 122, 155

Cacophony: in Isaiah, 180; urban, 169–70, 173, 179
Calendar, French, 119
Campanella, Tommaso, 90
Canaan, 12, 13
Cardanus's Comfort (Bedingfield), 182
Carroll, Joseph, 3–4
Cartesian dualism, 6
Casaubon, Isaac, 93
Catholicism, 151
Causality, 157; cause and effect, relationship between, 144, 150, 161, 163; Locke's theory of, 160; Newton's understanding of, 128–29; pulsebeat as cause of the moment, 159; spiritual cause *versus* natural cause, 141; in "The Tyger," 127, 128; transferentiality and, 163
Celestial mechanics, 20, 55; and language of desire, 156. *See also* Universe
Celestial order, 28
Chailley, Jacques, 71
Charters, 105–108, 113, 117, 120, 125, 179

Chaucer, Geoffrey, 18, 60, 159, 197n.30
Chemistry, 93, 97
"Chimney Sweeper, The," 175–76
Christ. *See* Jesus Christ
Christianity, 88, 102; gnosticism and, 91, 92, 104; metric system as threat to, 119; perversion of, 25
Chronology, Bishop Ussher's, 11, 52, 159
Chronology of Ancient Kingdoms Amended, The (Newton), 52
Circle, 55
City. *See* Urban landscape
Class struggle, 87, 182, 183, 184, 233n.18
Clockwork universe, 129, 130, 131, 134, 143–44, 152, 219n.19
Codes, sacred, 171
Codex Askewianus, 93
Codex Brucianus, 93
Cognition, origin of, 55
Coinage: false, 116; standards of, 111
Comenius, Johann Amos, 96
Consciousness, 50, 98, 99. *See also* Creative consciousness
Conservation, law of, 165
Consolation of Philosophy, The (Boethius), 150
Constitution, English, 120
Contingency, 9–10
Contraction, 53, 194n.12, 195n.16
Contraries, 125
Conventions. *See* Standards
Conversation, 22, 23, 188, 189
Corinthians, First Epistle of Paul to the, 15, 174
Corinthians, Second Epistle of Paul to the, 174, 189–90
Corn Laws, 232n.17
Corpuscular matter, 33, 34, 37, 39, 41, 42, 51, 88, 106, 117, 153, 221n.2, 226n.34; attributes of, 54;

Index

Index

Emanations, 146–47, 163–66, 191

Empiricism, 167

End of time, 188

Ends, causes and, 129

Enion, 165

Enitharmon, 24, 32, 33, 34, 49, 186

Enlightenment, 15–16, 157; anti-Newtonianism, 39–40; Freemasonry's influence in, 58–59; and tyrants of reason, 76

Ensoulment, 18, 95, 178, 180, 187; Newton's marginalization of, 218n.12

Epiphanius of Salamis, Saint, 92

Epistemology, 4–6, 15, 16, 86; demise of, 205n.4; Locke's globule and, 160

Erdman, David V., 106, 107, 109, 113, 171

Essay Concerning Human Understanding, An (Locke), 152, 160, 167

Essay on Man (Pope), 41

Essick, Robert N., 144, 184

Eternity, 12, 159, 162, 163, 196n.22

Ethereal medium, 218n.13

Eucharist, 34, 63

Europe, 97; frontispiece to, 66, 67, 68, *70*

Eve, 36; after the Fall, 157, 177

Everard, John, 93, 94, 95, 99

"Everlasting Gospel, The," 69, 70

Evil, 40, 95, 96; Goethe's response to problem of, 206n.16, 207n.21

Exodus (Bible), 7, 8, 9

Experiment and experience, 130, 143, 156

Ezekiel, 17, 25, 36

Fall, the, 29, 36, 53, 99, 112, 157, 179; alienation following, 177; and full speech, 162; and language, 43; moment of naming and, 144–45

False coinage, 116

Ferber, Michael, 94, 105, 115, 148, 149

Figurative language, 16; literalization of figuration, 144

Final cause, 128–29

Fineman, Joel, 217n.7

Firm perswasion, 25–26, 36, 49

First cause, 144; metonymic effects of, 152; Newton's understanding of God as, 128–29; in "The Tyger," 127; transcendence, 143

Fludd, Robert, 93, 95, 96

Fluxions, Newton's theory of, 158

Food crisis (1800), 232n.17

Force and body, synthesis of, 54

Forge, 116, 172

Forgetfulness, 45, 46

Forms, 130, 143, 145, 146; and desire, 166

Foucault, Michel, 15

Four Zoas, 20, 162, 164, 198n.7; conversion of, 56–57; death and rebirth, 72, 75; desire restrained, 146; firm perswasion, 25; language, Blake's account of, 22, 23; space and time, creation of, 30

Four Zoas, The, 18, 132–35; creation story, retelling of the, 29; erotic and thanatic, amalgamation of, 165–66; pity and wrath, reunion of, 165

Fragmentation, 32–37

Freedom, 22

Freemasonry, 17, 58–59; Blake's allusions to, 60–63, 66–72, 75, 84; Blake's problems with, 60, 75, 76, 77, 80; initiation rite, 66; prescriptive nature of, 77; rituals of rebirth and fellowship, 71; Solomon's Temple, significance of, 78–79

Free will, problem of, 40

245

Index

Index

Humanity: body-soul relationship, 43–45; Newtonian view of, 41–42; as one person, 52

Hume, David, 15, 153–54

Hutchinson, William, 61

Huxley, T. H., 3–4

Hypothesis, 22

Ideas, cause of, 160

Ideology, 148–50; historicization of, 150–54; of the natural, Blake as prophet against, 154–68

Immanence, 42, 94–98, 100, 101, 102, 104, 115, 117, 123, 124, 160; of creative principle, 130; of Genius, 162

Incarnation, 130, 131

Incommensurability, 105, 124, 125, 156

Individuality, standardization and, 114

Induction, 22, 33

Infoldment, Bacon's notion of, 153

Invention, 17–18, 196n.29

Irenaeus, Saint, 92, 102

Iron tablets, 194n.14

Isaiah, 17, 25, 36, 98, 180–81

J-account of creation and fall (Bible), 128, 140, 178

Jachin, 62, 63, 77

Jachin and Boaz, 60

Jacob, Margaret C., 21, 58

Jameson, Fredric, 87

Jehovah, 140, 141, 158, 161, 165, 168, 177, 178, 179, 187, 188

Jerusalem, 10, 11, 17, 18, 27, 34, *74*, 132, 159, 160, 164, 167, 168; Blake's negative view of nature in, 139–40, 145; Breath Divine, 123, 188; children of, 64; conversion of the Four Zoas, 56, 57; death and rebirth in, 71–72,

74–75; Emanations, Name of, 191; epigraph, 24; eternity, 162; fellowship of divine and human in, 72; forgetfulness, battle against, 45; Freemasonry references in, 60, 71, 72; language, alienation of, 179–80, 185, 186; language, reclaiming of, 187; language as basis of knowledge, 42; language properly spoken, 22, 23; Los, labor of, 235n.27; metaphor, nature of, 45, 142; particularity, 145; space and time, creation of, 30; urban landscape in, 169; wind in, 156

Jerusalem (city), in Blake's visionary scheme, 78–81, 83

Jesus Christ: and Blake's notion of invention, 17, 18; crucifixion of, 138; Elijah as typological anticipation of, 143; figure of, in *A Vision of the Last Judgment*, 62, 63; in gnosticism, 102; as God made manifest in the world, 9–10; in *Jerusalem*, 71; as Logos, 141, 194n.12; Priestley's view of, 100–101; resurrection of, 180; situation in discourse of, 14; in *Songs of Innocence*, 174, 175, 176; as source of Poetic Genius, 130, 189

John, Gospel According to, 101, 138, 180, 194n.12; *Logos*, 141, 181

John of Patmos, 132, 153, 174, 175, 176

Johnson, Joseph, 61

Johnson, Samuel, 21, 79, 80, 96, 236n.32

Jones, William Powell, 27, 28

Justin Martyr, 101

King Edward the Third, 107–10, 113, 114, 115

Index

Index

and metonymy, 144; naturalization, 145; Poetic Genius, 146; sacramental potential in, 142; spurious dichotomies, 171; standardization, 112–13; textualization, process of, 171–72

Marxism, 86, 92, 233n.18; ideology, Marxist definition of, 148

Masonic lodge, design of, 77

Masonic Master's apron, 63, *64*, *69*

Masonry. *See* Freemasonry

Material and spiritual, relationship of the bases of, 157

Materialism, 38, 39, 56, 96, 139; standardization and, 113

Material priority, delusion of, 46, 47, 49, 50, 76, 77, 78, 115, 164

Material world, delusory existence of, 165

Mathematical Principles (Newton), 129

Mathematics, 75; Newton's notion of limits of, 54

Matter: and beauty, 140; and divine immanence, 123; spirit's primacy over, 52, 168; theories of, 33, 39, 48, 49, 51, 88, 96, 98

Meaning, 23; signification *versus*, 227n.48

Measures. *See* Weights and measures

Mellor, Anne K., 62

"Memorable Fancy," of *The Marriage of Heaven and Hell*, 98

"Mental Traveller, The," 82

Mercantilism, standardization and, 113, 114

Metalepsis, 18, 141–42, 155

Metapherein (Greek term), 142

Metaphor, 16, 17, 43–46, 49, 50, 87, 137, 222n.5; Blake's notion of, 142; creation as making of, 77; full speech, 163; for immanent basis of life and humanity, 166; invention as, 18; language's basis in, 155; as metalepsis, 141–42; and metonymy, 131, 144, 167, 217n.7, 223n.16; moment of time, 159; origin of, 55; the sacramental and, 142; speech as, 162, 163; in "The Tyger," 127; wind, 157

Metaphysics, Newtonian, 21, 27

Metonymic logic, 127–29, 131, 134

Metonymy, 87, 88, 89, 102, 103, 137; alienated speech of, 163; Blake's view of nature, 97; cause and effect relationship, 144; defined, 163; Eco's notion of, 217n.8; ideology and, 149, 150; in "London," 110; and metaphor, 131, 144, 167, 217n.7, 223n.16; moment of time, 159; nature's womb, 158; and synecdoche, 223n.16, 224n.22; in "The Tyger," 127, 128; wool, 157

Metric system, 118, 119, 120

Midian, 12, 13, 14

Milton, 9–12, 14, 37, *73*, 133, 195n.14; among the graves of the dead, 167; architectural task in, 80–83; bodying forth, limits to, 53; breathing fields, 164; builder's task in, 78, *79*; creation story, retelling of the, 29–32; divestiture, metaphors of, 56, 167; *ecstasis*, attainment of, 55–56; gnomes, 117; goal of prophecy in, 161; institutionalized art, condemnation of, 62; language, boundary condition of, 156; language, reclaiming of, 187; linen, casting off of, 63–64; looking within, 54–55; metaphor and metalepsis, 142; metonymy in, 128; Newtonian thought,

249

Index

materialism, 38, 39, 96, 125; mathematical limits, 54; matter, theory of, 33, 51; metaphysics, 21, 27; metonymic logic and natural theology of, 127, 128–29, 134; mind-body model, 41; Pantocrator, 35, 37, 59, 143, 159, 165, 210n.39, 218n.12; Priestley's view of, 97–98; reasoning, rules of, 33, 128–29; selfhood and repudiation of, 24; space, notions of, 32; standards of coinage, 111; universe, model of the, 20, 28, 34, 40–41, 55, 88; Urizen, association with, 29–33; Ussher's chronology and, 52. *See also Principia*

Nicolson, Marjorie Hope, 19, 21, 27
Nimrod, 66
Nimrod's Tower, 66
Nothing, characterization of, 226n.42
Numbers (Bible), 13, 168
Number symbolism, Blake's, 28
Numerology, Biblical, 131

Oholiab. *See* Aholiab
Old Charges (Masonic instructions), 58–59, 66, 78
Ololon, 28, 147, 156, 167
Omniscience, 10
Ontology, 4, 5, 6; individual and God, relationship of, 143; of Moses, 8; situatedness and contingency, 9–10
"On Virgil," 75
Oothoon, 146, 159
Opacity, 49, 53, 195n.16
Optical phenomena, 41, 42, 124–25
Opticks (Newton), 27, 129, 153, 201n.9
Organic perception, 131–32, 144
Origen, 92
O'Sullivan, Gerry, 5

P-account of creation and fall (Bible), 128, 133, 140, 177, 178, 181
Pagels, Elaine, 91, 102, 104
Pagliaro, Harold, 127, 135
Paine, Thomas, 61, 106–109
Palamabron, 49–52, 164, 172
Paleness, 32
Paley, Morton D., 110, 126
Paley, William, 129
Pantocrator, 41; Newton's, 35, 37, 59, 143, 159, 165, 210n.39, 218n.12
Paradise Lost (Milton), 35, 36, 54, 79, 80, 194n.14
Parliament, 172
Parsimony, Newton's law of, 128, 150
Particularization, 34, 35, 36, 145
Pathos, 81, 82
Patriarchy, 88
Paul, Saint, 14, 15, 174–75, 179, 189–90
Pease, Donald, 80
Penny, 111
Perception, 140, 157; basis of, 160; organic, 131–32, 144
Perversity, 132, 133
Philo Judaeus, 101
Phlogiston theory, 98, 210n.36
Physics, Newtonian, 20, 21, 22, 27
Piper, the, in *Songs of Innocence*, 174, 175
Pitt, William, the Younger, 122, 172, 216n.48
Pity, 50, 51, 82, 159, 164, 165
Plato, 4–5, 10, 15, 182
Plow, 49
Pneuma, 98, 99, 102, 115, 117, 123. *See also* Soul
Poetical Sketches, 107, 174, 194n.14, 195n.17
Poetic genius, 11, 44, 45, 77, 78, 80, 81, 82, 114–17, 125, 130, 131, 132, 143, 146; and Freemasonry, 75, 76; Jesus as, 189

Index

Index

Index

world by, 99, 100, 133, 134, 135;
creative consciousness, denial of,
46–47; in frontispiece to *Europe*,
67, 68, 70; perversity of, 132,
133; secrets in nature's womb,
157–58; spear of, 138;
standardization, implications of,
109–10, 112; tigers, image of, 134
Urthona, 161
Ussher, Bishop James, 11, 52, 159
Usurpation, motif of, 108, 109

Vico, Giambattista, 15, 16, 39, 40,
42, 43, 44, 46, 48
Vision of the Last Judgment, A, 49,
52, 54, 65, 66, 77; false coinage,
116; Freemasonry references in, 62
"Vision of the Science of the
Elohim," 125, 158
Visions of the Daughters of Albion,
146–47
Vital energy, 94, 95
Voegelin, Eric, 91
Voltaire, 15, 16, 17, 59, 123
Vortex, 12, 13, 54–55

Weights and measures, 105, 106, 107,
109, 111–14, 117, 123, 124, 125;

French, 118–21; in Mosaic law,
213n.17
Wheatley, Francis, 184
White, Gilbert, 154
White, Hayden V., 15–16
Will of the Immortal, 53
Winchester, 185, 186, 237n.39
Wind, the, 155, 156, 157
Winstanley, Gerrard, 94
Wollstonecraft, Mary, 149
Womb imagery, 52, 153, 157–58
Wool, 155, 156–57
Word (*Logos*). *See Logos*
Wordsworth, William, 96, 170
Work. *See* Labor
World, historical duration of, 159
Worshipful use of God's gifts, 152
Wrath, 50, 51, 52; Blake's notion of
science of, 165

Yaldabaoth, 210–11n.39
Yates, Frances, 162
Young, Thomas, 124

Zoa, 163. *See also* Four Zoas
Zupko, Ronald Edward, 111, 112, 113

255